Data Structures, Algorithms, and Invariants

A Practical Guide

FIRST EDITION

Robin Hillyard

Northeastern University

Bassim Hamadeh, CEO and Publisher
John Remington, Managing Executive Editor
Gem Rabanera, Senior Project Editor
Susana Christie, Senior Developmental Editor
Abbey Hastings, Senior Production Editor
Emely Villavicencio, Senior Graphic Designer
JoHannah McDonald, Licensing Coordinator
Natalie Piccotti, Director of Marketing
Kassie Graves, Senior Vice President, Editorial
Alia Bales, Director, Project Editorial and Production

Printed in the United States of America.

Brief Contents

Detailed Contents

Preface

I have perhaps three credentials to justify my authorship of this book. The most obvious is that I've been teaching the subject for 8 years and have helped hundreds of students grapple with the topics herein. The second is that the very first program I wrote back in 1968, long before WYSIWYG editors and Integrated Development Environments, actually worked the first time. My third credential, and perhaps the most important, is that in the intervening years, I am confident that I have made every possible programming error that it is possible to make. So, I understand, perhaps in a way that some of my more illustrious colleagues do not, what it is to struggle with the concepts of computational complexity.

Let me tell you a story that I hope will illustrate the importance of understanding complexity and the responsibility implicit in the wielding of powerful computer resources. My dissertation was about dimensions and tolerances in computer-aided design. In particular, it revolved around *solid modeling*, the geometrical representation of solid objects. The work coined a new term: "variational geometry." It shouldn't come as a surprise that two-dimensional representations in which we typically pick two objects to be associated tend to result in complexities that are quadratic. Three-dimensional representations tend to result in cubic complexity. Of course, the biggest challenge is to tame these unwieldy computations.

My first job after graduating was at a company developing a solid modeling system. Early testing of the system indicated that the hardware being employed, the newly developed VAX-780, was capable of doing the work we needed. Unfortunately, as our models got more complex—more edges, vertices, and faces—the time taken became unbearably slow. I sought out the cause. There was a quadratic process that, in its inner loop, invoked a process that, internally, was of cubic complexity. Yes, the complexity of our system was $O(n^5)$! I don't remember the chief culprit—the whole team, I suspect. Suffice it to say, I've tried to be very careful about runaway complexity ever since.

What is the best defense against such a travesty? An Application Programming Interface (API) for every Abstract Data Type (ADT) that clearly states the complexity of each method. When did you last see such an API? In any case, even if the API is perfectly clear, the client programmer must be sufficiently knowledgeable to interpret the details and ensure that the ADT is indeed the most suitable for the given use case. A common example is the injudicious use of a hash table. Hash tables are the favorite ADT of all beginning programmers—and most senior programmers. If there is the possibility of employing a hash table, you can be almost sure that it will be chosen. And yet it is not always ideal. I have often seen code in which the construction of a hash table of perhaps 1,000 key-value pairs is followed by the enumeration of those pairs—in key order. If you are going to sort the entries by key at any point, you might as well use an ordered symbol table such as a red-black tree from the outset.

The purpose of this book, therefore, is to give students of data structures and algorithms the *understanding* they need to make sensible decisions regarding the choice of an ADT for a particular use case. Many ADTs are discussed in detail and, moreover, are available on the companion website https://github.com/rchillyard/DSAIPG. However, the book is not intended to be a compendium of algorithms. The emphasis is, instead, on teaching the student to understand how to solve problems in general.

WEB LINK: https://github.com/rchillyard/DSAIPG

Introduction

What Is This Book About?

Imagine that you are constructing a scene from LEGO Bricks. There are currently 3,764 different LEGO elements to choose from. Creating a "sculpture" consists, mostly, of fitting elements together. Each element has a "behavior" you can readily visualize just by looking at it. But perhaps you aren't familiar with all the different elements, and you'd like to search a catalog for just the right piece (e.g., https://brickarchitect.com/bricks/). You would need a language with which to describe (and thus to query) the catalog. The form of the element might be defined in terms of the length of the sides.

Building a software application is not all that different from constructing with LEGOs. Instead of bricks, the pieces you fit together are instances of abstract data types (ADTs). Some ADTs are seemingly very simple, an integer, for example. Depending on the language you are using, there may be some differences in the exact behavior of the integer type. In the Java world (Java, Scala, Kotlin, Groovy, etc.), an *int* is a 32-bit signed twos-complement integer and supports the following operations: +, -, *, /, %, <, <=, ==, >=, >. Ideally, programmers can relax, confident in the knowledge that the language, and the particular ADT (i.e., *int)* would take care of all eventualities. In order to use *int* successfully, the programmer needs to know quite a few details about the actual representation (in bits). In practice, there are issues with the use of any ADT that the programmer should know about. For example, if you add one to the number 2147483647, the result will be -2147483648. Surprise! In the terminology of computer science, *int* is considered a data type, but not an *abstract* data type, because its implementation details are not hidden—they are in full view. All ADTs have these behavioral limitations and performance characteristics that ought to be fully explained in the application programming interface (API) for the ADT. Sadly, this is not always the case. The frequent dearth of information is one of the reasons for this book.

ABSTRACT DATA TYPE

An abstract data type (ADT) is a mathematical model for data types. An abstract data type is defined by its behavior from the point of view of a *user*, of the data, specifically in terms of possible values, possible operations on data of this type, and the behavior of these operations.

Suppose that you have been tasked with writing a utility library dealing with prime numbers. The requirement is that such a number could be up to 512 bits long. Obviously, an *int* isn't going to do the job. How about a *long*? In Java, that will give you 64 bits. That's still a long way short of what you need. If you knew nothing at all about ADTs, you might give up at this point. However, you should probably expect that such an ADT exists and maybe you could find it in the equivalent of the LEGO brick catalog. I'm not sure that such a catalog exists, at least not in a form that is easily searchable. Using Google to search for "512 bit integer java" will, however, give you several references to the Java class *BigInteger*. This API document tells you everything you need to know if you plan on using the class. Practically speaking, you do not need to be aware of any internal implementation details. In that sense, *BigInteger* is an abstract data type: Its API is directed to you, the user of the type.

Algorithms

Any book, such as this one, that discusses details of searching, sorting, graphs, and so forth will inevitably be labeled as a book on *algorithms*. But what exactly is an algorithm? An algorithm is like a recipe for chocolate chip cookies. It is a sequence of steps that, assuming the starting state (your ingredients) is correct, and assuming that the recipe is followed accurately, will end in the desired end state (in this case, cookies). A computer algorithm works the same way: transforms a starting state (represented by bits in memory) into the expected end state. If the sequence of steps (the program), and the end state, are *predictable*, we call it a deterministic algorithm. If either the sequence or the end state is not predictable, we call it a nondeterministic algorithm.

What about something like the "Facebook algorithm" or the "YouTube algorithm"? We live in a world where almost everyone has heard of these algorithms. But they are not algorithms in the computer science sense of the word (as used in this book). They are not sequences of instructions (like the cookie recipe). Instead, they are machine-learning models that are *trained*—not programmed.

Attacking Complexity

An important aspect of software design is the struggle between the designer and the forces of complexity. We desire order and predictability, but nature seems to want chaos. Therefore, one of the most important tasks of the software developer is to tame or limit complexity. In other words, we typically want to know how to improve the performance of some component. I don't mean to suggest that performance improvement is the main job of a software developer. It isn't. But, when performance is a problem, a good developer should know the appropriate techniques.

Here are the broad categories of optimization that we will cover in this book:

- The "dictionary principle": Taking advantage of order (Chapter 1)
- The "filing system principle": Classifying elements to minimize searching (Chapter 4)
- Memoization: Caching of results—avoiding having to evaluate something more than once (Chapter 5)
- Lazy evaluation: Avoiding unnecessary work—or deferring it until it can be performed more efficiently (Chapter 5)
- Flexibility: Adding degrees of freedom to make structures less rigid (Chapter 6)
- Reduction: Including "divide and conquer" (Chapter 1) and dynamic programming (Chapter 10)
- The arbitrary substitution principle: Insights from red flags (Chapter 1)

We will omit discussion of other performance techniques, such as parallel or asynchronous processing, as they are beyond the scope of this book.

Who Should Read This Book?

This book is aimed at information science (data science) and programming students who need to know about ADTs to use them effectively. It is not explicitly intended for students who aim for a position that expects to implement ADTs. However, this book does provide a solid understanding of the data structures and algorithms involved with ADTs, and as such would be a good foundation for learning about, and perhaps implementing, some of the more esoteric algorithms.

CHAPTER

1

Solving Problems

Introduction to the Chapter

We use computers to solve problems. Whatever our application, the software that is helping us will solve a series of problems. In this chapter, we will look at many aspects of solving problems. Along the way, we will introduce the concept of an abstract data type—but we won't talk about them in detail until Chapter 3.

Concept Review and Note

Scan the code to access a video that will provide a review of logarithms (yes, it is essential that you have a good understanding of logarithms for this course):

WEB LINK: https://youtu.be/habHK6wLkic

Note that we will use $ln\,x$ to represent the natural logarithm of x, and $lg\,x$ to represent the binary logarithm of x, viz. $\log_2 x$. This is contrary to international standards but is customary in the United States.

Learning Objectives

In this chapter students will learn about the following:

1. Reduction and state
2. Recursion and iteration
3. The master theorem
4. The arbitrary substitution principle

Key Terms

The following important terms will be introduced in this chapter:

- **Search problem:** A problem that entails finding one satisfactory solution among many candidates
- **Reduction:** The recasting of a problem into a set of easier problems
- **Recursion:** Solving a problem by solving smaller or easier subsets of the problem
- **Iteration:** Solving a problem by processing one element at a time
- **Invariant:** A property or a combination of properties that remains unchanged between states of a solution

Search Problems

We start with the concept of a **search problem**. Such a problem searches for a valid solution among a "space" of candidate solutions. Each candidate solution can be tested to determine if it is valid by applying a *predicate* (a function that yields a truth—or Boolean—value). Such a problem also has a name: a *decision problem*. Note that a problem that requires we search for a key within a data structure is only coincidentally a "search problem." Almost all problems in the world of computation are search problems, including sorting. When sorting an array of n distinct elements x_i, for example, we seek the one solution from among all n! candidate solutions when, for all i from 1 to $n-1$, the identity $x_{i-1} < x_i$ holds.

When each candidate solution solves the original, unreduced, problem, we refer to such a strategy as a *brute-force solution*. Brute force sounds bad—and usually we do try to find a better method. But sometimes it's the only known way to solve a particular problem. In the case of sorting, the brute-force solution would consist of testing each of the $n!$ candidates—each one a permutation—until one is found that satisfies the identity shown. This has exponential complexity and is the method, more or less, of the infamous *Bogosort*. Clearly, we must be able to do better than that!

Most search problems can be *reduced* to a set of simpler problems, perhaps by remodeling the problem. Take, for example, the sorting problem. The clue is in the *invariant* described that every adjacent pair in the array must be in its proper order. In this case, if every adjacent pair must be in order, *every* pair must be in order. Perhaps we can remodel the sorting problem as a problem about *pairs of elements* rather than think about all possible permutations of the array.

How many pairs are there? Well, we can choose any of n elements for the first element and any of $n-1$ elements for the second element. A pair is a pair—it doesn't really matter what order the elements are in (apart from reversing the sense of the comparison). So, the total number of pairs is $\frac{n(n-1)}{2}$, typically written in the following "binomial" notation: $\binom{n}{2}$.

We can immediately improve our sorting solution by visiting every pair and swapping the elements if they're inverted (out of order). We've gone from a solution with exponential complexity ($n!$) to a solution with quadratic complexity (n^2). As we will see later, we can improve on this, but we'll still base the solution on the remodeled problem of considering pairs.

Reduction

When a problem cannot be solved trivially (i.e., the answer is known without much more effort than thinking about it) we must **reduce** the problem into an *equivalent* set of easier problems. As humans, we do this so naturally that it barely warrants a special name. But, in the world of computation, we need to define this process rather carefully.

Modeling the Problem

If we want to solve a problem, it is often necessary to *model* it in a way that is not always intuitive. A case in point is sorting an array of length n, which we will cover in great detail in later chapters. As we saw, if we concentrate on the ordering of individual elements—as seems intuitive—we are in danger of applying a solution that grows exponentially with size because the number of possible permutations to consider is *n*!. However, we can remodel the problem by looking at *pairs* of elements. If all pairs are in the proper sequence, it follows that all elements are in the proper sequence. Thus, remodeling is a way of solving a set of *other* problems whose combined solution is equivalent to the solution of the original problem. We say that we have *reduced* our original problem to the set of other problems.

There are three stages in the reduction of problem *A*:

1. Remodel problem *A* as an *equivalent* set of easier problems **B**.
2. Solve each problem in **B**, resulting in a set of solutions: **B***.
3. Transform the solutions **B*** back into the solution of the original problem: *A**.

Sometimes, the problems of set **B** are of a quite different nature from *A*. For example, one way to calculate the median of an array (problem *A*) would be to recast it as a set of exactly one problem *B*: sorting the array (step 1). Once we have a solution *B** (step 2), we just need to select the middle element of the solution (step 3) to give us the solution to the original problem (i.e., *A**). This idea of remodeling the problem by arranging to work with a *sorted* sequence is common. After all, it's the basis of binary search. However, most examples of reduction remodel the problem only in terms of size. That's to say that the **B** problems are essentially the same as problem *A*, but smaller and therefore less complex.

Divide and Conquer and Defeat in Detail

Significant gains in performance can be achieved when set **B** consists of problems exactly like *A*, only smaller and therefore easier. There are two obvious ways to divide a problem involving *n* elements:

- Divide and conquer (DnC): Partition the *n* elements into *k* partitions, each of $\frac{n}{k}$ elements; if a partition is trivially solvable, solve it; otherwise, repeat the process (i.e., divide and conquer recursively).
- Defeat in detail (DnD): Partition the *n* elements into two partitions, one of $n-1$ elements and one of 1 element. Iterate until each division has been processed. In computer science texts, DnD is often referred to as *elementary* reduction.

HISTORICAL NOTE

DnD is an archaic military term that is often lumped together with *divide and conquer*. The latter term suggests an even division (usually into two parts), whereas the former suggests an iterative approach. See, for example, the Battle of Sluys (1340), one of the first great victories of the English navy due mostly to the French ships being chained together and thus unmaneuverable, allowing the English ships to defeat them "in detail" (i.e. one target ship at a time).

WEB LINK: https://www.youtube.com/watch?v=pfSysxGQPnw

In the world of sorting, as we will see in more detail in Chapter 7, merge sort is an example of DnC, while insertion sort is an example of DnD. We will later learn that **iteration** and **recursion** are in many ways equivalent. Generally speaking, DnC uses recursion, while DnD uses iteration. However, this is not an absolute rule. You can also think of these as solving a tree-shaped reduction versus a list-shaped reduction. Later on (Chapter 10), we will talk about another kind of reduction based on a (directed) graph: *dynamic programming*.

TABLE 1.1 Reductions

NAME	GEOMETRY OF SOLUTION	PRIMARY MECHANISM
Defeat-in-Detail	List	Iteration
Divide-and-Conquer	Tree	Recursion
Dynamic Programming	Directed graph	Shortest path traversal

The Master Theorem

The DnC approach is governed by a not-very-aptly-named law called the *master theorem*. This method of reduction is so important in the study of algorithms that it is worth a little time to study it in more detail. As you will see, logarithms are an essential part of the master theorem. If you have forgotten how they work, see the review at the start of this Chapter. However, the symbols used to represent logarithms in this book follow standard U.S. practice, which is contrary to international standards:

- lg *x* represents the "binary" logarithm of *x*, viz., $\log_2 x$.
- ln *x* represents the "natural" logarithm of *x*., viz., $\log_e x$.
- We use log *x* when we are talking about growth, so don't really need to define the base.

Suppose that we have a problem *P*(*n*) of size *n* that we can reduce into *k* problems $P(\frac{n}{k})$, together with a merge (step 3), which takes time *f*(*n*). Thus, by using this reduction, we can write the following, where *T*(*n*) is the total time to solve problem *P*(*n*):

$$T(n) = aT\left(\frac{n}{k}\right) + f(n), T(1) = 0$$

In this expression, *a* is just a constant. In pure DnC, *a* and *k* will be the same. *f*(*n*) is not worse than a "polynomial function." A polynomial function is just a function that is made up of powers of *n*, possibly multiplied by $\log n$ or $\log\log n$, for example, n^d or $n^d \log n$. As you will see in the next chapter, we typically are only concerned with the fastest growing term in the polynomial. Since this polynomial function limits the time taken (for the merge step), we often abbreviate it to "poly-time."

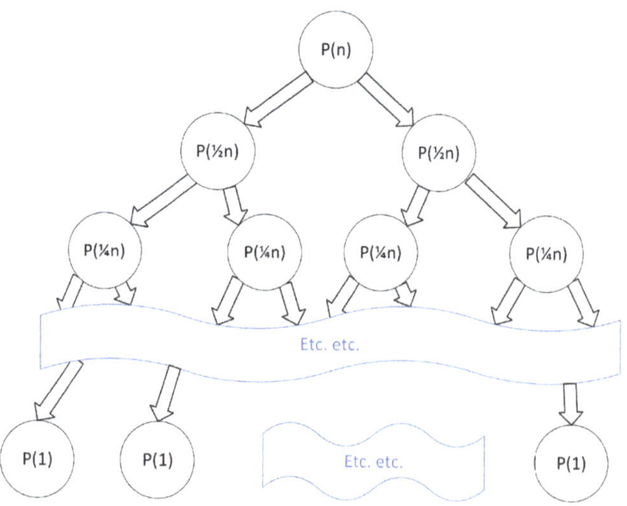

FIGURE 1.1. Divide and conquer.

In a pure DnC solution, $a = k$. The solution "tree" has the root (at the top) corresponding to *P(n)* and a number of levels down to the leaf nodes, each of which is a trivial solution, *P*(1), and which requires no time to solve. We've tacitly assumed, for simplicity, that $n = k^h$ (where *h* is the height or depth of the tree), but such an assumption is not necessary. How many levels of the tree will there be? There will be $h = \log_k n$ levels, and each level must process *n* elements, thus (in this example) taking a total of *nhc* time, where *c* is a constant (the time to process one element). Because we are mostly interested in the growth of time as *n* increases, we will typically ignore the constant (set it to 1). The total time to solve *P*(*n*), therefore is

$$T(n) = n \log_k n.$$

As an example, let's say that $a = k = 2$ and $f(n) = n$. We'll see in Chapter 7 that this is the situation that pertains to merge sort. Therefore, the time taken to merge sort *n* elements is, approximately

$$T(n) = n \log_2 n.$$

Note that nowhere in this expression does it depend on the time to solve *P*(*n*) *without* reduction—that it is, somewhat surprisingly, irrelevant.

In general, however, the master theorem analyzes the solution time according to the relative magnitudes of *f*(*n*) and $\log_b a$. Details can be found online, for example, in this video:

WEB LINK: https://youtu.be/T68vN1FNY4o

P and NP

In the theory of computation, the sets **P** and **NP** are used to denote the following:

- **P:** The set of all search problems that can be solved in polynomial time, when the solution time is no worse than $t \sim n^p$, where *p* is some power. Note that this does not include problems that require exponential time.
- **NP:** The set of all search problems that can be solved in nondeterministic polynomial time. From a practical point of view, these are the problems that we can't solve except by getting "lucky."

We call problems *NP-complete* when all possible reductions are themselves in **NP**. This is all we will say about these advanced topics—it's probably all you need to know.

Invariants

Often, we can gain insight into the solution of a problem by considering what does and does not change as we solve its sub-problems. For example, consider insertion sort. The ith sub-problem, where i runs from 1 through $n-1$, consists of inserting the ith element into the (sorted) elements in positions $0..i-1$. The fact that said elements are in order is an **invariant** of insertion sort. The algorithm progresses by the fact that, at each iteration of the outer loop, the size of this ordered partition increases until it spans the whole array. We will cover insertion sort in much more detail in Chapter 7.

As an example of the use of an invariant to *solve* a problem, look at the unexpectedly hard windmill problem by 3Blue1Brown.

WEB LINK: https://www.youtube.com/watch?v=M64HUIJFTZM

The Arbitrary Substitution Principle

When we "reduce" a problem into sub-problems, it often will not matter which we tackle first. Take DnC, for example, where each partition (sub-problem) is independent of the others; it will not matter whether we process left before right or right before left.

But there are many situations when the sub-problems are *not* independent. If we discover a solution that is sequenced left then right, we should always consider what might happen if we substitute right for left and left for right. If the result is the same (sub-problems were independent), unless it's completely obvious, we should comment our code to the effect that order is immaterial. If, on the other hand, the order does matter, we have violated the arbitrary substitution principle (ASP).

So what? If it works, it works, right? Not necessarily. We will cover a few examples in this book when it appears not to matter but when, if we take note of the red flag arising from the ASP, we might be able to improve our solution. This principle has, potentially, many applications, yet it is not well covered by either programming books or algorithm books. We can summarize this important principle of software design as follows:

> If an expression can be written using any of two or more apparently interchangeable but programmatically nonequivalent formulations, the program should be written in such a way as to clarify that one form cannot be arbitrarily substituted for another. Typically, such an expression involves a noncommutative operator.

As a trivial example, consider the following two expressions involving integer division:

(a) $11/3 * 2$
(b) $11 * 2/3$

It is readily apparent that these two expressions are not interchangeable: (a) and (b) evaluate to 6 and 7, respectively. That's to say, we cannot arbitrarily substitute (b) for (a) without changing the value.

In this case, it is clear what's going on. But note that, if the expression was instead $a * b/c$, it would not be so obvious that its value might *sometimes* be different from that of $a/c * b$. This would be especially true if the types of a, b, and c were not declared near the expression itself. Note that floating point arithmetic is not immune from this problem. For example, you might want to check the difference—on your system—between $10.0/3 * 3$ and $10.0 * 3/3$.

Another common context—typically when the author has deliberately chosen an asymmetric expression—is in the use of so-called "short-circuit" operations such as && and || in Java. As far as I know, there is no annotation for this in Java or any other language. I would suggest @asp. Without such an annotation, attention can be drawn to the problem with a comment. An expression that *is* symmetric, such as 1 + 2, does not need any annotation because there is no ambiguity since the operands can be inverted without changing the value.

Is this discussion perhaps a case of much ado about nothing? No, because it is at these @asp situations that we may find we have overlooked a bug—or at least an opportunity for a performance improvement. We will see examples of this in Chapter 6 (Hibbard deletion) and again in the final chapter when we discuss the *union-find* problem.

Representing State

Modeling the Solution to a Problem

As described, we solve problems by *reduction*. We repeatedly solve problems that are typically of the same general nature but differing in size. The repetition is either iterative or recursive. But we did not explicitly discuss how to represent the result of each of the repetitive steps, the solutions, **B***.

In practice, we model the solution process by representing its *state*. The state begins as 100% problem (no knowledge) and ends as 100% solution (everything is known). In other words, we go from a state of maximum entropy (see below) to a state of zero entropy.

The simplest kind of reduction is one for which we solve our problem element by element. For example, we want to know the largest element in an array *xs* of size *n*. If *n* is large, we will not be able to solve this problem trivially. Let's break it up. To begin, we look at only the first element (index 0 of the array). It is the largest of its own sub-array because it is the *only* element. Now, let's increment our index by one. We have the largest *known* value (i.e., the largest element of the subarray $xs[0:0]$) and the value of $xs[i]$, where *i* is one. All we need do is to compare them to get the largest value of $xs[0:i]$. In other words, we have reduced the problem to a series of $n-1$ sub-problems whereby we compare the value of *xs[i]* with *largest(xs[0:i-1])*. In practice, we can implement this either recursively or iteratively. The choice depends to some extent on the language paradigm: functional or imperative, respectively.

The data structure that we require to implement the iterative version of this solution is just two variables: the index and the largest value. But we cannot do it without those two variables. It is admittedly a minimal data structure, but it is required. If we wanted to draw this solution as a flowchart, we could draw it as a linear list of boxes.

Let's take another simple example: binary search. We start with an ordered array *xs* of size *n*, which we represent here, conventionally, as $xs[0:n]$, where *n* is the index of the first element that we are *not* interested in. We wish to find the index of element χ. First, we divide the array into two sub-arrays: $xs[0:\frac{n}{2}]$ and $xs[\frac{n}{2}:n]$. If $\chi < xs[\frac{n}{2}]$, we know to continue looking in the left partition; if $\chi = xs[\frac{n}{2}]$, we return $\frac{n}{2}$ as the result; otherwise, we continue looking in the right partition. Either we have terminated or we have halved the size of the problem. If we were to draw this as a flowchart, it would look like a tree. This is an example of that very common kind of reduction: DnC. We will have more to say on this later in the chapter.

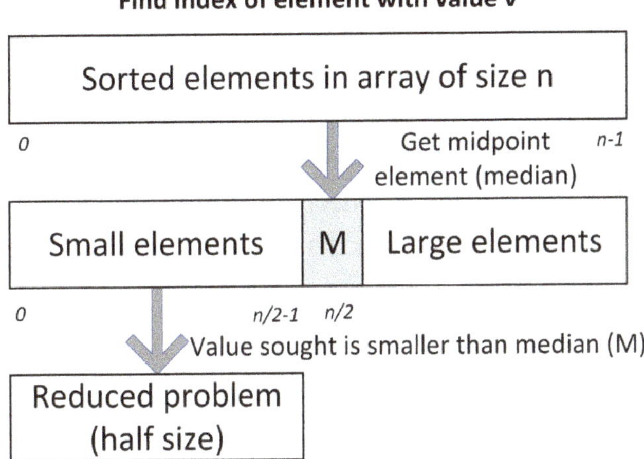

FIGURE 1.2. Modeling the solution to a problem.

Abstract Data Types

Data Structure, Invariant, and Algorithm

The state must be represented by a *data structure* in the computer's memory. The state will vary between stages of the solution, but there will typically be a unifying invariant that applies to the data structure at each stage, as noted for insertion sort. To transform the data structure from one stage to the next, we define a (sub-) algorithm. The logic that transforms the data structure from the problem to the solution is the complete algorithm. Typically, there will be different sub-algorithms required for different state transitions.

Sometimes, the solution to a problem is a series of independent steps. For example, we require an ordered representation of key-value pairs that support insertion and deletion (see Chapter 6). The overall problem is maintaining the search tree. However individual sub-problems are the various insertions, and deletions and are under the control of the client code—not the search tree itself. Each of these different types of sub-problem will be implemented by a different (sub-) algorithm.

Maintaining order is the role of the invariant(s). For example, in the search tree, the invariant will be *symmetric order*: The left sub-tree of a node contains keys smaller than *k* (the key of the node), while the right sub-tree of a node contains keys larger than *k*. The definition is appropriate for a tree of discrete keys. If there are duplicates, we would say that the left sub-tree contains keys that are not larger than *k* and that the right sub-tree contains keys that are not smaller than *k*.

Together, the data structure, invariant(s), and algorithm(s) form an *abstract data type*. We will go into much more detail on this subject in Chapters 3, 4, 5, 6, and 9.

Variables and Collections

The simplest representational state is a single variable. Examples include finding a root of an equation using the Newton–Raphson method. In this standard technique, we take an equation and transform it into the following form:

$$f(x) = 0$$

Then we iterate, beginning with a guess of the independent variable x of the function, and at each iteration, we try to improve x by writing

$$x' = x - \frac{f(x)}{f'(x)}.$$

When the value of $f(x)$ is sufficiently small, we return the current value of x. For this algorithm, we only need one variable: x. This represents the entire state of the solution. The only snag is that, if our initial guess is not well chosen, the value of x will not converge. We can improve the algorithm by adding another variable representing the number of guesses. When it exceeds a threshold, we admit defeat. Alternatively, we could keep the previous value of $f(x)$ in an attempt to ensure that it is always decreasing. Each of these "improvements" has its problems, but we don't need to go into that much detail here.

Generally speaking, solution states will be more complex. For example, suppose we wish to find the largest value in an array. For that, we will again need two variables. One is an index that allows us to visit every element in turn. The other is a representation of the current largest value (initialized at negative infinity).

Of course, the representations of states of the types of interesting problems we care about will generally be much more complex. Typically, we will need to keep track of a *collection* of values. This might be in the form of an array, a linked list, or some other data structure. We will cover more details in Chapter 3.

Degrees of Freedom and Constraints

You should be familiar with the concepts of degrees of freedom (DoF) and constraints from simple classical mechanics. In general, a stationary, rigid body will have as many constraints as it has DoF. In data structures, there is a similar setup. A mutable value has a degree of freedom; fixing that value by making it immutable is a constraint. Consider a linked list made up of node pointers. There is typically a pointer to the head (a node) of the list, and each node will have a next pointer and a value. For a list of n nodes, there will be $n+1$ pointers and n values (typically also pointers), therefore. However, because of the repetitive nature of the list, we are more likely to think in terms of three pointers: the head, the value of the head, and the head's next pointer. Each of these (or all or none) may be constrained. An "immutable" list will constrain the node value and next pointers, while the pointer to the head may or may not be mutable. A (mutable) stack, for example, will require that pointer to be mutable. But an immutable stack (or list) will keep that pointer fixed. As we will see, from one variable, we can systematically add degrees of freedom and appropriate constraints to build all the abstract data types that we need. Our ultimate data type will be the graph.

An Important Reduction

Let's finish this chapter with arguably the most important type of reduction.

Binary Search (the Dictionary Principle)

A naïve approach to searching would be to iterate over all elements of a collection (whether array, list, etc.) until the desired element is found. The time required for this task is of course proportional to the size of the collection. On average, we must search $\frac{n}{2}$ elements. Linear time doesn't sound so bad. But, if the collection is in an *ordered array*, we can do very much better.

The problem, $P(n)$, that we begin with is to find the index of the element with the required value. Let us try the DnC approach. First, we divide the array into two equal partitions. Then, we search the left-hand partition. If it's not found, we search the right-hand partition. Wait! That can't be right—there would be no advantage because the total time of searching would be the same as without the partition.

What if we only needed to search one of the partitions? That would do it! But how do we know which partition to search and which to ignore? That's where the fact that we are dealing with an array makes a difference. We can find the value of the middle element in *constant* time! All we have to do is to compare the value we seek with the value of the middle element. If we seek a larger value, we must throw away the left-hand partition and repeat the process in the right-hand partition. If we seek a small value, it's the other way around. If the value we seek is the same as the middle element, then we're done! This is what is meant by *binary search*.

There's just one snag. This idea only works for an ordered (sorted) array because we must be able to rely on the fact that all elements in the right-hand partition are larger than the middle element and all elements in the left-hand partition are smaller.

Won't the initial sort make this method of searching much more expensive than a simple linear search? Well, yes. If you only plan on searching once, it would be madness to sort first. But as you search the same collection more and more, the initial outlay for sorting the array becomes smaller and smaller relative to the time you save.

We can apply the master theorem to analyze binary search. But it's so simple to think about. What's the maximum number of times that we can divide the array into two partitions? It's $\lceil \log_2 n \rceil$. And at each division, we perform just one comparison. Therefore, the maximum number of comparisons is $\lceil \log_2 n \rceil + 1$ because we still have to check that the only remaining element is indeed the one we're seeking. You can always check this type of expression by substituting an easy value for n such as 1. log1 is of course zero, but we must do at least one comparison.

EXERCISE

If an array of n elements is to be searched m times, for what value of $\boldsymbol{m}$ will the effort expended sorting the array (assume $\boldsymbol{n \lg n}$ comparisons) be balanced by the saving of comparisons while searching?

This process is so important that we give it a special name: the *dictionary principle*. By that, we mean sorting first and then searching many times. That's how dictionaries work. Imagine a dictionary that wasn't sorted. With hundreds of thousands of words in the language, how would you ever find the meaning of a word? When we buy a dictionary, it's already been sorted by the publisher. So, we are spared the decision of whether to sort. However, the mechanism for finding a word is identical to binary search. We narrow down the pages of interest to half, then a quarter, then an eighth, and so on until we find the one page on which our word can be found.

Takeaways

Following is a list of the main ideas to take away from this chapter:

- Problems are normally solved by remodeling the problem as a set of easier problems (reduction).
- Divide and conquer is one of the most common ways of solving a problem.

- For some problems, the easiest approach may be to order the input data first.
- For other problems, classification is a way to reduce the scale of a problem.
- The master theorem governs the efficacy of size-based reductions.
- There are other optimization principles that we will cover in future chapters.
- The dictionary principle takes account of both the time saved in a binary search and the outlay of effort required to sort the array.

Chapter Review Questions

Directions: Refer to what you learned in this chapter to respond to the following questions and prompts:

1. What is an invariant? Is it just another name for a variable whose value is fixed?
2. DnC must be done using recursion, while DnD requires iteration. Discuss.
3. The term "search problem" covers only those problems that involve finding a particular element of a collection. True or false?

CHAPTER

2

Complexity

What Is an ADT's Cost in Terms of Resources?

Introduction to the Chapter

Is it necessary for every programmer or data scientist to understand the details of every abstract data type that they employ in their work? No. But they do need to understand the appropriate use cases for the ADT in question, and that implies that they have a basic understanding of its growth in terms of resources as the size of the problem increases. This topic, as far as this text is concerned, can be summed up by the term *complexity*.

Here's a case in point: A programmer heard that a hash table is generally faster than a tree for storing and retrieving key-value pairs. They, therefore, build a hash table. Finally, when the hash table is complete, they want to present all the key-value pairs on a dashboard. Naturally, they sort the keys first.

This sounds perfectly normal. We've probably all done this at one time or another. However, if we sum the construction time (and any update/search times) to the sorting time, we will probably find that the overall time will be about the same—or possibly longer—than the time to do everything with a red-black tree (e.g., Java's *TreeSet*). In other words, the red-black tree is *designed* for this use case; the hash table is not. Having a good understanding of the complexity of abstract data types will help you make these kinds of choices.

Concept Review and Note

Scan the code to access a video that will review aspects of the master theorem and introduce some of the concepts of complexity.

WEB LINK: https://youtu.be/frT1UPiJUO0

Learning Objectives

In this chapter students will learn about the following:

1. The true cost of accessing memory
2. The concepts of best case and worst case
3. Asymptotic notation
4. How to look at code and deduce its growth in time and memory usage
5. Complexity and the choice of an abstract data type for a particular use case

Key Terms

The following Important terms will be introduced in this chapter:

- **Tilde** ("~")**:** An approximate evaluator of a function as size tends to infinity
- **Big O** ("O")**:** A guarantee that resources for a particular solution to a problem will grow no faster than a given function
- **Big Omega** ("Ω")**:** A guarantee that resources for any possible solution to a problem will grow at least as fast as a given function

Resources: Space and Time

Time is money, as the old saying goes. But, in computer programming, space *is* time. What's that? The memory used determines the execution time? Surely, it's the number of operations that counts. Well, no. The most accurate predictor of the execution time of an algorithm is, usually, the number of memory accesses. That's because, while generally fast, memory access can be excruciatingly slow compared with clock speed. While the architecture of any two machines may differ, it is a fact that the time to execute a simple instruction such as subtraction (required for comparison) may be something like half a nano-second for 64-bit integers. The time to *fetch* from memory is *at best* about the same and, at worst, around 100 nanoseconds, assuming that you don't have to go out to secondary storage (disk). In practice, fetch time will average somewhere between these limits: faster if you are sequentially accessing elements of an array and slower if you are accessing elements of an array at random. Clearly, the sizes and speeds of the various caches are crucial to making a real estimate.

In later chapters, we will use a slightly different concept for an array access, which, for the purposes of this book, we will call a "hit." How does a hit differ from an array access? Array accesses that are known to be in cache are not counted as hits. For example, when we invoke a conditional swap (more on this when we get to Chapter 7), we first compare two elements, and then, if they are inverted, we swap them. But once the two elements have been compared, they must be in the cache, and therefore subsequent array accesses, for swap purposes, will not incur a (amortized) cache page fault. Another example is the merge process for merge sort. Here, elements are copied from a source array to a (different) destination array. The copy operation for an element requires two array accesses and the same number of hits. That's because the arrays are separate areas of memory. However, such hits are not equal in terms of time. Consider copying an element from one array to another (equally large) array, counted as two hits. Now consider swapping two elements within an array, also counted as two hits. Note that in the swap there will be four array accesses, but two of those are guaranteed to be in cache. In the swapping scenario, whatever the probability of a cache page fault, that probability will be doubled for the copying case. This is why merge sort runs more slowly than quick sort, even though quick sort appears to require more hits. Counting such hits still overestimates the time for implementation if the elements are accessed in sequence (as they usually are), whereas random access might be more accurately estimated with hits.

There is one more complication: Operations such as comparison require us to follow object pointers to the heap. We will call this a *lookup* and cover it in more detail in Chapter 7.

Armed with the exact details of the architecture of your machine, it is perfectly possible to predict the precise time taken for an algorithm. However, it is extremely difficult in practice and requires expertise that is far beyond that of most developers. Will the performance of algorithms continue to be a mystery forever, then? Hardly. We have the means to determine performance under any conditions we choose—simply by benchmarking.

Benchmarking

Benchmarking is the process of timing the execution of a program in terms of *clock time*. By clock time, we mean—at least theoretically—*real time*, not time as measured by the computer's clock. We can use a stopwatch to measure clock time. However, an external device such as a stopwatch must necessarily introduce additional variables, for example, the reaction time of the observer. In practice, then, it is much more convenient and, importantly, much more precise to use the computer's own clock for this purpose.

However, there are still many apparently random effects that will impact your observations. In the Java virtual machine, you must take the following into account:

- Bytecode is loaded from disk on demand—the first time a class is referenced.
- Instructions are generated from bytecode by a just-in-time compiler.
- Memory is recovered from the heap by a process called garbage collection, which, practically speaking, occurs at random times.

When running an experiment, you should try to "warm up" your benchmark *before* you start timing. You can control garbage collection too, although that is beyond the scope of this book.

How should an analyst go about benchmarking? We may be particularly interested in the time to solve a problem of a specific size. However, in general, we want to use benchmarking to help us gain insights into possible optimizations—and then measure the effect of those optimizations. This last step may seem obvious, but it is extremely common in practice to "optimize" code *without* actually verifying that it improves the performance.

One possible strategy is to pick problem sizes at random and then measure the performance for each size. You could then draw a graph of time versus size and try to fit a curve through it. That's an excellent way to do it, provided that your random sizes cover the appropriate range (it would be best to choose a size that is 2 raised to the power of the random value). However, you will find it difficult to interpret the graph.

A simpler strategy is to use doubling. First, run a series of experiments for a small number of elements, say 16. You might run 10,000 such experiments. Then do the same thing for 32 elements, perhaps only 5,000 experiments this time, and so on. Now, determine the mean time for each problem size and take its logarithm (to base two if you're doubling the size each time). The difference between the results for successive problem sizes will give the power to which *n* is raised for your particular solution. Consider Table 2.1 showing benchmark times for Shellsort.

TABLE 2.1 The Doubling Method

n	T (μsec)	lg T	diff
1,000	192	7.588	--
2,000	452	8.819	1.231
4,000	1,030	10.009	1.190
8,000	2,330	11.186	1.177

The average difference of the *lg T* values is 1.2, which suggests that the growth of time for Shellsort (see Chapter 7) is $\sim n^{1.2}$, which is to say $\sim n^{\frac{6}{5}}$.

Growth of Resource Usage

Search Problems

A "search problem" is any problem for which we search for valid candidate solutions from among a solution "space." Each candidate is validated using a predicate (a function that returns a Boolean value), also known as a "decision problem."

This definition is intended to be broad. It includes almost every possible problem that can be solved by a (true) computer algorithm, including sorting (ordering), discrete Fourier transforms, finding the prime factors of a number, and so on. Understanding the prime factors problem is helpful. It is a common feature of cryptography, that being able to factor large numbers can be the means of gaining access to the cipher. The validation step is simple: Given the known product *N*, and given two possible factors, f_1 and f_2, the decision problem becomes $N = f_1 f_2$, simple (albeit long) multiplication followed by comparison with *N*. It is the asymmetry in costs that ensures the integrity and utility of such ciphers:

- the small cost of validation versus
- the enormous cost of validating all candidate pairs of factors in the solution space

The obvious solution to a search problem is to validate all candidate solutions. Those that are valid make up the solution. We call such a search a *brute-force* solution. Given sufficient time, the solution will be successful. The reason that encryption, using TLS (Transport Layer Security) for example, is safe is that a key is typically valid for only a short time. A brute-force attack would have to use resources that are not economic when compared with the potential gain.

Sorting as a Search Problem

There is a humorous sorting algorithm called Bogosort. There are variations of it, of course, but the essence is that a search problem validates each and every possible permutation, stopping when it finds the permutation such that all elements are in sequence. In other words, every possible permutation is considered as a candidate. Thus, Bogosort is the true brute-force approach to sorting. The factors that make it so bad, compared to legitimate brute-force solutions to other problems, are, for *n* discrete elements,

- the exponential nature of the number of permutations, viz. $n!$ and
- the relatively slow validation step, viz. *n*.

As we will see in Chapter 7, we can reduce the sorting problem to one which, instead of considering all elements at once—as Bogosort does—models sorting as a problem of ordering *pairs* of elements.

If we do indeed implement sorting by comparing pairs of elements, can we determine the *minimum* number of comparisons? Let's reason as follows: First, let's consider how many pairs of elements there are. There are *n* possibilities for choosing the first element of the pair and $n-1$ possibilities for choosing the second element. But it doesn't really matter which element comes first—the pair {7, 13} is the same as the pair {7, 13}. Thus, there are $\frac{n(n-1)}{2}$ pairs. Since this is the number of ways to choose two elements from n distinct elements, we write it in binomial notation as $\binom{n}{2}$.

If we can arrange for each of these pairs of elements to be in their proper order (left-most element is not larger than right-most element), we will have sorted all n elements. However, to achieve that, we will have performed approximately $\frac{n^2}{2}$ comparisons, assuming that $n \gg 1$. For the pair model of the problem (as opposed to the permutation model), this is the brute-force approach.

Suppose that we start with a random collection of n elements. As we already know, there are $n!$ possible permutations. Let's divide this rather large number of candidates into two piles according to the order of one randomly chosen pair: $\frac{n!}{2}$ candidates have the pair in order, while the others do not. Let's discard the pile that's out of order. We repeat the process until we have just one candidate left whereby all pairs (and therefore all elements) must be in order. What's the *minimum* number of comparisons that we will need to complete this? (In practice, we typically do considerably more comparisons because we chose the pairs at random—and therefore many comparisons will be redundant).

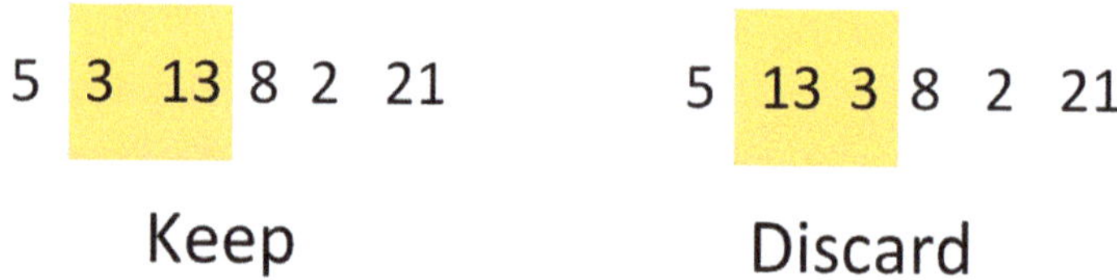

FIGURE 2.1. Discarding inversions.

That number is given by $m = \log_2(n!)$. That's because $n!$ can be halved m times (from the definition of logarithms). But that's not super helpful. We can develop an *upper bound* for m (i.e., guarantee that it is less than a certain function of n) as follows:

$$\mathrm{m} = \log_2(n!) = \sum_{i=1}^{n} \log_2 i \leq \sum_{i=1}^{n} \log_2 n$$

Therefore, $m \leq n\log_2 n$. In other words, the minimum number of comparisons that we *must* perform to comparison sort n elements is no greater than $n\log_2 n$. This is an important result, and we will revisit it many times in this book. If we can find an actual solution to the sorting problem that requires approximately $n\log_2 n$ comparisons (we can), we will have improved the pair-based brute-force workload from $\frac{n^2}{2}$ to an optimal $n\log_2 n$.

Logarithms

HISTORY NOTES

In the 21st century, it's easy to forget that multiplication is much harder than addition. Why? Because when we add two m-digit numbers together, it will require $2m-1$ separate additions. But if we multiply two m-digit numbers, we must perform m^2 products and additions. In the 17th century, it was all too obvious. John Napier first described how to use the addition of logarithms as a substitute for multiplication in 1614. During this author's lifetime, it was still normal to do everyday multiplication by logarithms—using the invaluable aid of a "slide rule."

First, let's review the main identities of logarithms:

1. If $x = b^p$, then $p = \log_b x$ where b is an (arbitrary) base. The bases of interest in this course are 2 and e (Euler's number).
   Additionally, if $y = b^q$, we can write $xy = b^p b^q = b^{p+q}$ and so $p + q = \log_b xy$.
2. Therefore, $\log_b xy = \log_b x + \log_b y$.

Logarithms play a crucial part in the study of complexity. This is because the most effective—and most common—optimization technique substitutes log n for n in expressions of complexity, an example of which we just saw in the section on search problems. This potentially dramatic improvement arises from presorting a collection of elements. For example, presorting 1,024 elements might result in an algorithm reducing its execution time by a factor of 512/10, or 50 in round numbers. That is a significant improvement! Because this optimization is so important, we give it a name: the *dictionary principle*.

The natural logarithm (i.e., $\log_e$)x is, as usual, denoted by $\ln x$. And, following general practice in the United States, we denote $\log_2 x$ as $\lg x$. This may come as a surprise to those of you who are used to following international standards.

The Dictionary Principle (revisited)

Imagine that you are holding in your hands an English dictionary (yes, a physical book of word definitions). You need to look up the meaning of a word, for example, *facetious*. Suppose that there are 838 pages. We look at the words on page 419 (halfway). They all begin with M, so we know that our word is in the first half of the dictionary. Let's check page 210—where we find words beginning with E. Now, we must find the midpoint of the higher page range: page 315, which is all H's. We continue with

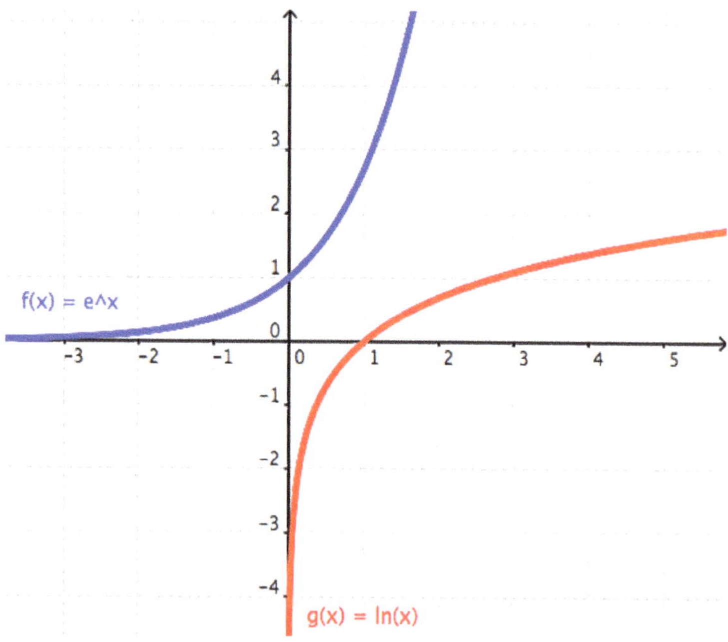

FIGURE 2.2. Natural logarithm and exponential function.

pages 262, 236, 223, 229, 226, 228. We had to check 9 pages (it would have been 10 if we had chosen 227 after 226). We call this search algorithm *binary search*. The dictionary principle can be summarized as follows: If you take the trouble to sort an array of elements, you will be able to speed up searching by performing binary search.

Note that we *halved* the size of the search space at each stage of the algorithm. How many times (h) can we halve a number n such that we end up with just one? The answer is $\log_2 n$. If $n = 2$, $h = 1$, and so on. In our dictionary search, $\log_2 838 = 9.71$, so we would expect either 9 or 10 steps in our search—exactly as we found. Sometimes, of course, we get lucky and find the word with fewer steps. If we'd been looking instead for *frivolous*, we'd have found it in only four steps.

But let's not forget the cost of sorting. How many operations (in particular, comparisons) does it take to sort n distinct elements? From the previous section, we know that it is, at a minimum, something like $n \log_2 n$. You will need to perform a considerable number of word searches to make up for the initial cost of the presort. Of course, when you buy a printed dictionary, part of the price of the purchase is for the sorting of the words.

You plan to sort a list of ***n*** words for an internal dictionary in your application. At least how many searches should you expect to do such that you break even in total comparisons performed?

Rocket Science

Another property of logarithms is related to the sum of the harmonic series:

$$S(k)=\sum_{i=1}^{k}\frac{1}{i}=1+\frac{1}{2}+\frac{1}{3}+\frac{1}{4}+\frac{1}{5}+\frac{1}{6}+\ldots+\frac{1}{k}$$

It can be shown that $\lim_{k\to\infty} S(k)=\ln(k)+\gamma$, where $\ln(k)$ is the natural logarithm of k (i.e., $\log_e k$) and where γ is the Euler-Mascheroni constant (approximately 0.58).

But are there any practical applications of this formula? Consider a space rocket made up of k stages. Each stage produces the same impulse ($\mathcal{I}$), the same increase in momentum. But, as each stage is depleted and falls away, the total mass of the vehicle is reduced, so each successive stage results in a greater change in the velocity (Δv) of the payload. If we assume that the mass (m) of the payload is the same as the (initial) mass of each stage, the $\Delta v_i = \frac{W}{k+1-i}$, where $W=\frac{\mathcal{I}}{m}$.

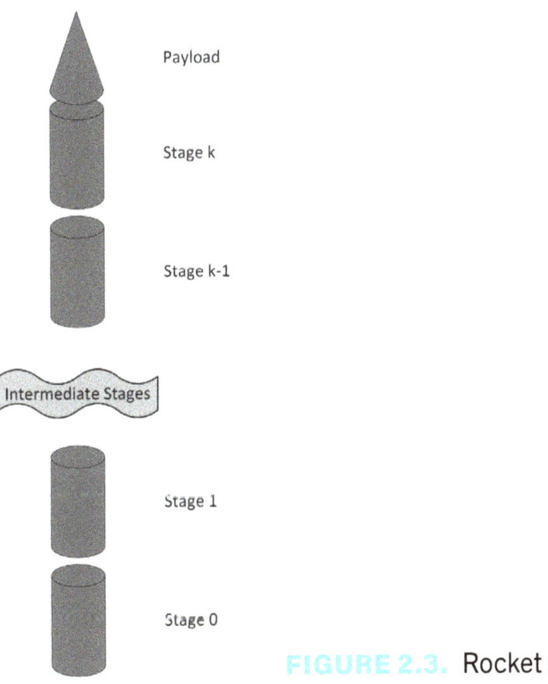

FIGURE 2.3. Rocket science.

Therefore, the final velocity of the payload is

$$V \sim \sum_0^{k-1}\Delta v_i \sim \sum_0^{k-1}\frac{W}{k+1-i} \sim \frac{W}{k+1}+\frac{W}{k}+\frac{W}{k-1}+\frac{W}{k-2}+\ldots+\frac{W}{2} \sim W(\ln(k+1)+\gamma-1).$$

Don't worry if this is a bit confusing—the idea is just to give you a visual appreciation of what logarithms are. We could also have considered another topic that people find tricky: compound interest.

Entropy

Information entropy (also known as Shannon entropy) is a measure of the expectation of information emanating from a random source. Like thermodynamic entropy, it is a measure of randomness or disorder.

Let $p(x)$ be the probability of event x occurring. Note that a certain event has $p(x)=1$, while an impossible event has $p(x)=0$. Let $q(x)$ be the information provided by event x. Since information is cumulative, we can state that $q(x)>0$.

A certain event provides no information when it occurs; an improbable event provides much information. Therefore, we expect the expression $\frac{dq}{dp}<0$. The only logical way that we can relate these quantities, given the constraints listed above, is if

$$q(x)=-\log p(x)$$

Entropy, that is, the expectation of information, is simply the product of $p(x)$ and $q(x)$ summed over all possible events. If all events are equally possible, the expression for entropy (h) simplifies to

$$h=-\sum_{i=0}^{n-1} p(x)\log p(x)=-\sum_{i=0}^{n-1}\frac{1}{n}\log\frac{1}{n}=\log n$$

For example, let us consider the roll of a true six-sided die. If we consider the die as a random source, its entropy is therefore *log*(6).

Thus far, we have not specified a base of logarithms. However, it is conventional to measure information entropy in terms of bits (yes/no decisions) and therefore the entropy for a six-sided die is $\log_2 6=2.585$ bits.

If your random source can produce n equally probable events, and you were to use it to generate one result that was invisible to me, I could still find out the result simply by asking either $\lfloor\log_2 n\rfloor or \lfloor\log_2 n\rfloor$ yes/no questions. For the die example, where $n=6$, I would need either two or three questions. Let's say you roll a 5. I ask you "Is the number odd?" and you respond, "Yes." There will now be three possibilities, 1, 3, or 5. There are two reasonable questions I can ask now: "Is the number greater than 1?" or "Is the number greater than 3?" If I choose the latter question (and the number is 5), you will answer yes, and I will know immediately that you rolled a 5. But if I happen to choose the former question, there will be two possibilities remaining: 3 or 5—so I must ask one further question.

An ordinary deck (pack) of 52 playing cards can be used as a random source if we shuffle it well and then ask someone to draw a card at random (and keep its identity hidden). How many questions must I ask the drawer before I too know the identity of the card? Give your answer as *p or q*. Hint: You will need the result we developed in "Sorting as a Search Problem."

In the game 20 Questions, the questioner thinks of some "thing." They tell you the category (animal, vegetable, or mineral) to which it belongs, and then you are allowed 20 yes/no questions to identify the thing. In round numbers, what's the greatest number of unique things such that you can reasonably expect to succeed?

Imagine that you are designing an encryption algorithm to protect passwords, and you require a source of random information. The two options you are considering are as follows:

- An integer formed from the number of nanoseconds elapsed since January 1, 1970. You may ignore the fact that approximately half of these bits aren't really random.
- Ask the user to shuffle an ordinary, deck (pack) of 52 playing cards and then deal 13 cards without replacing the cards back into the deck. The user then enters the identities of the 13 cards, in the order they were selected. Hint: You can approximate the answer with sufficient accuracy if you pretend that the cards are replaced in the deck (i.e., the entropy provided by each of the 13 cards is the same).

Estimate the entropy of each source and determine which provides the most.

Making Use of Entropy

How can we make use of entropy when solving problems? We can use it as a guide to the complexity of the best possible solution to a problem. For example, suppose that we have an array of n elements. The operation that we will perform on this array to sort it is the compare-and-maybe-swap ("coswap") operation applied to a pair of elements (not necessarily adjacent). What's the minimum number of coswaps required to sort the array?

Each coswap removes one bit of entropy from our problem. How much entropy do we start with? The array can be in any of $n!$ permutations to start with. If we choose our coswap operations with no redundancy, each one will result in separating the search space into two piles: those with the pair in order, and those with the pair inverted. The minimum number of coswaps to achieve perfect order will therefore be $\lg n!$ In Chapter 7 (Optimal Sorting), we will see that this is approximately $n \lg n$.

Asymptotic Bounds

When studying problems and their solutions, it is usually much too difficult to derive a precise expression for the growth of the resource (time and/or memory) required. Instead, we usually are content to describe the bounds of the growth as the size of the problem gets larger and larger. These bounds are known as *asymptotic* because they apply to the situation when $n \to \infty$. First, we must carefully consider whether we are bounding the problem or one of its solutions.

Big Omega

In order to get an idea of the complexity of a *problem*, we think about the minimum possible number of operations required to solve the problem (as we did above in Making Use of Entropy). There are two cases we care about: the *best case*, when the input is favorable, and the *average case*, when the input is random.

Suppose that we have a list of n elements and we want to find an element with a particular value. At the moment we are not concerned with any particular solution. What's the best possible case? We find the element in the first place we look. But that situation is not really intrinsic to the problem because we don't know in advance about this favorable situation. It's more a consequence of a solution that just happens to get lucky. So, for this problem, we conclude that there really is no best case.

How can we express the growth of the problem as n increases? If we double the size of the problem, it's clear that, however we go about solving the problem, the growth of the resources required is also going to double. In practice, there are probably many possible solutions to this simple problem, but, because potentially we must see every element and, recognizing that some solutions might actually be somewhat inefficient, we can describe the problem by saying that

$$r(n) = cn + \varepsilon(n)$$

where $r(n)$ represents the required resources for any solution to the problem, c is a constant, and $\varepsilon(n)$ represents some unknown function of n which grows more slowly than n. Regardless of the size of $\varepsilon(n)$ when $n = 1$; because $\varepsilon(n)$ grows more slowly than n, it will eventually be insignificant compared with cn. In other words, we can write

$$r(n) \to cn \text{ as } n \to \infty, \text{ while } r(n) > cn \text{ otherwise.}$$

There is a convenient and well-understood shorthand for this expression:

$$r(n) = \Omega(n),$$

which is pronounced "$r(n)$ equals **big Omega** of n." Note that since c is a constant, it doesn't affect the *rate* of growth, and since these asymptotic bounds are concerned only with growth, we do not include c inside the big Omega function.

Generalizing this concept for other problems, we will normally say that a problem is $\Omega(f(n))$, where $f(n)$ is some growth function that cannot be bettered by any solution. Note that determining such a function $f(n)$ is not always so easy! History is full of such mistakes.

HISTORY NOTES

In 1960, world-renowned Soviet mathematician Andrey Kolmogorov posed a series of mathematical problems, one of which stated that the problem of multiplying two $\boldsymbol{n}$-digit numbers must require $\Omega(\boldsymbol{n}^2)$ operations. Within a week, 23-year-old student Anatoly Karatsuba had found a solution whose growth of operations was $\boldsymbol{n}^{\log_2 3}$, thus falsifying Kolmogorov's conjecture. The story continues as Kolmogorov wrote and published a paper on the solution—not with his own name as author but with Karatsuba's!

Big O

Now that we think we know the lower bounds for a problem, we need to see if we can find a solution that matches those bounds. If we find such a solution, it is called *optimal*.

For a solution, we are particularly interested in the worst case. If possible, we want to bound the resources required, thus providing a *guarantee* that the resources cannot possibly be worse than the bounding function. In general, for a solution, we want to say

$$r(n) = f(n) - \varepsilon(n),$$

where *f*(*n*) grows more rapidly than $\varepsilon(n)$, such that $r(n) \to f(n)$ as $n \to \infty$ while $r(n) < f(n)$ otherwise.

As we did before, we introduce a shorthand for this expression:

$$r(n) = \mathrm{O}(f(n)).$$

More succinctly, we say that a particular solution "is" O(*f*(*n*)), pronounced "big Oh of *f*(*n*)" (rather than big Omicron).

Except for trivial problems, the solution to all practical problems involves reduction. To find a suitable reduction, we must model the problem. For searching a list, we might be tempted to model the list as a sorted array. This entails a reduction that first converts the list to an array, then sorts the list, and then uses binary search. Would this solution be optimal? No, because one of the steps grows according to $\Omega(n \log n)$ and thus the overall growth is $\Omega(n \log n)$, which grows more rapidly than *n*.

How about simply traversing the list element by element (modeling the problem as is)? In this case, the average number of elements we must examine before finding the right one is $\frac{n}{2}$, but the worst case (corresponding to our guarantee) is n. As with big Omega, we do not include any constants in our function *f*(*n*).

The purpose of **big O** (and big Omega) is to *classify* solutions (and problems) according to their growth. A *O*(log *n*) solution is fundamentally different from a *O*(*n*) solution, which in turn is fundamentally different from a *O*(*n* log *n*) solution. Thus, they belong to different classes of solution. It is similar for problems and big Omega.

Big Theta

We should not entirely neglect Theta because you will encounter it occasionally. It is used similarly to a combination of big O and big Omega:

$$r(n) = f(n) \pm \varepsilon(n),$$

which we write as

$$r(n) = \Theta(f(n)).$$

This is like saying that $r(n) = O(f(n))$ & $\Omega(f(n))$. In practice, its use is similar to that of ~, but we ignore any constant factors.

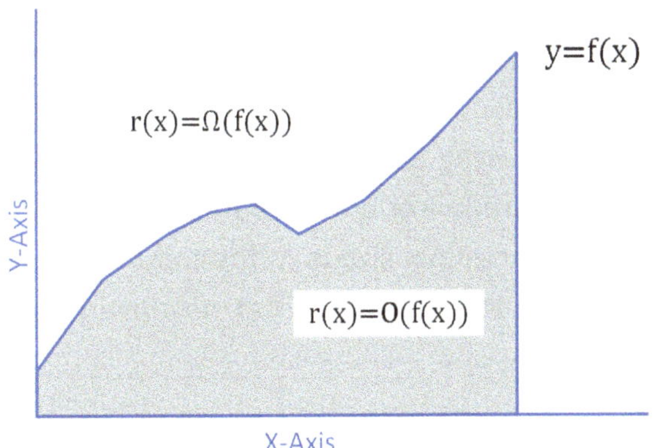

FIGURE 2.4. Asymptotic bounds.

In Figure 2.4, the possible functions *r*(*n*) where $r(n) = O(f(n))$ all lie below the curve for *f*(*n*) while *r*(*n*) is always above the curve where $r(n) = \Omega(f(n))$. It's harder to show big Theta, but you can think of possible *r*(*n*) functions as being close to, but not necessarily on, *f*(*n*) where $r(n) = \Theta(f(n))$. As with big O and big Omega, $r(n) \rightarrow f(n)$ as $n \rightarrow \infty$. In all these situations, don't forget that any constant coefficients are eliminated from the relevant functions.

Tilde

Another measure of growth that is more of an approximation, and that does not attempt to bound the growth in either direction, is **tilde** (~). Formally,

$$\text{if } f(n) \sim g(n) \text{ then } \frac{f(n)}{g(n)} \rightarrow 1 \text{ as } n \rightarrow \infty$$

Note that this definition implies that constants are significant when using ~. For example, we benchmark a sorting algorithm, and it appears that $t \sim 20 n \lg n$ nanoseconds. The result is empirical, and we have no basis for any kind of guarantee of performance, so instead of big O, we employ "~".

Amortized Cost

Sometimes the cost of an operation is described as *amortized*; for example, the amortized cost of adding an element to a resizable array is $O(1)$ (i.e., constant time). The meaning is that, over a large number of operations, such as addition, the total cost can be spread out among each of the operations. This amortized cost can indeed be considered constant time even though individual additions incur a significant resizing. We must still be careful, however. In the case of resizing an array, suppose that we resize the array by adding *m* elements to the current size (*n*) whenever the array is full. Then $m-1$ additions will incur a cost of $a(m-1)$, where *a* is the cost of one array access. The last addition will incur a cost of at least $2nma$, yielding an average—or amortized—cost of $\sim 2na$. If $N = km$ so that *k* resizings take place and the final size is *N*, the total cost is $\sim kaN$, which does indeed work out to $\sim ka$ as the amortized cost, assuming that $k \gg 1$.

Multivariate Complexity

It is common to encounter a measure of complexity that involves a different variable that is a choice of the algorithm rather than determined by the size of the problem. For example, in the previous section on amortized cost, we ended up with $\sim ka$. In this case, *k* is the subject of a choice, while *a* is truly a constant.

The asymptotic bounds notations $O(f(n)), \Omega(g(n))$, and so on, focus on *n* only. Yet, many solutions do involve a second algorithm-specific value, *k*. Since *k* is chosen for the algorithm, for example, the load factor for a hash table, it will not appear in the asymptotic bounds. However, when comparing two solutions with the same growth rate, it does make sense to consider such a *k* value.

3SUM Case Study

3SUM is a classic problem and an excellent exemplar of the process of optimization. While there are legitimate applications of the 3SUM problem, its importance lies in the fact that it is representative of many similar problems involving computational complexity. We will study it here as an illustration of problem solving.

Given a set of *n* real numbers, identify all the triples that sum to zero. It should be clear that a brute-force approach to this problem is going to take $O(n^3)$ time because we must validate each of $\binom{n}{3}$ triples. That is, the number of ways we can choose three from *n* distinct objects: $\frac{n(n-1)(n-2)}{6}$. (Note that we can treat them as distinct because they are real numbers.)

Let us now give some thought to the problem rather than any particular solution. We can model the problem as choosing a pair and a singleton. The absolute minimum possible growth must therefore depend on the number of ways of choosing a pair, $\binom{n}{2}$ or $\frac{n(n-1)}{2}$. Although it's not yet clear how we might solve this model of the problem, let's assume for now that the 3SUM problem is $\Omega(n^2)$ and see if we can find a solution that is $O(n^2)$, and thus optimal.

What about memory usage? If we can find a solution that avoids storing each pair of elements, we may be able to avoid any extra memory at all, other than the result. However, we are likely to need to sort the elements and if so we might need $\Omega(n)$ extra memory if we end up using merge sort. A memory-optimal solution would therefore be $O(n)$.

Quadrithmic Solution

Let's start by building a table of all pairs of elements, finding their sums, and then, for each entry (sum $\rightarrow$ pair), add it to an ordered symbol table. Then, for each element, we look to see if there are any complementary sums (such that the element and the pair would sum to zero) and retrieve the list of matching pairs. We call this the *quadrithmic* solution by extension from a *linearithmic* solution. What would be the complexity of this solution?

Phase 1: Identify and sum each pair: $O(n^2)$ for both memory and operations.

Phase 2: Build the ordered symbol table, assuming insertion time is logarithmic: $O(n^2 \log(n^2)) \sim O(n^2 \log(n))$.

Phase 3: For each element, find any complementary pairs (assume search time is logarithmic): $O(n \log n)$.

The total time for the solution is $O(n \log n + n^2 + n^2 \log n)$. Of these, the dominant term is $O(n^2 \log n)$. The total memory required is $O(n^2)$. Clearly, this is not an optimal solution either by memory or operations.

The Principle of Complementary Pairs

The dictionary principle reduces complexity from n to $\log n$, or n^2 to $n \log n$. But there is a technique whereby we can reduce the number of interesting pairs from $O(n^2)$ to $O(n)$ provided that the collection is ordered and we have a function that can determine if two elements are complementary. Actually, we need the function to also indicate—when two elements are not complementary—whether we should aim up or down in the order to find the next complementary pair. The simplest example of this is when the elements are integers and complementary, which implies that their sum is zero. If the sum of two elements is nonzero, we know in which direction to proceed based on whether the sum is positive or negative.

Quadratic Solution

Let's try to improve our quadrithmic solution by using the principle of complementary pairs. For that we will need to sort the elements first, taking time $O(n \log n)$.

Let our outer loop (j) run linearly over all the elements and divide the array into two partitions. Then we apply our complementary pair function to the two partitions starting with $i = j-1$ and $k = j+1$; we run the inner loop as long as $i \geq 0$ and $k < n$. Inside this inner loop, we evaluate the sum (s) of the triple from indices $\{i, j, k\}$. If $s = 0$, add it to the resulting list and increment k. If $s < 0$, increment k; otherwise ($s > 0$), decrement i. This works (in linear time) because, if we don't get a triple, we only ever change one index at a time and only in the direction that suggests that we will succeed.

-38	-23	-15	-12	-6	17	18	37	42	43
0	1	2	3	4	5	6	7	8	0
			i	j		k			

FIGURE 2.5. Solution of 3SUM

In Figure 2.5, we have an array of 10 elements, each a random integer between −49 and +50. Consider the situation when $j = 4$ (the fifth pass of the outer loop). The inner loop begins with $i = 3$ and $k = 5$. The sum is –1, and thus we increment k such that the sum is now zero—we have found a triple. Indeed, this is the only triple that sums to zero.

The outer loop is linear over n, and the inner loop is linear over n; therefore, the search phase is $O(n^2)$. The initial sorting phase is $O(n \log n)$, but that grows more slowly than the search phase and therefore becomes insignificant.

Our complementary pairs solution is indeed optimal for operations (quadratic) and memory (we don't need any extra memory except perhaps in the sorting phase). Note that this method works for any general function $f(i, j, k)$ provided that the result has three states: less than zero, zero, and greater than zero.

HISTORY NOTES

Until 2014, it was widely assumed that 3SUM was $\Omega(n^2)$. But, as with Kolmogorov and multiplication, it turns out that we can do better. Such algorithms are beyond the scope of this book.

Conclusion

We have prepared the ground for the next chapter (on abstract data types). ADTs are the basic building blocks of software development. But it's important to understand how they behave, especially as the size *n* of the data structure grows to very large numbers.

You learned how we tend to use ~ expressions for generally describing the complexity of a solution, particularly considering the average (random) case. But you also learned how to guarantee that the growth of complexity cannot be worse than a certain function of *n* (using big O) and how, for a given problem, we can at least try to show that there is a function of *n* (using big Omega) such that no solution can grow less than the function. You also saw how we can try to solve a problem (in this case 3SUM) by estimating the best possible growth for any solution and then iterating over actual solutions until you find one that is optimal.

Looking ahead to the chapter on abstract data types, here is a teaser that regards various ADTs as "solutions" to hypothetical problems and shows the expected complexity.

TABLE 2.2 The Bigger Picture: The Costs of Data Types

ABSTRACT DATA TYPE WITH CAPACITY n	ADDITIONAL MEMORY	ACCESS WITHIN CACHE	INSERT/ DELETE	SEARCH	SHARE WITH SAFETY
Array	$O(1)$	$O(1)$	$O(1)$	$O(n)$	$O(n)$
Ordered Array	$O(1)$		$O(n)$	$O(\lg n)$	$O(n)$
Binary Heap	$O(1)$		$O(\lg n)$		
Linked List/Stack	$O(n)$	$O(n)$	$O(1)$ at head	$O(n)$	$O(1)$
Red-Black Tree	$O(n)$		$O(\lg n)$	$O(\log n)$	
Hash Table	$O(n)$		$\Theta(1)$	$\Theta(1)$	

Takeaways

Following is a list of the main ideas to take away from this chapter:

- Complexity is an important aspect of abstract data types because it is impossible to estimate how long a task will take without understanding the complexity of the ADT in question.
- Benchmarking is the most practical way of measuring the complexity of an ADT, even if you think you know it from theoretical considerations.
- The time required to execute a process depends primarily on its memory usage and secondarily on its instructions (although a large number of floating-point instructions might slow things down). Furthermore, the circumstances of memory access are significant: Is it simply accessing an element in an array? Or is it additionally having to look up a reference on the heap?
- Big Ω and big O should properly be applied to problems and solutions, respectively.
- The dictionary principle recognizes that there is a significant cost incurred when sorting that can only be recouped with sufficient search operations.

Chapter Review Questions

Directions: Refer to what you learned in this chapter to respond to the questions and prompts:

- The definition of information entropy comes directly from the requirement that combining probabilities requires multiplication while combining information requires addition. Can you repeat the steps that Claude Shannon took almost 100 years ago?
- Why do we consider constant factors when using the ~ (tilde) operator but not when using the asymptotic operators such as big O?
- What is the key to using the principle of complementary pairs?
- Under what circumstances can we share a linked list "safely" in constant time? Why can't we share an array safely in constant time?

CHAPTER

3

What Are Abstract Data Types?

And Why Do We Need Them?

Introduction to the Chapter

We have reached perhaps the most important chapter in our book. Why do we care about abstract data types? What do they actually do for us? And why do they have such a complicated name? We need ADTs to represent the *state* of the solution to a (sub)-problem. Furthermore, we need to understand their behaviors so that we can use them efficiently and for the appropriate use cases.

Abstract data types are the LEGO Bricks of the software development world and, as such, take on an enormously important role in the development of (computer) applications. They are the basic reusable software component and can save developers a lot of time—if properly understood. Developers do not take as much advantage of the ADTs that are already written and tested.

Learning Objectives

In this chapter students will learn about the following:

1. How we represent states of the solution to a problem
2. What options we have for storing information
3. What is meant by the term abstract data type (ADT)
4. The role of abstract data types in problem solving

5. The three key attributes of an abstract data type: data structure, algorithms, invariants
6. How to choose from among similar ADTs for a particular use case
7. How to read/write an application programming interface (API) such that the advantages and disadvantages of an ADT are clear

Key Terms

The following important terms will be introduced in this chapter:

- **State:** An information model which is represented by a data structure
- **Algorithm:** A series of steps required to transform one state into another
- **Abstract Data Type (ADT):** A composite type that embodies a data structure (state), algorithm(s), and invariant(s)
- **Explicit:** A data structure that uses pointers that define specific relationships between elements
- **Implicit:** A data structure that does not use pointers but relationships between elements are based on their actual positions (indexes)
- **Array:** A fixed-length, contiguous, mutable collection of elements of a particular type
- **List:** A variable-length, noncontiguous, immutable collection of elements of a particular type
- **Application Programming Interface** (API)**:** A contract between the developer and a user of an ADT

Representing State

INSIGHT

"Show me your flowcharts and conceal your tables, and I shall continue to be mystified. Show me your tables, and I won't usually need your flowcharts; they'll be obvious" (Brooks, 1975, Chapter 9: Representation is the Essence of Programming).

These days, we would probably substitute **algorithms** for flowcharts and data structures for tables, but the message is as true today as it was almost 50 years ago. Of the triad of data structures, invariants, and algorithms, we should always be able to infer one from the other two. The easiest of these inferences is, I believe, data structure + invariants => algorithms. If any part of programming is amenable to automated code generation, this should be it.

Recall from Chapter 1 that an essential part of problem solving is representing the **state** of the solution. This follows directly from the concept of *reduction*. Of course, our state will be made up of bits and bytes in some organized manner. Each independent component of state—whether it's an index, a scalar, an **array**, or some other collection—must be *typed*. We need to know how to interpret the bits and bytes as higher level objects—indexes, scalars, and so on. Note that not every programming language requires an explicit type; compilers are good at inferring types. In what follows, we will cover the concepts of state and types in more detail.

A state may be simple (e.g., a single Boolean value) or complex (e.g., a complete relational model of a database in memory). However, for an application to be considered well written, the granularity of the ADTs should be such that each ADT *does one thing—and does it well*. You should generally resist the temptation to throw more stuff into an ADT.

Ideally, there will be a finite number of possible states (a finite state machine) because that makes the state easier to reason about. As an example, an empty stack is a state; a stack with one element is another state; and so on. There are exactly two transitions required to implement the transitions between states of a stack:

- push, which increases the number of elements on the stack
- pop, which decreases the number of elements on the stack

You already know about the most basic data structures: arrays and **lists**. We will consider these in some detail here. And you are familiar with the standard simple data types: integers, floating point numbers ("double"), bytes, Booleans. But, in the real world, we need to be able to handle aggregations of information at the same time (i.e., with *one* reference). This is because we want to be able to apply logic to these more complex groupings of data such that the logic is applied appropriately to all individual elements of such a grouping.

Data Types

Some data types are very well known and understood. Of these, Boolean is the simplest. The cardinality of its domain is two: the only values are *true* and *false*. There is thus only one operator that can be applied to a single Boolean, and that is negate (!). We can create a truth table for this: $!true \Leftrightarrow false$. With two Booleans, we will need a two-dimensional truth table (Table 3.1).

TABLE 3.1 Truth Table for Two Booleans

	TRUE	**FALSE**
true	true	$f \Rightarrow true,$ $g \Rightarrow false$
false	$f \Rightarrow true,$ $g \Rightarrow false$	false

Leaving aside the exclusive-or (XOR) operation for now (which can be composed of the other operators), we can reasonably assume that two truths must yield true and two falsehoods must yield false. But we have a choice when it comes to the true/false combinations: function *f* (which always yields true) or function *g* (which always yields false). Since logic tells us that if *either a or b* is true, the result is true; and, similarly, the result is true only if *both a and b* are true; therefore, *f* must correspond to *or* ($\vee$), and *g* must correspond to *and* ($\wedge$). Thus, there are only three operators and two values that completely define Boolean algebra. Here we've defined an algebraic data type (another kind of ADT), which is a similar concept but not the focus of our attention.

We can apply similar arguments to the *byte* data type. A byte is just eight bits, each of which can be considered a Boolean. Thus, we can also apply logic operators to bytes. A byte doesn't have a value in the sense of something we all agree on. It can be converted to a *character* (or, at least, a partial character), given a particular encoding. And a sequence of bytes requires a direction ("bigendian" versus "littleendian"). Nevertheless, bytes have been sufficiently universal that, for decades, they have been the chief mechanism for inter-system communication.

And so on to integers: We have to define their actual bit lengths and bit patterns because these will have a profound effect. If we choose 32 two-complement bits, with a "sign bit" at the high end, we can represent all the integers from $-2^{31} \ldots 2^{31}-1$. But this representation has the drawback that if we add one to $2^{31}-1$, we get the result: -2^{31}. That's not ideal but, because the integer type is so well known and understood, we can live with it.

HISTORICAL NOTE

The binary search implementation of Java fell foul of this issue until it was noted and resolved in 2006. When determining the integer index at the midpoint of an array, it matters whether you evaluate $\frac{(lo+hi)}{2}$ or $lo+\frac{(hi-lo)}{2}$. Can you see why?

Floating-point numbers are another well-known data type. Their representation and operations are typically defined by standards (IEEE 754 in particular). Beyond these and a few other basic data types that might vary between languages, two data types are sufficiently fundamental that we can consider them to be well known: (a) the array and (b) the pointer (memory reference). But, because they are the building blocks of aggregate data structures, we will discuss them in more detail later.

Composite Data Types

The definition of data type might have given the impression that the value is always a simple value, like an integer. Depending on the language used, it could be any union of values, each itself from a data type, in which case the domain will be the Cartesian product of the individual domains. But perhaps the most common and obvious composite data type is an array. Each element of the array will itself be a value of some data type, for example, an array of integers.

What all these data types have in common is that the programmer needs to understand not only the domain and operators but also the representation itself because this will inform proper usage. A data type such that the programmer does not need to know the details of either the representation or the algorithms is called an **abstract data type (ADT)**.

Abstract Data Types

The simple data types mentioned are not going to be sufficient for object-oriented programming. A language like FORTRAN (up through FORTRAN 77, at least), which was unable to define structures more complex than arrays, was severely limited in the kinds of programs that could be built.

DEFINITION

An abstract data type defines a class of abstract objects that is completely characterized by the operations available on those objects. This means that an abstract data type can be defined by defining the characterizing operations for that type (Liskov & Zilles, 1974).

What is abstract about an abstract data type? There are, in general, many implementations—both in terms of algorithms and data structures—that can satisfy the API. From the programmer's point of view, such details are (or should be) unimportant. Even when there is only one possible implementation, an ADT might still be abstract if it is based on a (nonconcrete) parametric type: its "underlying" type (e.g., the type of individual elements). In the Java language, these are called "generic" types. The reason for having generic types for structures like *List* is that we want to follow the *Don't repeat yourself* (DRY) principle of programming. Finding the length of a list, for example, shouldn't depend on the type of elements in the list. The code should be written once and used for all lists. Hence the need for parametric (generic) types. If we draw a Venn diagram with *all types* as the union of the simple and well-known "data types," as well as other data types, we need a label for these others. For our purposes, we will call them "abstract data types."

So far, we have observed that of all the data types available, some are well known and understood (the simple **data types**). Now we will talk about everything else. Some authors suggest that the difference between a data type and an *abstract* data type has to do with knowledge of the internals. However, that is not a distinction that has much merit.

There is, of course, an infinitude of different abstract data types. They are limited only by your imagination and perhaps the memory constraints of your computer. And many of them are known by well-known names. However, because such names can have varying implementations, it is not safe to consider these to be well-known data types. So, how do we know what defines the domain, the properties, and the behaviors of an ADT? It must be defined somewhere! By convention, it is defined in the **application programming interface (API)**. This is a strange name for the concept because the term *application* has been coopted to mean a complete program. But, here, *application* simply refers to any client code that *applies* the ADT in some way.

HISTORICAL NOTE

In the early days of programming (we didn't call it software development or coding in those days), large software projects almost always ended up being late or failing. See, for example, Fred Brooks's (1975) *The Mythical Man-Month*. The problem was that complex programs could not be easily reasoned about. The development of languages with procedures and blocks enabled teams to write programs in smaller modules—which could be reasoned about, understood, and tested. One of the key contributions in this field was made by Barbara Liskov, recipient of the 2008 Turing Award. The idea of ADTs was introduced in 1974 in the paper "Programming With Abstract Data Types" (Liskov & Zilles, 1974).

READ AT: https://dl.acm.org/doi/10.1145/942572.807045

Invariants

Invariants are the properties, or combinations of properties, of an ADT that do not change from one state to the next. Note that it is normal and expected that these invariants may change while the ADT is in transition between states. There are at least two types of invariant: (1) API invariant, and (2) internal invariant (often referred to as a loop invariant). The invariants of the first type determine exactly how a data structure supports the various operations required by the API. Thus, when an ADT is at rest, all API invariants will apply. Conversely, while an algorithm of the ADT is running, API invariants will generally not be maintained. Similarly, internal invariants will apply when some internal procedure is not running. This internal procedure might be a private method, a loop, or—potentially—any change of scope. The further inside an invariant applies, the narrower its scope will be. For example, insertion sort, which operates on an array, has an inner loop that inserts a transitional element into its proper place in the ordered sub-array. The loop invariant can be characterized as saying that, when that inner loop is not running, elements on the left of the outer loop index are in the imposed order, while the elements to the right of that index are still in their original order. Only when the outer loop of insertion sort terminates and control is returned to the caller, do we expect the entire array to be in the proper order (the API invariant).

The most significant invariant, when present, is the order of placement of elements in the data structure. Many, perhaps most, useful ADTs impose an order of some sort. Some have no concept of order. Usually, the first question you need to ask yourself when considering which ADT to employ is "Do I need the elements to be ordered in some way?" By *order*, we mean something more significant than placement. A FIFO queue might be said to be ordered—first come, first served—but that is an ordering based on when an element was inserted. A priority queue, on the other hand, is not concerned much with the order in which elements are added; instead it will always yield the highest priority item, even if that element has only just joined the queue.

Let's consider an ADT that is to replace a simple filing system for customer accounts. A small company may have only a few customers, and therefore a single filing cabinet drawer is sufficient to hold the files. When a new customer is added, the file is placed in its appropriate place according to alphabetical order. This makes lookup extremely efficient so that if a customer calls on the phone, their file can quickly be located. Using the dictionary principle, we can retrieve a file in time proportional to the logarithm of the number of customers. However, the total amount of work required to arrange the files in the drawer is quadratic in the number of customers! Quadratic operations do not scale, as we saw in Chapter 2. But, in our example, all that work can be spread out over several years, so it is not a burden. You may be thinking that we can locate the appropriate place to insert the new customer in logarithmic time, just like retrieval. This is true, but we may need to make room for the customer, and this is typically a linear process—perhaps not in the simple filing cabinet situation, but it would be the case with the customers arranged in an array.

However, a new product has increased the number of customers tenfold, and the replacement system must satisfy both the rapid insertion of new customers and the location of existing customers. Yes, we should probably also be concerned about losing customers. Whatever we choose, we know that the ADT we require will be ordered. Should we stick with an ordered array (the equivalent of our filing cabinet drawer)? It has the advantage of simplicity, and if the expected number of customers is modest, the insertion time will not be excessive. However, here we come to another of the big questions that we must answer: Can we afford the additional memory required for an index in the form of a tree? If we can, then we should. This will give us logarithmic insertion time, as well as logarithmic retrieval time. In other words, we will have created an ADT that maintains order while minimizing insertion and retrieval times. The notion of sorting, as when we sorted the ordered array, no longer applies to this ADT. The ordering is implicit in the structure of the tree. (We will examine this in more detail in Chapter 6.) Therefore, the most significant invariant that we should consider for an ADT—according to our use case—is whether it should be ordered.

Data Structures

We postponed our discussion of arrays and pointers from the section on data types to this section. A pointer is a reference to a location in memory that holds a value of some sort. On its own, this doesn't sound very exciting. But pointers can be arranged in serial or parallel fashion to allow for lists and trees. Indeed, the active memory locations in the so-called heap form a directed graph of associations. Each edge of the graph (each pointer) also carries with it, at least in an object-oriented context, the type being referenced. Thus, the pointer mechanism is the most powerful and flexible tool we have for creating data structures.

The other primary mechanism for creating data structures is the array. It is really like a pointer with a length, as it also can carry information about the type of the elements in the array. We will discuss arrays, together with the structures that can be built from pointers, in the next section.

In the last chapter, we saw that when large data sets are involved, the number of memory accesses (hits) is a good predictor of execution time. That's because large data sets don't entirely fit in cache and the time to service a cache page fault can be amortized over all the memory accesses of the page.

We note that arithmetic operations on indexes and other (singleton) variables do not contribute much to the overall execution time and can generally be ignored. Therefore, we should concentrate on the use of bulk memory (collections). There are two fundamentally different types of collection, from which all others are derived. These are **implicit** and **explicit** data structures, typified by the notions of arrays and lists.

Indeed, the choice between using an implicit (array-like) and explicit (list-like) data structure boils down to the classic space versus time trade-off. Pointer-based (explicit) structures use more memory, but they are also much more flexible. To make a proper decision you must carefully consider your use case: What operations will typically be required to build and maintain the data structure?

Arrays and Lists

An *implicit* data structure is one where the space used by the structure is dedicated to values. The classic example of an implicit data structure is the *array*. An array of sixteen 4-byte integers will take 64 bytes. In an *explicit* data structure, some of the space used is required for pointers. A linked list of sixteen 4-byte integers would require the same 64 bytes as for the array, plus space for the sixteen pointers (at least another 64 bytes).

Arrays

Let's start with the array since it relates most closely to a block of memory. It's just a pointer to the start of the block, together with a length and a stride (the latter being the size in bytes required for each element). In typed languages, each element of an array will be of the same type (or a sub-type). In effect, an array is a contiguous collection of variables. An array has some big advantages with a few, relatively minor, disadvantages:

- Implicit: No space is "wasted" by pointers. There may be an implied relationship between elements according to their positions. Perhaps successive elements are placed in the order they were inserted; or, in another scenario, the array has been sorted and the elements are in their natural order.

Constant time access to any random element; that is, the time to access any element—with a known index—is not dependent on the length of the array. Strictly speaking, this is not quite accurate. Any array that is too large for the cache will require extra time whenever an element is addressed that is not currently in the cache. This extra time can be minimized if we access the elements in sequence (forward or backward) rather than purely at random since random access will tend to generate more page faults. We can also "amortize" the time taken for cache page faults, and thus we can consider access time to be constant.

- Mutability: Arrays are the perfect data structure for swapping the order of elements (as happens in sorting) or updating key-value pairs in a hash table, because arrays are designed for this type of work.

Arrays can be indexed only by a positive integer in a certain range: violations of this range will throw an exception. Other keys—when required for access—must first be converted into an integer in the given range (*hashing*). If an array is to be copied, it is typically inadvisable to simply copy the reference (starting address). This is because another method or thread may need to update its copy of the array. If both code fragments address the same memory, conflicts may arise. Therefore, for a safe copy of an array, the elements of the entire array must be copied. This will take time proportional to the length of the array (i.e., linear).

Arrays are allocated with a fixed length and cannot be trivially resized later. This is a consequence of the way data structures are packed into the memory "heap." Therefore, to "grow" an array, for example, a new (larger) array must be allocated and the original copied, element by element, into the new array. This will take linear time.

Lists

In this section, we take "list" to mean any data structure that is based on pointers rather than indexes. Lists therefore include trees and other pointer-based structures. Lists are the opposite of arrays, as we will see. We will discuss simple linked lists that can, generally speaking, be considered a head element followed by a tail, which is itself a (possibly empty) list.

- Explicit: Lists require pointers (*directed edges* in graph theory). The relationship between any two elements is characterized by the pointers that must be followed from one to the other.
- Constant time: Access to the head of the list, but linear time access to the other elements in the list. If you need access to an element that is not at the head of a list (and might be at the end of the list), you will in general have to spend time proportional to the length of the list. If required, random access to list elements can be implemented with an additional index (see, e.g., Java's ArrayList).
- Immutability: Whereas arrays are designed to allow for elements to change value, lists are designed to facilitate referencing sub-lists, with immutable elements. Of course, it's possible to have mutable lists, but doing so loses some of the advantages of lists.
- Extensibility: Lists are infinitely extensible subject to memory limitations. They have no fixed size.
- Shareability: Lists never need to be copied, assuming that they are immutable. A list is just a pointer that can safely be shared with other threads or methods. Sharing a list, then, is a constant-time operation because no copying is required.

- Generalization: The concept of a list—which is made up of elements, each with a value and a pointer—can easily be extended to trees and graphs.
- Performance: Lists are not as cache-friendly as arrays since an element is an object that must be instantiated somewhere on the heap but with no direct control over where in the heap it will be found. Therefore, traversing a list might trigger many cache page faults.

Because of the significant differences in properties between arrays and lists, they necessarily have different use cases. Arrays are well suited to sorting and hash tables, or any kind of lookup table where we can look up the properties of an element that is indexed by an integer zero through $n-1$. There is also a type of data structure called, somewhat confusingly, a "heap" wherein an array is used to represent a tree (see Chapter 6). Such a heap is typically used for a priority queue, which suggests, though does not require, a structure that does not need to grow in size. Arrays can also be used to implement a circular queue (see Chapter 5), although, like a hash table, it will sometimes be necessary to "grow" the array.

On the other hand, lists (and trees) do not require the size of a data structure to be known at construction time. This situation is common in practice because it's frequently the case that we don't know the size of something when we start reading it. For example, suppose you are reading a CSV (comma-separated values) file. Such files do not come with the number of rows defined in meta-data (unlike, e.g., a Parquet file).

Application Programming Interface

Applications

An application, regarding an abstract data type, is any client code that uses the ADT. However, we also use the word more broadly as the entire solution to a problem, which may depend on several ADTs as sub-solutions. The code that interacts with the ADTs will itself have state, and this state will *model* some aspect(s) of the real world. For example, suppose that you are programming a ticket agency. You will need to model at least two independent—but related—states: the set of unsold tickets and the corresponding set of sold tickets, each associated with its appropriate financial transaction data. Typically, each of these will be handled by an ADT. The job of the complete application is to ensure that changes to these ADTs are balanced: The sale of a block of tickets must be precisely balanced by adding a financial instrument such as a credit card transaction.

DISCUSSION

You might argue that you could combine these two states into one, and indeed you could. The drawback is that you will necessarily have to make the state mutable (i.e., some fields of your state will have to change their value during the execution of the ticket agency). This isn't necessarily a bad thing, but it can hinder the easy debugging of what is necessarily going to be a concurrent system.

API

As we've seen, a user (in this context, we mean programmer) interacts with an ADT through the API. You may think of this document as a legal contract between two parties: the developer and the user, or, if you prefer, between the implementation and the client code. Like any other contract, it may be the result of a process of negotiation. The odd thing is that, in practice, the content of the API is usually embedded in the code itself. In Java, for example, the API is extracted from the source code into a separate (but derivative) document by parsing block comments, the so-called "Javadoc." This makes it quite easy for the developer to change the API unilaterally. Perhaps a separate blockchain-based document would be preferable. In any case, the API should list all public methods, including any constructors, and carefully describe the following:

- the input parameters—including any preconditions
- the result, mentioning any error conditions that might arise (in Java, these are called *exceptions*)

It is also very likely that an API might refer to its super-API. For example, a *List* API might define only two methods: *next* and *value*. However, a MutableList API might include methods to update the *next* and *value* fields. But it will also extend the *List* API because a mutable list still needs to be traversed in the same way as any other list.

Ideally, the API should stipulate which packages it may be invoked from (this is defined by the architecture of the application). Furthermore, the API should have a version history, but that gets too much into the details of software engineering.

Benefits of ADTs

There are four major benefits of representing state with an ADT:

- Encapsulation: This is the essence of *abstraction*: the suppression of implementation details from the API.
- Localization: This is a byproduct of encapsulation. Internal changes to an implementation class do not affect code that relies only on the API. Even changing the name of a concrete class will not be felt outside the appropriate factory code.
- Flexibility: This is particularly important during development and testing. A surrogate implementation (including a "mock" object) can be substituted until the correct implementation is ready to be used. The surrogate may be a particularly inefficient or system-dependent implementation of the API.
- Validity: An ADT can enforce the domain of a type in a way that a (simple) data type cannot. For example, an integer (an ADT) can ensure that the bounds of the integer domain are respected. An exception might be thrown if the range $-2^{31} \ldots 2^{31} - 1$ is exceeded. In general, simple data types such as Java's primitives do not respect these bounds.

Classification of ADTs

Given the scope of this book, we do not intend to go into the more esoteric details of different kinds of data types, such as algebraic data types. But there are two major divisions we need to discuss: order and mutability.

Order

Order is a significant distinction. Generally speaking, ADTs fall into three kinds according to how information about the ADT may be traversed and/or presented:

- Unordered: For an unordered ADT, there is no ordering; there may be no concept of sequence in such an ADT (i.e., it may not be *iterable)*. Examples include these:
  - bag
  - hash table
  - graph
  - pseudo-random number generator.

- Positional: A structure based on the actual position of elements within the data structure, which is often dependent on the order of insertion of elements. Examples include these:
  - linked list (and, therefore, stack)
  - double-ended queue
  - array
  - string
- Ordered: An ordered ADT is based on a comparison function for the elements. Examples include these:
  - binary search tree, red-black tree, B-tree
  - priority queue
  - sorted array suitable for binary search

This taxonomy will form the basis for this book.

Mutability

From a practical point of view of learning about ADTs, mutability is of less concern to us than order. Nevertheless, we should discuss the issue here because if you are designing an ADT (and its API), you will need to make clear whether the ADT is mutable (it's a property, after all).

Many readers will have come at programming via a distinctly nonmathematical approach. Why should this be? It's primarily because of the way programming started: machine code instructions executed by a microprocessor. At its most basic level, a microprocessor is made up of memory locations that can change their value (i.e., they mutate). Why should this be so? Whether we construct our processor, as in the early days of computers, using valves or, today, with transistors, it doesn't really matter. Both of these devices work, essentially, the same way. The output (voltage levels) depends on two other quantities: the input and the control. That output can be measured and considered as a "bit" of information (high voltage is a 1, low voltage is a 0, or something like that). That bit represents a state of something. Since it can so easily change its value, as often as once every clock cycle, it is by definition *mutable*. Early programmers could cause the processor to execute a series of steps by writing in machine code. Each step would likely change (mutate) the state of the program. Thus, the notion of variables and arrays was naturally born. Most programming languages have retained this notion of mutable state as if it was religious dogma.

Mutable state has its advantages, but it is not something we find in mathematics. If a mathematician says "Let *x* be a positive integer," *x* may take on, in conceptual terms, any positive value. You might even say that it represents all positive values at once as if there was an infinite number of parallel universes, each with a different value of *x*. But what *x* does *not* do is to take on the value of 5, say, and later change it to 2. Thus, what we call variables in algebra are nevertheless immutable. They're not so much variable in time, but in (mathematical) space. Why would we want to base programming on mathematics? If we wish to prove our program's correctness, for example, we should depend on proofs and axioms rather than the quantum effects of semiconductors.

In mathematics, one of the major techniques for solving problems is called *reduction*. If we can solve problem A by solving problem B, we say that problem A *reduces* to problem B. We will talk about this more in the next chapter. When problem B is simply a smaller version of problem A, we need to use a recurrence relation, *recursion* in programming terms. This is the problem-solving counterpart to the method of mathematical proof called *induction*. If we want to find the value of 5! (5 "factorial"), we can use the relationship $f(n) = if\ n \leq 1\ then\ 1 else\ n f(n-1)$. We do not need a (mutable) variable that runs from 1 to *n*, as we might try if our approach to programming is computer centric rather than mathematics centric. But surely we need some mutable variables? Not really. If a list is defined as a head element followed by a tail (another list), anything we want to do with a list, such as summing its elements can be done using the following expression:

```
sum(List xs) = if xs.empty then 0 else xs.head + sum(tail)
```

Surely, this is less efficient than having a variable *sum* and incrementing it for each element of the list? Not if it is well implemented. It should take exactly the same amount of time.

Instead of starting with the idea of mutable variables and collections accessed by iteration, let's start with immutable variables and collections accessed by recursion. What would be the advantages and disadvantages of each approach? The major advantage of immutability is the lack of redundancy. A list that is 0, 1, 2, 3, 4 can be implemented simply as a head element 0 together with a pointer to the list 1, 2, 3, 4. If, for some reason, we need another reference to the list 1, 2, 3, 4, it simply shares the pointer with no additional storage space cost, other than the pointer itself. Where this pays off is in concurrent (i.e., multithreaded) programming. If your collections are mutable, another thread may mutate a variable or element of a list without your thread being aware of it. This necessitates a very complex discipline of coding involving "mutex" locks. Not only is this kind of program almost impossible to debug, but the locks can slow things down considerably. Frequently, programmers resort to making actual copies of collections just so that they can guarantee no other thread can mutate the collection.

This regime of immutability is particularly favored in functional programming but is increasingly important in ordinary OOP given that parallel processing and concurrency are the only way for modern computers to increase their throughput. However, let's talk about some situations when immutability does not perform well. Suppose that you have two (immutable) strings to concatenate, "Hello" and "World!" One way is to build a string s, "HelloWorld!," and have the string "Hello" be the substring of s from char 0 to char 5 (exclusive), while the string "World!" is the substring of s from char 5 to 11. This is how Java did things before **Java 7u6**. But that resulted in lots of junk on the heap, which couldn't be garbage collected. Now, all three strings are separate entities, resulting in "H" being stored twice, and so on. Strings are thus still immutable, but we are not getting much benefit from that immutability. Indeed, the total time to concatenate two strings is proportional to the sum of their lengths. This means that, if you create a log file message, for instance, by concatenating many strings together, the total time can be more like the length squared! To alleviate this problem, a mutable ADT called *StringBuilder* is used. In other words, mutable structures can sometimes be used to optimize certain immutable operations. But do note that this isn't because *String* is immutable. It's because, even though it is immutable, the concatenation operator doesn't take any advantage of that immutability.

However, there is one very important mutable construct that is most definitely essential, and that is for implementing a sort method because on compare-and-maybe-swap (e.g., quicksort, insertion sort). To make this work efficiently, we need a (mutable) array that enables swapping in constant time.

Conclusion

ADTs are the reusable components of the software world. Each individual ADT, of which there is an unlimited number, including hundreds of "standard" ADTs, has its own characteristics, behavior, and—most importantly—appropriate use cases. Just as you would not try to force a nonfitting LEGO Brick into your construction, you should not force an ADT to serve a use case for which it is not suited.

While it may be tempting to think of the separate aspects of an ADT (data structure, algorithms, invariants) as independent entities, this would miss the point entirely. An ADT does its job because of the synergy between the three components.

Takeaways

Following is a list of the main ideas to take away from this chapter:

- ADTs are the building blocks of software applications.
- There are significant differences between the operation of implicit data structures and explicit data structures, and these generally result in different performance characteristics.

Chapter Review Questions

Directions: Refer to what you learned in this chapter to respond to the questions and prompts:

1. Enumerate the differences between an array and a linked list.
2. Is it possible to write a sort algorithm for a list? Or can we only sort arrays?

References

Brooks, F. P., Jr. (1975). *The mythical man-month.* Addison-Wesley.

Likov, B., & Zilles, S. (1974). *Programming with abstract data types.* https://dl.acm.org/doi/pdf/10.1145/800233.807045

CHAPTER

4

Unordered ADTs

Introduction to the Chapter

This chapter discusses those ADTs that do not impose any particular ordering on their elements. We start with a simple object. This is then expanded to accommodate *n* similar objects arranged in an *array*. Linked lists are described in the next chapter because, although their elements may not be ordered in the sense of being sorted, the list is constructed in such a way that the list retains the order of insertion. The next unordered ADT is the *bag or multiset*. A bag is similar to a *set b*ut allows for duplicates. Finally, we describe hash tables, which are data structures based on the array but designed for fast storage and retrieval of key-value pairs.

Learning Objectives

In this chapter students will learn about the following:

1. Objects, sets and multisets (bags)
2. The filing system principle (classification)
3. Hash tables and hashing
4. Different implementations of hash tables

Key Terms

The following important terms will be introduced in this chapter.

- **Iterator:** A mutable object that navigates a collection such that each element is visited once and once only
- **Bag:** A multiset
- **Classification:** A technique that can improve the efficiency of searching data by a constant factor
- **Symbol table:** An abstract data type suitable for storage and retrieval of key-value pairs, where "symbol" is really just a synonym for "key"
- **Hash table:** A commonly used type of symbol table that allows for constant-time insertion and searching

Object

An *object*, or to use a more old-fashioned word *struct*, is a general data structure. It could be as simple as a *Boolean* or it could be an instance of a more complex class, for example, a *Person*, which might have fields of *name*, *date-of-birth*, and *identifier*. The set of all possible instances of such a class is called its *domain*. For a class with no additional constraints, the domain will be the Cartesian product of the domains of its fields. Additionally, a class will have a set of invariants that are essentially validity, or membership, rules. And it will have its own API that client code (code that interacts with it) must follow. It is indeed an abstract data type, but it is not something we can describe here because it is too general.

An object on its own—typically represented as a variable—is of interest mostly inside loops of code. But what is generally of greater interest to software developers is a *collection* of objects. With a collection, we can manipulate many objects with the same logic. This is a very powerful and ubiquitous concept in programming, and every ADT that we will look at in this and the following chapters houses a collection of objects.

There is another type of nonsimple object that we will not cover in this book but is worth mentioning here by way of contrast: a *container* (or wrapper)—a concept more appropriate for a book on functional programming. For example, we might want to express an object as being *optional:* It is either present (with a value) or not present.

Set

A *set* is a mathematical concept that is defined in terms of membership. It is a collection of members (objects) with the same type, but each having a different set of properties. For example, if we have a type *Colorful*, we might have a set of colorful objects such that each of its members has a color that is a different shade of blue. Similarly, we might have a set whereby each is a shade of green, and so on. A set has no obvious identifier; it is only the *membership* that is significant.

Elements in a set are not ordered. However, something has to be said about the interface java.util.Set<T> (which does not imply any ordering of T elements) and, in particular, the class java.util.TreeSet<T> (a common concrete type for Set, which does require an order for T elements). TreeSet will only behave appropriately when either a Comparator is passed into its constructor or when the generic type T is Comparable. Otherwise, a ClassCastException will be thrown (!!).

Bag

A **bag** of elements is also known as a multiset and is similar to a set where duplicates are allowed. Why is it called a bag? It is the data equivalent of a bag or purse: a stretchable container that can hold any number of objects, such as coins. It's also malleable so that we can knead or shake up the contents such that the positions of individual bricks are not retained. Finally, and perhaps the key attribute, it's opaque so that we cannot see the contents when we insert a hand to withdraw an object. Thus, when we remove an element we do so at random.

The API of a bag must include the *add* method. As usual, we need to be able to find out if the bag is empty. Do we need anything else? Yes, we need a way to process each element nondestructively. This is the equivalent of dumping the contents onto a table and doing something to each element, for example counting, and then putting everything back in the bag. We will emulate this process with the **iterator** method, which returns an *Iterator*. See Chapter 5 for a discussion of iterators. In the case of a bag, we really should populate the iterator at random since we have no reason to put the elements in any particular order. What about an *extract* (*remove*) method? It would not be as useful as the equivalent *Set* method because we wouldn't know how many times we should invoke the method before all traces of an object have gone. You're free to implement your own *remove* method of course. Java doesn't have a *Bag* (*Multiset*) class, although there's one in the *guava* library.

There is a good use case for a *Bag*. It is for the connections of a vertex of a graph, noting that there may be identical connections between any pair of vertices. A tenet of graph theory is that, when traversing the connections for a particular node (vertex), the connections should not be visited in any particular order.

The Filing System Principle: Classification

The requirements for using the dictionary principle are that elements of a collection must be orderable and that the collection is relatively static (although even dictionaries must periodically incorporate new words in new editions). An orderable collection requires an (orderable) key that we can sort by. What if we don't have such a key? Or what if the collection is sufficiently dynamic that it is considered too expensive to maintain it in order?

The traditional solution is a filing system that "classifies" each item by identifying it as belonging to a "file." The items in each file do not need to be kept in order (though they can be—at an additional cost). The point is that the file contains only as many items as can be linearly searched in a short time. If there are n items and r classes, the average number of items that will be searched is $\frac{n}{2r}$. This is a performance improvement by a factor of r over a straight linear search, assuming that the **classification** process itself is a constant-time operation. It is possible to sort each class and use binary search within a class, but the break-even point for the number of searches is approximately proportional to r and so, for practical purposes, when a small number of searches is required, the standard filing system is the most efficient. If it were not, filing systems would have been abandoned long ago.

Of course, the big question is how to classify items. For that, we need a *classifier*. If an entry is a numeric value x, the classifier might be something simple such as $\frac{x}{10}$, or alternatively $x \, mod \, 10$. This latter operation gives us the "units" (the final digit) of the integer x. And the number of classes (r) would be 10. If we were looking for, say, the number 42, we would search in the 2's class. With this scheme, we would reduce the average search time from $\frac{n}{2}$ to $\frac{n}{20}$. This is how a physical filing system works, whereby the most common classifier is probably the initial letter of the appropriate name.

In general, a classifier can be based on any subset of properties of an item. A common classifier in the English-speaking world is last name (surname or family name). If there are likely to be duplicates, we might consider a composite classifier such as first name + last name. Whenever there is a possibility of duplicates (e.g., John Adams), we need to handle collisions (the term for duplicates in this context). For more detail on a common application of classification in the context of storage and retrieval of information, see the Hash Tables section. A method of sorting—bucket sort—employs the same principle (as we will see in Chapter 8) to reduce the number of inversions of an array. Indeed, all noncomparison sorts are based on classification.

Another way to look at classification is that it works by reducing entropy by moving similar elements closer to each other. As we saw in Chapter 2, the entropy of an array for classification-sorting purposes is only $n \log r$ when there are r classes that are more or less evenly populated. That's because we can't tell the difference between members of a class, and therefore they will be sorted into the same general location. That, obviously, requires less work than sorting all individual elements in order. Note that this concept of a classifier acts, for the filing system principle, in the same way as a key acts for the dictionary principle.

Classifiers

Not every type of object is amenable to easy classification because not all objects have an obvious classifier. This is particularly true when there are several properties with the same relative importance, particularly when each property is likely to be nondistinct. An example is color. Colors are generally defined by three different parameters such as red, blue, green, or perhaps hue, chroma, and saturation. In computer graphics, these are generally represented with integer values (and therefore nondistinct). But which is the most significant value? We have no obvious way to order colors—unless we choose an arbitrary scheme such as the Sherwin-Williams color code.

For objects with no intrinsic classifier—and sometimes even when we do have one—we must combine several classifiers into one classifier. Most typically, this classifier will result in a non-negative, finite number i, where $0 \leq i \leq r$, which can be used as the index or label of a class. Because of the artificial and nonrecognizable nature of this type of class, we will use the term *bucket* instead of class. Given that the total information content of an object may be many megabytes and that the resulting index might be just a few bytes in length, we call such a function a *digest* or *hash* function.

Hash Table

A **hash table** is a type of **symbol table** whereby we use an associated key to store and retrieve a value. It has various names in different languages, including *associative array*, *dictionary*, and *map*. In this sense of the word key, there is no implication of any ordering; it is used in the more general sense of an object that can be associated with some other object for storage and retrieval. In some cases, the key can be directly inferred from the value but, generally speaking, a hash table stores key-value pairs. Once we know the key, we can store or retrieve its associated value. An array is a special case of such a symbol table whereby the index of an element is its key. But, in practice, it is unusual to want to look objects up with a positive integer whose value is between 0 and $n - 1$.

DISCUSSION

Why is it unusual? Don't we do that all the time in software? Yes. But what about real life? There aren't many examples of integer keys in real life. At least, not where the numbers are sufficiently small to be easily memorable. Here's a counterexample: the numbers of London bus routes (currently around 544).

In the next chapter, we will look at *ordered* ADTs, which can also be used as efficient symbol tables. But in every such case, we must be able to compare two keys and use the result to help navigate our way to the appropriate value. What if the type of key we are dealing with, for example color, has no intrinsic order? Are we destined to use linear search to find the value we are looking for? No—we already know we can use a filing system.

Hashing

Let's say we have an object that consists of three binary fields: a Boolean (1 bit), an integer (32 bits), and a three-character code in extended ASCII (24 bits). That's a total of 57 bits of information. Again, we suppose that the number of buckets we plan for is 256 (8 bits). How can we condense 57 bits into 8 bits in such a way that each field of an object contributes to this 8-bit *hash?* We need to choose a *hash function*. It would be ideal if each of the 2^{57} possible objects was equally likely to result in one of the 256 different hash values because we want each of the buckets to have approximately the same number of elements, viz. $\frac{n}{256}$.

We will go into more detail about hash functions after having presented the two basic methods of devising a hash table. What follows is a description of these two methods. However, the API to a hash table is the same, regardless of the implementation method. We will require the following methods as a minimum:

`put(key, value) -> void` # Adds a key-value pair or updates the value for an existing key
`get(key) -> value` # Returns the value for the key if present, else null (or other nonresult)

Buckets (Separate Chaining)

The filing system, whereby we classify objects into buckets, can be used directly for a hash table. This method is sometimes referred to as *separate chaining*. As described previously, the method still requires linear time for searching because we considered r, the number of classes, to be fixed. But we can arrange for r to grow as n (the number of objects) grows, and that is one of the chief differences that transforms a filing system into a hash table. The other major difference is that a hash function is chosen as the classifier that tries to ensure that each class is equally probable.

A separate chaining hash table is basically an array of m elements (in the context of hash tables, we usually use m instead of r), each of which is a pointer to a bucket, usually implemented as a linked list. Because we maintain m in proportion to n, lookups (and insertions) take constant time. Whatever the value of n, finding the correct bucket can still be done in constant time because array lookups are constant-time operations. If m is very large, lookups may incur a cache page fault, but we will ignore that for now.

Each bucket is made up of a linked list of nodes. When a key-value pair is added to a bucket, by invoking the method $put(k, v)$, it is placed at the head of the linked list as that can be accomplished in constant time. If it turns out that the key is already in the bucket, this arrangement will also ensure that the most recently added value is the one that will be retrieved. However, in practice, this mechanism will result in buckets that are longer than necessary because they hold irrelevant key-value pairs. Instead, we want to look for the key first which, if absent, will require a complete scan of the bucket. If we find the key, we update its value to the value (v) that we have been given. If we don't find the key, we add a newly formed node to the head of the linked list.

To retrieve a value associated with a particular key, we first find the appropriate bucket based on the hash of the key and then search the linked list for a key-value pair whose key matches. If it is not found, we return an appropriate indication (null in Java).

A node, typically called an *entry node*, in the linked list represents the key, the value, and a pointer to the following node. Thus, there is some overhead, due to the pointers, amounting to $n+m$ words when we include the bucket array itself.

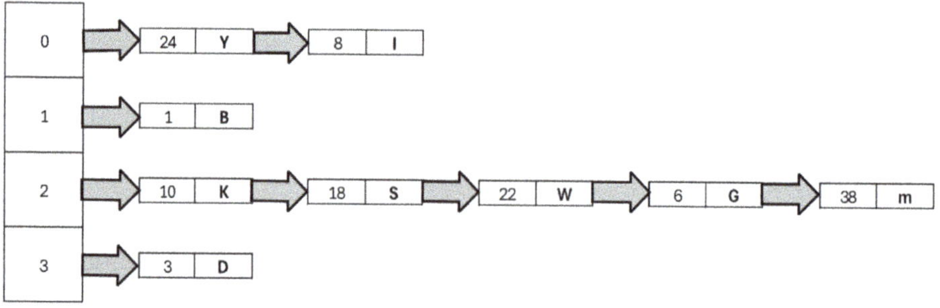

Simple Hash Function: key % 4
{1,B; 10,K; 18,S; 22,W; 6,G; 24,Y; 3,D; 8,I; 38,m}

FIGURE 4.1. Bucket-based hash table.

How can we maintain this situation as we increase *n*? By keeping track of the ratio $\alpha = \frac{n}{m}$, where α is the mean bucket size. If it exceeds some threshold, say 8, we can grow the array and rehash the existing elements. Of course, this process will take time proportional to *n*, but we expect to recoup that cost with more efficient future searches.

What is the distribution of the bucket sizes and what is the most likely size? The distribution will be a binomial distribution $B(n,\alpha)$ and the modal (most frequent) size is given by $\lfloor \alpha(n+1) \rfloor$ which simplifies to *m*.

Removing a key is easy. We simply search for the appropriate node and delete it from the linked list, a constant-time operation. No other bucket is affected.

So far, we have not talked about *collisions*, when two different objects hash to the same index. It sounds like an unfortunate and rare occurrence. Nothing could be further from the truth. Recall that we set out to divide the objects into *m* buckets by arranging for one bucket to contain all the objects that hashed to the same index, so such collisions are exactly what we expected would happen. Nevertheless, *collision* is the term used and, when we look at open addressing, we will see that there is a slightly negative connotation to a collision.

Open Addressing (Linear Probing)

In *open addressing*, we use a completely different strategy. The array on which we base the hash table must be larger than the maximum number of elements to be stored in the hash table. The array itself stores the entry nodes, though does not necessarily need a node pointer (this is implementation dependent).

When inserting a key-value pair, as with bucketing, we must first look to discover if the key already exists, in which case we simply update the value. While we have not found the key, we must keep probing until we encounter an empty slot. When searching for a key, we first get the index based on the hash of the key. If we encounter an empty element, the key does not exist, and we return null. If we find that the key of the entry node is equal to the key we seek, we simply return the corresponding value. Otherwise, we continue to probe.

	0	1	2	3	4	5	6	7	8	9	10	11	12	13	14	15
key		1	18	3			22	6	24	8	10	38				
value		B	S	D			W	G	Y	I	K	m				

Simple Hash Function: key % 16
{1,B; 10,K; 18,S; 22,W; 6,G; 24,Y; 3,D; 8,I; 38,m}

FIGURE 4.2. Open-addressing hash table.

When probing finds an entry node whose key is not what we're looking for, we implement the appropriate probing scheme. In the simplest linear probing implementation, we simply increment the index (modulo *m*, the length of the array) and continue probing. Whenever we encounter an empty element, we know that the key is not in the hash table. Note that it is a grave error to allow the array to fill. As long as only successful searches are attempted, no harm will result. However, as soon as a caller requests the value for a nonexistent key, the algorithm will continue forever because whenever probing reaches the end of the array, the next probe occurs at the start of the array. Note that, when probing, all index calculations must be made modulo *m*.

There exist many different algorithms for resolving collisions for open addressing. The method described, whereby the index is increased linearly, gives rise to the term *linear probing*. For the following discussion of the performance aspects of open addressing, we will assume linear probing.

In the normal course of insertions and searches, clusters will develop. Each cluster is terminated by an empty slot. However, the elements of a cluster will not necessarily have the same hash value. When inserting (or searching for a nonexistent key), it is the average cluster size that determines the performance. Clusters will get unreasonably long when the array gets close to being full—or when the hash function is nonuniform.

As before, we use α to represent the ratio $\frac{n}{m}$. However, in this case, α will always be a fraction. The space overhead for open addressing consists of the empty elements in the array. If the array is half full (i.e., $\alpha = \frac{1}{2}$), that implies that the length of the array is $m = 2n$, thus the unused space is simply n. In general, the space overhead is $n(\frac{1}{\alpha} - 1)$. How many probes can we expect under such circumstances? A mathematical analysis (Knuth, 1998) yields the following approximations for the expected number of probes p in a successful or unsuccessful search:

Successful search: $p_s \approx \frac{1}{2}\left(1 + \left(\frac{1}{1-\alpha}\right)\right)$

Unsuccessful search: $p_u \approx \frac{1}{2}\left(1 + \left(\frac{1}{1-\alpha}\right)^2\right)$

Thus, when $\alpha = \frac{1}{2}$, $p_s \approx \frac{3}{2}$ and $p_u \approx \frac{5}{2}$. When there is exactly one vacant space, an unsuccessful search will require on average $p_u = \frac{m+1}{2}$.

Removal of a key-value pair is a little more complicated than for the bucket scheme. This is because keys are, to some extent, used for navigation. If a slot in a cluster is removed from anywhere other than the last element of the cluster, keys that are downstream of the slot may become inaccessible. For this reason, all such keys must be deleted and re-inserted.

One advantage of the open addressing scheme is *locality of reference*. This is just a fancy way of saying that the probability of invoking a cache page fault is small because much of the information we require for navigation is in the array itself.

The Hash Function

The most important property of a hash function is repeatability. Thus, we require that $hash(x) = hash(x)$. While it's tempting to use randomness in the hash algorithm, that would destroy repeatability.

A desirable property of the hash function is that any of the possible keys is equally likely to hash to any of the possible hash values. Such a scheme also means that it is impossible to reconstruct the original key from the hash itself without knowing some details of the hash function. It also follows that the slightest change in the key will result in an unpredictable change to the hash. Cryptographic hashes have (or should have) this property. In practice, noncryptographic hash functions are designed more for speed and simplicity.

A typical hash function uses multiplication of a prime number to mix the hash values of each of the fields (properties) into the result. A commonly used factor is 31 i.e., $2^5 - 1$. If the current pattern in the hash is x, the result is $\sim(\sim(x \ll 5) + x)$, where $\ll$ denotes shift-left and $\sim$ denotes bit-flip (negation). This results in a bit pattern that has the original pattern shifted five bits to the left and, in the lowest five places, the complement of the original low-order bits. Often, we initialize our hash calculations with another prime number: 17. Thus, for our object of three fields, where $a, b,$ and c represent the hash values of each of the three fields,

$$hash = \left(\left(17 \cdot 31 + a\right) \cdot 31 + b\right) \cdot 31 + c$$

Similarly, to evaluate the hash value for a string, list, or array, we extend the method to allow for each character or element to contribute in the same way.

The Birthday Paradox

Given a randomly chosen key object, what is the probability of the hash function resulting in any particular value? It is obviously $\frac{1}{m}$. But, given k keys, what is the probability that they all hash to different values? It's a little more complicated and usually referred to as the "birthday problem."

The probability that k keys do not hash to different values is $1 - p(m,k)$, where $p(m,k)$ is the probability that all k values are distinct. The probability that any particular pair has different hash values is $\frac{m-1}{m}$, as the first of the pair can take any of the m values, while the second must be one of the other $m-1$ values. Now, let's add a third key. The probability that all hash values are different is $\frac{m-1}{m}\frac{m-2}{m}$. By extending this to k keys, we get

$$p(m,k) = \frac{m!}{m^k (m-k)!} = \frac{k!\binom{m}{k}}{m^k}.$$

The reason this is known as the birthday problem is that it is quite surprising how few people are needed to have at least an even chance of there being a common birthday among them (we ignore years in the birthdays). That's to say, what is the value of k such that $p(365,k) \sim \frac{1}{2}$? An approximation to $p(m,k)$ when $k \ll m$ is $e^{-\frac{k^2}{2m}}$. This leads to a further approximation, so we can say that the probability $\mathcal{P}$ of a collision (i.e., $1-p(m,k)$) is $\sim \frac{k^2}{2m}$. Note, however, that this is a very poor approximation unless $k^2 \ll m$.

QUESTION

How many people are needed to have an even chance of a common birthday? Use the approximation given (although this is quite a bit off the true number).

The Coupon Collector

Another topic of interest when designing a hash table is to know how many keys need to be hashed before we can expect every hash value to have been used at least once. This is known as the coupon collector problem. This is similar to the birthday problem but requires a lot more mathematics to derive: We will simply state without derivation that $C_m = m \ln m$. For a hash table of a thousand elements, we would expect each value to have been used at least once after approximately 7,000 hashes (a good approximation to the natural logarithm of 1000 is 7).

DISCUSSION

Compare the coupon collector expression for C_m with the Prime Number Theorem (PNT), which provides an approximation of how many numbers you will have to consider before you encounter the mth prime number. That's to say $m \ln m$. Admittedly, the PNT takes a very long time to converge on the given expression. Coincidence?

Buckets versus Open Addressing

Which scheme is best? As usual, there are trade-offs. But when we observe that the standard libraries of different languages can't all agree, we're forced to conclude that there isn't much in it.

For ease of implementation, buckets are preferred, especially code for the removal of a key-value pair. The performance will steadily downgrade for buckets, and although open addressing will be efficient when the load factor is quite small, it will blow up as the array gets close to being full. Therefore, open addressing is an excellent solution when the scope of the problem (i.e., the number of key-value pairs to be stored) is known in advance. If we do have to grow (or shrink) the array, each scheme requires about the same amount of work when rehashing all entries. Note, however, that by knowing the keys are unique (as we do when rehashing), we can simply add each entry at the head of its bucket (a constant-time operation). Similarly, when open addressing is used, we can insert it at the first vacant slot.

TABLE 4.1 Buckets versus Open Addressing

	BUCKETS	**OPEN ADDRESSING**
Implementation	Simple	Somewhat more complex
Performance	Steady degradation	Blows up when full
Hash Sensitivity	Some degradation when nonuniform	Clustering when nonuniform: significant degradation
Deletion	Easy	Requires some re-hashing
Use Case	Eventual loading unknown	Predictable loading
Cache Performance	Not good: heap pointers	Good: array
Space Overhead	$N\left(\frac{1}{\alpha}+1\right)$	$N\left(\frac{1}{\alpha}-1\right)$
Typical Overhead	$1.25N$	N

Conclusion

There are other collision-resolution schemes available, including open addressing with alternative probing schemes. However, they are beyond the scope of this book. Which of the two schemes described should be used? When should you choose a tree-based versus a hash-based symbol table? Are your keys comparable? If so, then all options are open. If not, you must use a hash table. If, once your proposed data structure has been completed, you plan to collect the key-value pairs in key order, you should use a tree. Otherwise, you should construct a hash table.

Takeaways

Following is a list of the main ideas to take away from this chapter:

- Arrays are efficient data structures with "constant" access time, given a known index.
- Arrays can form the basis of a key-value store (an ADT) by using a hash function to generate an index.
- Bags and sets are important abstract data types.

Chapter Review Questions

Directions: Refer to what you learned in this chapter to respond to the questions and prompts:

1. If 10 buckets (classes) are used, and if it takes 10 seconds on average to find an entry by linear search, how long will it take using bucket search (i.e., a filing system)?
2. A common use case for a hash table is to store key-value pairs and then get a (sorted) set of all the keys. Does this sound like a good use of a hash table?
3. Which type of hash table uses the least amount of memory?
4. Which type of hash table will blow up, performance wise, when it gets to be almost full?
5. What are the appropriate use cases for each type of hash table?

Reference

Knuth, D. E. (1998). *Art of Computer Programming, volume 3: Sorting and searching, 2nd edition: 6.4 Hashing, p 528.* Addison-Wesley Professional.

CHAPTER

5

Positional ADTs

Introduction to the Chapter

In the last chapter, we looked at ADTs, which were not ordered in any particular way. In this chapter, we will introduce ADTs that maintain an order that is not based on any intrinsic property of its elements but, instead, are solely based on the order of insertion into the ADT, or perhaps subsequent rearrangements. The most important of these are lists, queues, and stacks. But we will also cover iterators and strings.

The ADTs in this chapter will consider the *position* of its elements to be significant in some way. For example, a list made up of the elements 1, 2, and 3 is not the same as a list made up of the elements 2, 3, and 1. We start with the simple linked list, which retains the order in which the elements were added. We then show how a simple linked list, with one or two extra invariants, is essentially the same thing as a stack. We then continue with nonstrict (lazy) ADTs and two types of queues. We finish up with strings.

Learning Objectives

In this chapter students will learn about the following:

1. The roles and relationships between linked lists and stacks
2. Strictness and laziness, including lazy lists
3. Double-ended and circular queues

4. Strings
5. Parsing and evaluating an infix expression
6. Why you shouldn't use a doubly linked list for a double-ended queue

Key Terms

The following important terms will be introduced in this chapter:

- **Pointer:** A reference to an (other) object, which may point to no object at all
- **Lazy:** A performance-enhancing technique used to avoid evaluations that are never needed
- **Strict:** Eager—the opposite of lazy
- **Queue:** A first-in, first-out data structure that can be used as a buffer between independent producers and consumers

Strict versus Nonstrict

Any abstract data type that represents multiple elements can choose whether to store the actual value of each element (**strict**) or not (nonstrict). Clearly, the values of the strict elements are available at any time—they are permanently "memoized." What about the nonstrict elements? How are they made available?

Let us consider the moment when we evaluate the ith element. None of the elements whose index is greater than *i* have yet been evaluated; they are unknown. What about the elements with index less than *i*? There are three possibilities:

- *Iterator:* Elements have been evaluated but are not memoized and so are unavailable.
- *Lazy collection:* Elements have been evaluated and *are* memoized and available.
- *View:* Elements may or may not have been evaluated and memoized.

In other words, a **lazy** collection (e.g., a lazy list) visits elements sequentially, evaluating each new element as it is encountered and storing (memoizing) each value. An iterator is like a lazy list but with a very short memory (only the current element can be recalled). A view is like a lazy list but without the requirement of accessing each element in sequence.

For all nonstrict ADTs, the following will be necessary:

- be backed by another ADT (strict or non-strict), optionally with a "decorating" function
- be defined by a function that takes a parameter
  - that's the index (typical for a view) or
  - that's the previous element's value (typical for a lazy list)

Java has always had an iterator. *Streams*, introduced in Java 8, are lazy by design.

Iterator

Whichever way we choose to group objects, there is one operation that is fundamental to many of the ADTs described in these chapters: *iteration*. Iteration is a nondestructive process whereby we *visit* each element of a collection in turn. An *iterator* is somewhat like a variable in an algebra book. It takes, in turn, the value of every object—once and once only—of the collection on which it is based. Despite its temporary nature, we consider an iterator an abstract data type since it fulfills the role of a representation of the current solution state for some problem. Each object is visited in turn by (a) testing to see if there are more items and (b), if so, getting the next item (the *next()* method in Java). Because Java didn't have an *Optional* class in the early days, the only safe, uniform way to terminate the iterator was through an auxiliary method called *hasNext()*.

The idea of an iterator is that the concept of iteration should be decoupled from the details of the underlying data structure. Each iterable ADT is free to implement its iterator in its own way. An iterator is conceptually a *nonstrict* (lazy) once-only data type. If you had an iterator based on 1,000 objects, but you were only interested in the first 10 of these, you would avoid evaluating 990 elements. What do we mean by "once-only?" An iterator is like a bus (or metro) ticket—once you've used it, you cannot use it again. If you need to iterate over a collection *m* separate times, you will need to create *m* iterators to accomplish the task.

In Java, we can construct an iterator on a collection by invoking its *iterator()* method, which returns an *Iterator<T>*, where *T* is the underlying type of the collection. The *iterator()* method is defined by the interface *Iterable<T>*. Note that, in Java, arrays are not iterable. There's one other peculiarity of Java to warn you about. There exists, in the *Iterator* interface, a method called *remove()*. The idea that an iterator should be mutable from the client's perspective is staggeringly bad. You would do well to forget that such a method exists. You may also ignore the *forEachRemaining* method (since 1.8).

Not every collection should be iterable. The presence of an iterator suggests that it is permissible to "see" every element in a collection. Also, strange things might happen if the iterator presents the elements in an unexpected order. Furthermore, if your collection is mutable, what will happen if the collection is modified by one thread while an iterator is active on another thread? When you define an API for an abstract data type, you should decide if you need to provide an iterator.

An iterator itself has a definite order even if the collection on which it is based does not—otherwise, it would be very difficult to guarantee that each element was contained exactly once. It is for this reason that iterators appear in this chapter. However, a subsequent iterator on the same collection will not necessarily yield the same order.

Array

An (unordered) array is simply a contiguous collection of *n* elements, each of which is of the same type (the type specified in the array declaration is required to be the super-type of all elements). In Java, elements may be primitives or objects. In the former case, the array is *efficient* in the sense that all the data for the array is contained in the array elements themselves. In the latter case (an array of objects), this means that the array is made up of references (**pointers**) to objects that might be anywhere in the heap. If we consider that the positions of the elements in the array are significant in some way, an array is also *implicit*.

An array is a "constant-time" random-access data structure because the time to read (or write) any element is the same, but this isn't really true, given what we know about data caching. For a small array, it will be true, or close to the truth. But for a large array (larger than a single cache page), accessing the elements sequentially is faster than accessing them randomly because sequential access will minimize the number of cache page faults.

We covered arrays quite extensively in Chapter 3, so there's not much to be added here. Of course, it's also possible to sort an array, in which case it will be an ordered array (see Chapter 6). Since an array is unordered, this section would fit Chapter 4 also. But it's here because the one feature of an array that is really important is its position.

Whether we should dignify an unordered array with the title "abstract data type" is somewhat questionable since there really are no true invariants or algorithms involved, provided that the index is within bounds. If the index is out of bounds, all bets are off. In Java, this condition throws an exception.

Lists

Linked Lists

Immutable List

An immutable list supports two primary operations: *cons* and *split* (you won't necessarily find these names used in your favorite language, of course). If we have a list of type *A*, *cons* takes two parameters: an object *a* of type *A* and a *List* (*a*) of type *A*. The result is a new list (of type A) whose head is *a* and whose tail is *as*. Split does the inverse: It takes a *List* of type *A* and splits it into its head (*a*) and tail (*as*).

Immutable lists are the backbone of functional programming but, if you're a Java programmer, it's possible that you haven't come across them because they were hard to create before Java 1.9. However, we can create our own immutable list type in Java (although it won't be as elegant as it would be in Scala):

```
public class List<T> implements java.lang.Iterable<T> {
 public static <U> List<U> cons(final U u, final List<U> tail) {
 return tail.prepend(u);
 }
 public static <U> List<U> empty() {
 return new List<>();
 }
 public static <U> List<U> of(final U … us) {
 List<U> result = new List<>();
 for (int i = us.length; i > 0; i--)
 result = result.prepend(us[i - 1]);
 return result;
 }
 public Split<T> split() {
 return list == null ? null : new Split<>(list.t, new
List<>(list.next));
 }
 public int size() {
 int result = 0;
 for (T t : this) result++;
```

```
return result;
}
public Iterator<T> iterator() {
return new Iterator<>() {
Node node = list;

@Override
public boolean hasNext() {
return node != null;
}

@Override
public T next() {
Node n = node;
node = node.next;
return n.t;
}
};
}
public List<T> prepend(final T t) {
return new List<>(new Node(t, list));
}
public List(final Node list) {
this.list = list;
}
public List() {
this(null);
}
class Node {
public Node(final T t, final Node next) {
this.t = t;
this.next = next;
}

private final T t;
private final Node next;
}
```

```
static class Split<X> {
public Split(final X head, final List<X> tail) {
this.head = head;
this.tail = tail;
}
final X head;
final List<X> tail;
}
private final Node list;
}
```

Perhaps the most important and flexible method on a list is *iterator()*. This creates an instance of another abstract data type: an *Iterator*.

ArrayList

Java provides a compromise abstract data type with the benefits of both an array and those of a list: the *ArrayList*. It is essentially a resizable array that also has the properties of a list and is one of the standard collections. Unlike an array, it is iterable. It supports (amortized) constant-time *add* but *insert* and *remove* are linear-time operations.

Stack

A stack is an abstract data type that is homologous to the type of linked list just described. The difference is in the names of the operations. Instead of *prepend* (or *add*) we call it *push*. And instead of *split* (or *remove*), we call it *pop*. But, in terms of behavior, a stack is equivalent to an immutable linked list.

A stack is often referred to as a last-in, first-out (LIFO) structure. One of the most obvious use cases for a stack is reversing the order of a collection. This is the same principle used when reversing the cars (trucks) of a train by sending the cars down a single dead-end siding and then pulling them along a separate connection (known as a Wye). But the true calling of a stack is in software for keeping track of nested (including recursive) method calls. We will see in Chapter 9 how essential stacks are for traversing graphs.

Another important use case for stacks is in parsing, particularly back-tracking parsers. A simple example of this sort of parsing is when evaluating a numerical expression in "infix" notation, for example (((3 + 4) * 7) + 1). This problem can be solved by establishing two stacks: an operand stack and an operator stack. Left-hand parentheses are essentially ignored (although they can be used to check that parentheses balance); values, such as 3, 4, and so on in the example are pushed onto the operand stack; operators (+, *, etc.) are pushed onto the operator stack. When a right-parenthesis is parsed, the top two elements of the operand stack are popped, as is the top element of the operator stack. The resulting operator is applied to the two values, and the result is pushed on to the operand stack. This is known as Dijkstra's shunting yard algorithm.

TABLE 5.1 The Two Stacks in Dijkstra's Shunting Yard Algorithm

3			
3			+
3	4		+
7			
7			*
7	7		*
49			
49	1		+
50			

Relaxing Constraints

If we make the *next* pointer mutable (remove the *final* keyword in Java) we have the additional ability of being able to insert (or delete) nodes that are not at the head of a list. We can also make the value of *t* mutable, in which case we can change the value at any node. For the most flexible of linked lists, we can make both mutable.

Lazy List

A lazy list is a nonstrict ADT. A true lazy list is one when the tail of the list is evaluated lazily (i.e. has its evaluation deferred until necessary).

Java doesn't support lazy lists as such, although *Stream* has most of the required properties of a lazy list. One notable exception is an indication of whether the stream is finite or infinite. This is crucial, for example when converting a lazy list to a (strict) list. The time to perform this operation is proportional to the length of the lazy list. If that is infinite, the time will be infinite (actually, the executing processor will throw an exception when it eventually runs out of memory). That is not a desirable property. A properly implemented lazy list has the behavior of *memoizing* all values that have been evaluated while not wasting resources on any value that has not been (and may never be) evaluated.

As an example of a useful lazy list, it is possible to define all the Fibonacci numbers, without limit. Of course, to do anything useful with such a lazy list—such as printing it—we must make the list finite. But making the list finite and defining the Fibonacci sequence are distinctly different aspects of the solution. A library function can define the (infinite) Fibonacci sequence, while clients of that function will determine how many elements are needed for their own particular use case.

HISTORY NOTES

Defining a Fibonacci function naïvely by using two recursions, as suggested by

$$f_n = f_{n-1} + f_{n-2},$$

is, as you may know already, a very bad idea. The reason is that the total number of operations to evaluate f_n is proportional to f_n. And, since f_n is exponential in complexity (of ***n***), it implies that the overall complexity is exponential.

Indeed, we must solve this problem only with the memoization of the Fibonacci numbers. Because of their memoizing properties, lazy lists are perfect for this type of application.

How do you like this bit of code written in Scala, a functional language that runs on the Java Virtual Machine?

```
val fibonacci: LazyList[BigInt] = 0L #:: fibonacci.scanLeft
                                    (BigInt(1L))(_ + _)
```

Because it is based on the unbounded numeric type *BigInt* (equivalent to Java's *BigInteger*), this is guaranteed to provide as many Fibonacci numbers as your computer has memory for.

Queues

A **queue** is necessary any time there are variations in the rates of production and consumption of a stream of objects. If production outpaces consumption, the queue grows; if consumption is faster than production, the queue shrinks. When discussing input/output utilities, a queue is also known as a *buffer*. Most queues, in particular the two we discuss in this chapter, follow the FIFO principle. The standard method names for enqueuing and dequeuing, at least in the Java world, are *offer* and *poll*. In the next chapter, we will discuss a different kind of queue: the *priority queue*, which is not a FIFO queue.

Double-Ended Queue

A double-ended queue is the standard "explicit," FIFO queue. Elements are offered (added) at the *tail* of the queue and polled (removed) from the *head* of the queue. From this definition, it's clear that we cannot use a single linked list for the queue, at least not without serious performance issues given that one end or the other would require traversing the whole list. What about using a doubly linked list? That would work, but it would also use significantly more space than necessary. However, we can efficiently use a linked list for the head and a single-element pointer for the tail. Let's see how this idea works.

When offering an element to the tail—that's to say the last element of the head list—we can simply add our new element to the tail of the head list and reset the tail pointer to the new element. Note that if we offer an element to an empty queue, there will be no current last element. When polling an element from the head, we simply perform the usual operation to remove the head of a list. Note that if the queue now becomes empty, we must also unset the tail pointer. In the following code section, the head list is called *oldest* while the tail pointer is called *newest:*

```
public void offer(Item item) {
 Element<Item> element = new Element<>(item);
 Element<Item> secondNewest = newest;
 if (oldest == null) oldest = element;
 else secondNewest.next = element;
 this.newest = element;
}
public Item poll() {
 if (oldest == null) return null;
 Item result = oldest.item;
 oldest = oldest.next;
 if (oldest == null) newest = null;
 return result;
}
```

Circular Queue

A circular queue is an implicit structure—based on an array. The array must have a size that is one more than the greatest possible number of elements to be stored in the queue, otherwise we cannot distinguish between an empty queue and a full queue. Of course, it's possible, though at an O(*n*) cost, to grow the array whenever necessary.

Assuming that the array is of length *n*, all indices are of course modulo *n*. We begin with two indices: *head* (*i*), and *tail* (*j*), where $i = j = k$ and where k is arbitrary but might as well be zero. The elements currently in the queue are those between *i* and *j* (exclusive), thus, initially, the queue is empty. The current size of the queue can be determined by $(j - i + n)\%n$.

The logic for *offer(x)* is simply: *q[j++]*$\leftarrow$x, while the logic for *poll()* is *q[i++]*. After an offer, we check to see if $i = j$. If so, we grow the array in preparation for the possible addition of new elements.

Construct an empty circular queue with 7 slots and $i = j = 3$:

			i, j			

Offer "A":

			i	j		
			A			

Offer "B":

			i		j	
			A	B		

Poll:

				i	j	
			A	B		

FIGURE 5.1. Circular queue operations.

String

A string is also an abstract data type. Because strings are so prevalent in almost all programming contexts, the implementation needs to be appropriately optimized. Logically, therefore, a *String* should be an immutable array of characters. Clearly, the position of the characters is significant. In Java, it is implemented as an array of bytes (not characters). Thus, a sequence of characters must be (internally) encoded according to the coding scheme (usually UTF16).

Because strings are immutable, it is possible to define substrings to point at a part of a longer string. Java went away from this idea during the lifetime of Java 6, however. For now, it's complicated.

Conclusion

In perhaps the majority of data structures, the position of each element is significant. We saw in this chapter how that positional information can be used to advantage in arrays, lists, and queues. Strings are similar in that the position of each character is significant. The fact that a data structure is positional does not, however, guarantee that the position is useful. We might have a list of objects whereby the position simply reflects the order in which the elements were added. In a queue or stack, the position of an element is crucial. And that is another reason stacks and linked lists are different abstract data types despite being implemented in an identical fashion.

List of Key Takeaways

Following is a list of the main ideas to take away from this chapter:

- Some abstract data types are accessed primarily by their position.
- Lazy data structures and algorithms can lead to improved performance.
- An important use case for a stack is the reversal of a sequence.
- The primary role of a queue is buffering—when providers/consumers are not perfectly matched.
- The most space-efficient type of double-ended queue has just two pointers.

Chapter Review Questions

Directions: Refer to what you learned in this chapter to respond to the questions and prompts:

1. Is it possible to create your own stack explicitly, or are you required always to use the system stack?
2. A queue can expand without limit. Under what conditions is this statement true?
3. An iterator is a memoizing data structure. True or false?
4. In Java, you don't have to trade off between the advantages of arrays versus lists. You can have the best of both worlds with an *ArrayList*. What are the costs/drawbacks involved in an *ArrayList?*

CHAPTER

6

Ordered ADTs

Introduction to the Chapter

In this chapter, we discuss abstract data types whose elements maintain order. Some will be *implicit* (i.e., based on an array), while others will be *explicit* (i.e., based on pointers). In all cases, it is required that a total ordering is defined: We must be able to take *any* pair of elements and determine which should come first.

Learning Objectives

In this chapter students will learn about the following:

1. Ordered arrays and binary heaps
2. Binary search trees and red-black trees
3. When to choose an ordered ADT

Key Terms

The following important terms will be introduced in this chapter:

- **Complete tree:** A tree where only the lowest level may be missing nodes
- **Heap order:** A property of a binary heap such that each branch is in order

- **In-order traversal:** A traversal of an ordered ADT such that the keys are returned in their correct order

Ordered ADTs

In this chapter, we will discuss abstract data types whose order is their chief feature. As soon as we impose the invariant of order on an ADT, we note that there may be a significant difference in the methods that we use to construct/update or to access the data. The reason is that any work required to impose an order on the data must happen at construction time and that accessing the data may be somewhat simpler. Our assumption is that we will access the data at least as frequently as we will update the data, and therefore if we must make a choice, we should aim to optimize the access methods rather than the construction methods. The relative frequencies of updates to accesses will be a chief factor in choosing an ordered ADT.

Clearly, these are only of interest in situations when order—and the preservation of order as elements are added and removed—is required. By way of contrast, there may be situations where a one-time ordering of a collection is sufficient for the simple reason that membership in the collection is fixed. For such an application, we can use an array and sort it once. This occurs in a dictionary, in its traditional meaning of a book of word definitions, or translations. The business model of such a book is that the list of words changes very slowly and that it is profitable to publish it and sell many copies before it is necessary to update the dictionary.

Perhaps the most obvious use case of a more dynamic collection kept ordered is that of a database index. The entire purpose of a database is to allow insertion and deletion of records on an ongoing basis, and with as little disruption and cost as possible. We will discuss such indexes briefly at the end of this chapter.

Ordered Array

Humans are particularly fond of two things: classification and sorting. We like to determine, for every object, which *class* it belongs to. For example, some of us are obsessed with deciding whether a bird we see in a forest is one or another of two visually almost identical species.

For factual presentations, we want to see things *in order* because we want to know the *rank* of an object. For example, we want to know the rank of our favorite team in some sporting competition. Or perhaps we are in a competition during which, after each round, half the players are eliminated. We want to know, not only whether we qualified, but *where* we ranked among the qualifiers. Perhaps the most obvious application of sorting, of interest to humans and computers alike, is looking things up, for example the definition of a word in a relatively fixed table such as a dictionary.

For this situation, we need to sort an n-element array so that we can use binary search. Our best possible sort will take $n \log n$ operations, allowing us to save $\frac{n}{2}$ operations per search (we ignore the $\log n$ operations per binary search because it is typically so much smaller). Thus, sorting is only worthwhile if we plan to do at least $\sim 2lgn$ searches *before the array changes*. That's a relatively unusual situation in a computer application—but it is typical in the noncomputer world of dictionaries (see the dictionary principle). A database, for example, that is frequently being updated (inserts, deletions, updates) does not store its items in an array. It stores them in a self-ordering *index*. Depending on the use case, this index might be a red-black tree, a B-tree, or even a hash table. But it will never (well, hardly ever) be an array.

Incidentally, there is one other reason that sorting algorithms is important to students of computer science: They represent a family of generally simple algorithms whose properties and performance characteristics are quite varied. In other words, they are very good pedagogical subjects.

Given that there is a need for an ordered array, we would expect to find such an abstract data type in a system library, such as that of Java. But we will look in vain. Yet, we should be able to find it because as soon as we impose the invariant of "sorted" to an array, it becomes more than just a data structure; it becomes an ADT. So, let's design its API.

Application Programming Interface

```
public class OrderedArray<K extends Comparable<K>> imple-
ments Iterable<K> {
    public K get(int i);
    public void set(int i, K k); // if our OrderedArray is
mutable.
    public int indexOf(K k);
    public void addElements(K[] addition); // if our Ordere-
dArray is mutable.
    public int getSize();
}
```

There are many details to decide here but the main requirements are as follows:

- Get the (ordered) i^{th} element (indices start at 0 with the smallest).
- Set the ith element (internally, this will force a re-sort).
- Finding the index of a particular element (using binary search).
- Add elements (which might involve growing the array) and re-sorting.
- Get the size.
- Get an iterator (defined by *Iterable<K>*).

Ideally, our internal sort algorithm will be *adaptive* (see Chapter 7) such that calls to *set* or *addElements* will require only partial sorts. This, in turn, suggests that our ADT should be *lazy* (see Chapter 3) for the definition of lazy and section *Lazy OrderedArray* for a more detailed description.

Having an *OrderedArray* available means that we will never try to apply binary search on an array that isn't actually ordered. Doing so is possible in Java because the binary search and sorting methods are unrelated. We postpone any further discussion of sorting until Chapter 7.

Lazy OrderedArray

We can easily create a lazy version of an *OrderedArray* by establishing two partitions:

- an ordered *archive* of elements
- an unordered *journal* of new elements that contains all the recent additions since the last search operation

All searches and gets operate on the eager version (where the journal is empty). That's to say, every type of search must first insert the journal entries into the archive. This is particularly suitable for any application where searches are less common than inserts.

To analyze this design, let's assume that, at any given moment, the number of elements is n and that the mean ratio of inserts to searches is r where $n \gg r \gg 1$. If we employ some sort of balanced tree, we can expect to perform $r \log n$ comparisons for the next inserts and $\log n$ comparisons for the search. The total is, therefore, $(r+1) \log n$, or simply $r \log n$.

Using our lazy *OrderedArray* design, we expect to perform

- r operations while adding to the journal
- $\frac{(rn+r^2)}{2}$ operations while eagerly merging the journal (based on the number of inversions)

The amortized (average) cost of each (eager) insertion is thus $\frac{(n+r)}{2}$, which can be simplified to $\frac{n}{2}$. This in turn implies that the total time to build up a table of n elements is $\frac{n^2}{4}$. However, the time to make a (lazy) insertion is $O(1)$. If two searches come together, the time for the second search is $\log n$ since we can use binary search.

Another variation on this idea is to make the merging operation occur only during "maintenance" time if it is acceptable for the system to go offline for a short time—for example, during the night. With this model, insertion is still constant time, while searching will take a total of $\log n + O(\frac{kr}{2})$, where k is the typical number of searches per maintenance interval.

Priority Queue

Imagine that you are in charge of scheduling patients in a health care situation (triage). As each patient enters, you assign them a priority and place them in a (virtual) queue. When a provider resource becomes free, the next patient is taken from the queue, and their treatment begins. However, that patient is not necessarily the one who was been waiting the longest—rather it is the patient with the highest clinical priority, as assigned by yourself when they arrived.

How should you maintain this queue? The most obvious way would be to keep a set of case numbers visible to the other staff in order of priority (say, highest priority at the top). You might do this with a set of writable magnets that you can move around easily. Whenever you place a new magnet into the list, other than at the bottom, you will need to take linear (i.e., $O(n)$) time to move the magnets being "bumped" down a place. Note that, because your list is ordered, you can find the insertion point in $O(log\ n)$ time by doing a binary search. Recall that you do this every time a patient joins the queue, giving rise to an overall growth of $O(n^2)$.

This doesn't sound too bad if your list is fairly small. But there are other scenarios, especially in the world of Big Data or graph theory, where n is simply too massive. It also would not benefit you much if you kept the list unsorted and then looked for the highest priority case when taking from the queue. Again, it would be quadratic. However, if you only kept the m highest priority cases, where $m \ll n$, and told the others to go back home (not a protocol that would work well in an emergency room scenario), you could actually gain a little by keeping the list unordered, for then the total amount of work you would have to do would be "only" $O(mn)$.

How can we reduce the total amount of work to $O(n \log n)$? As usual, we must take our linear list and turn it into a tree of some sort. Thus, when we insert or remove an item from this tree-like priority queue, we must do work that is $O(\log n)$. How can we do that? If you consider the width of any level of the tree, it will be proportional to n at the bottom of the tree. Indeed, if we have a full binary tree, that lowest level would have $\frac{n}{2}$ items. Clearly, it makes no sense to try to impose any order in the horizontal direction.

What about the vertical direction? The depth (or height) of the tree is $O(\log n)$, so if we maintained order in the vertical direction only, we could achieve our goal. This idea gives rise to one of the most elegant instances from the pantheon of abstract data types: the "binary heap."

Binary Heap

A binary heap is an implicit data structure whose invariant, called **heap order**, is that it is ordered only in each branch of the tree. There is no relationship or implied ordering between nodes on different branches.

HEAP ORDER

A parent node must have at least as high a priority as any of its children.

By following this invariant to its logical conclusion, we see that the root of the tree *must* hold the element with the highest priority. What if our binary heap gets out of order somehow (we will see in a moment how this arises)? For example, suppose that a child has a higher priority than its parent. The simple solution is that we swap the child and its parent. We call this operation "promote" (or "bubble-up," "up-heap," "swim-up," "sift-up," etc.) if, from the point of view of an element, it is moving to a higher level (i.e., closer to the root). Promote requires just one comparison per level. What if the parent has lower priority than one or more of it children? In that case, we make sure that we swap the parent with the larger of its children. We call this latter operation "demote" ("down-heap," sink-down," "sift-down," etc.) because the parent goes to a lower level. Demotion therefore requires two comparisons.

In general, we will have to perform multiple swaps. But here's the crucial point: There are at most $\log n$ levels, so these promotion/demotion operations only need to be repeated at most $log\, n$ times. Thus, this mechanism satisfies our requirement for logarithmic performance.

Implementation

How should we store this binary heap structure? We have the usual two choices: implicit or explicit. Let's say we try an ordinary binary tree based on pointers (explicit). We need a pointer for each child so that we can descend the tree. But we also need a pointer to each node's parent so that we can ascend the tree. That's two pointers per node, plus any null pointers at the leaves. That's a lot of memory overhead.

What about the alternative (i.e., implicit) array? How can we represent a parent-child relationship in an array? Does this even make sense? Just try drawing our tree on top of an array, *a*. You can see that, if we represent the root node in *a*[1], the parent of element *k* is at $\frac{k}{2}$, while the children of element *k* are at $2k(+1)$. This makes traversal—and swapping—of the binary heap very simple.

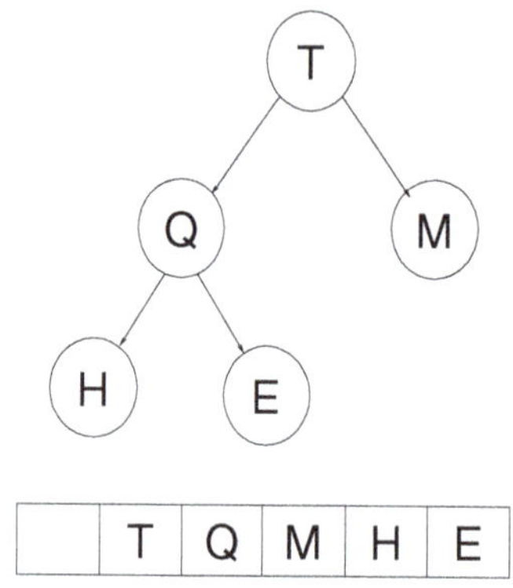

FIGURE 6.1. Binary heap in order

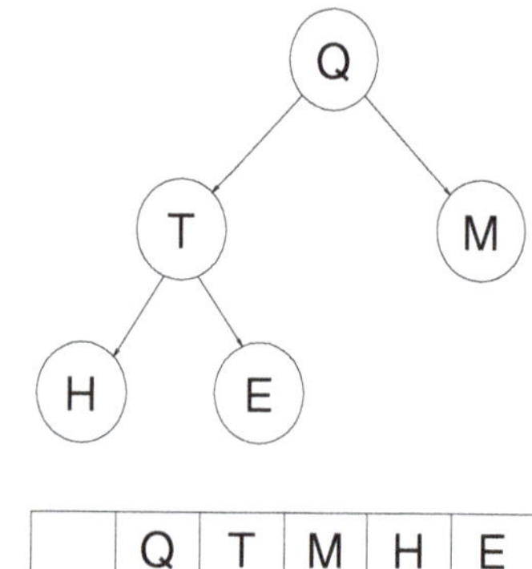

FIGURE 6.2. Binary heap transition.

But we must also be careful. If we are not, we might construct a very deep tree indeed. Imagine that the root has only a left-child, and that node has only a left-child, and so on. The depth of our heap will now be *n*, and performance for insertion/removal will therefore be $O(n)$. In addition to the heap-order invariant, we must also require that any gaps in the array (and thus missing nodes) be at the end of the array. Technically, a tree in such a form—where all levels are full except possibly the lowest level—is called a **complete tree**.

Insertion

When we insert an element into the binary heap, there is only one place we can put it, according to our complete-tree invariant: at the first available empty slot. Starting with our heap-ordered tree from Figure 6.1, that place is the left-child of the node containing *M*. At this time, we also update the count of elements in the heap.

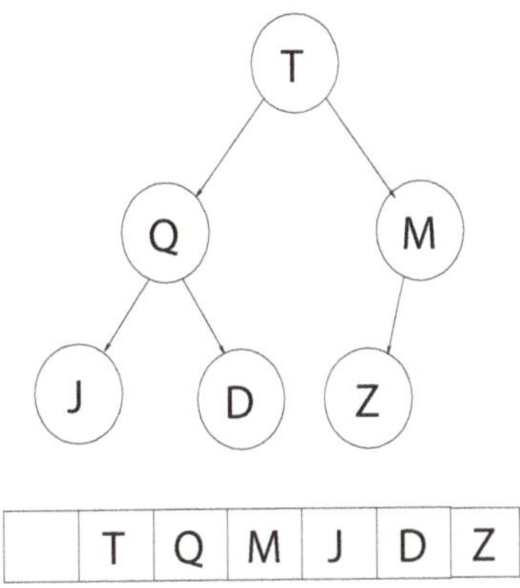

FIGURE 6.3. Heap insertion.

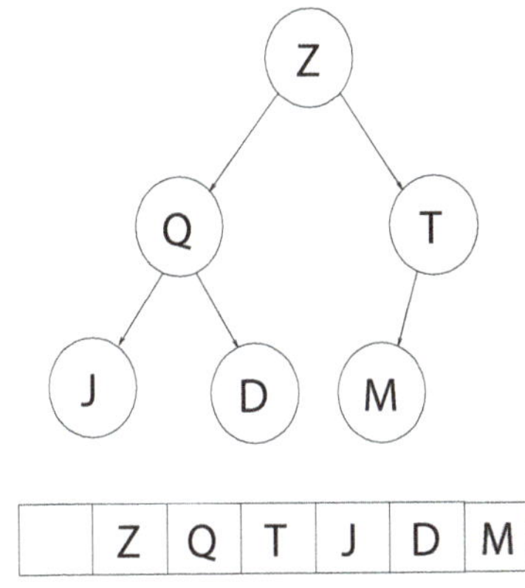

FIGURE 6.4. Heap order restored.

In order to restore heap-order—as we are currently in a transitional state in Figure 6.3 —we must bubble-up the new element *Z* as appropriate. *Z* has higher priority than *M*, and therefore *Z* and *M* must swap. However, the promote process is not yet finished: *Z* exceeds *T*, and therefore *Z* and *T* must swap. *Z* becomes the new root.

We must now address the issue of whether our binary heap should have a fixed size or should grow as necessary. If we expect to process a limited number of elements, there would be little purpose in allowing the heap to grow. Insertion (and removal) would suffer increasing execution time for no good reason. But, if we decline to accept any new elements when our binary heap is full, we run the risk of ignoring a high-priority item.

What if we compare the incoming element with that in the last slot and accept it if it has higher priority? It's easy to imagine that the last slot always holds the lowest priority item, but this is simply not true. Look at the heap in Figure 6.5. This is a valid heap, but the element in the last slot is in fact the third highest priority item. If a new element *R*, a potential fourth highest, is presented for insertion, it would not displace the *S*, but it would nevertheless be lost forever. This suggests that it is prudent to accommodate at least one more level in the heap, thus doubling the minimum memory required but adding only one additional comparison to the insertion time.

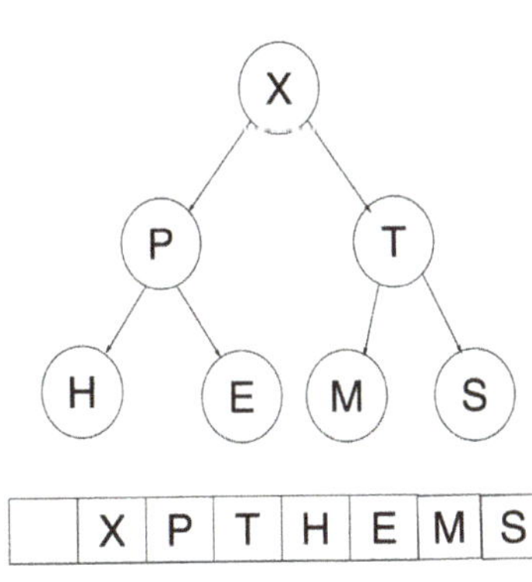

FIGURE 6.5. Full heap.

Removal

The removal operation has various names, *remove*, *deleteMax*, and so on, but the idea is the same: We need to take out the highest priority item which, of course, is at the root. That's not a convenient place for manipulating the heap, so we first swap it with the last item. But now a low-priority item is in root position, so we must slide it down. When the element has reached its proper place, which may be quite distant from its original place, we will conclude the process by passing back the highest element, reducing the count, and clearing the last place.

Let's observe while we're here that the element originally in last place that was thrust into the root position and then sunk to its proper place is somewhat more likely than not to belong in one of the lowest levels. Could we save some comparisons by sending it express to the lowest level (think *Snakes and Ladders*, *Moksha Patam*, or—as it is known in the United States—Chutes and Ladders) and then letting it bubble up as appropriate? We can save a comparison at each stage on the way down by forcing it to swap with the larger child. This optimization, known as Floyd's trick, does work, although it increases the number of swaps. However, swaps are usually at least as efficient as comparisons and often more so. Thus, Floyd's trick can save overall time.

EXERCISE

Given a heap with h levels, with at least one available space in the lowest level, and counting the root as level 1, if the final resting place of the element is in level k, how many comparisons can we save? How many additional swaps will be required? To decide if this idea will be useful overall, you will first have to determine the expectation of k, the level in which the element is most likely to end up.

What about other optimizations? The depth of our binary heap will be $\log_2 n$, but if we were to use an r-ary heap where $r > 2$, we could flatten the heap somewhat. Insertions would be faster, but removals, which require sliding down, may not be faster because, at each level, we must perform r comparisons.

Binary Search and Half-Swaps

There is one other optimization that we will study in a little detail because it will appear again when we visit insertion sort: "binary search and half-swaps." When you consider the promotion process, there is only one possible path from the insertion point up to the root. Observe that these elements, while not contiguous, are nevertheless ordered. Given such an ordering, we can use binary search to discover the proper place for our new element to bubble up to. That will reduce the number of comparisons from $\log n$ to $\log \log n$. Unfortunately, we still must do $\log n$ swaps. But we can optimize that a little using "half-swaps."

Let's say that we need to insert an element into an array, and that causes us to move l elements each by one place. Swapping the normal way requires $4l$ array accesses. But these aren't l independent swaps; they are logically dependent. Think of a sorted array *a* of length four. We wish to move the element at index 3 down to index 0 and move the others up one place. Here is some pseudo-code:

```
temp := a[3]
for (i <= {2, 1, 0}) a[i+1] := a[i]
a[0] := temp
```

Instead of requiring 12 array access in total, we only require 8. This is the case when $l = 3$ and the "normal" way of swapping takes $4l$ array accesses but the half-swap method requires only $2(l+1)$. As we've noted before, the first array access at an index is the potentially expensive one (when the cache suffers a page fault). The second access is much less expensive. However, it still isn't free, so halving the number of array accesses is a good thing to do.

Before leaving binary heaps, we should also note that the way that elements are arranged in the array is not ideal from the point of view of caching. Other variations on the basic heap theme are slightly faster because they arrange the elements to be more optimized for caching.

HISTORY NOTES

J. W. J. Williams developed the binary heap in 1964, first as a useful data structure in its own right and then as the basis for the implementation of heapsort. Williams was a Welsh computer scientist working for the Elliott computer company in the United Kingdom. It was an Elliott computer that inspired Tony Hoare to invent Quicksort 4 years earlier.

There is one final point: For a binary heap with capacity *m*, we need an array of size $m+1$, assuming that we leave the 0th element vacant. We did this to optimize the calculation of parent and child indexes. While that might have been significant in the early days of computers, the extra calculation required when the root is in the 0th element takes essentially no more time, given modern pipelined and/or parallel processors, especially given the time that it will take to retrieve the value from an array element. A much more significant point is that, for heapsort, we don't have any spare elements! Thus, binary heaps do generally start at element 0 and not element 1 as suggested earlier.

Analysis

Let's think about a suitable value of d and whether Floyd's trick is a good idea. The number of comparisons saved using the trick is one per level (independent of d). Assuming that the expectation of the final resting place of an element is at the level above the lowest level, we will do two additional swaps. The number of comparisons saved can readily be seen as $h-3$. Thus, the minimum heap depth at which Floyd's trick breaks even is $h=5$.

Given that the number of elements that can be accommodated in a heap of depth h: $n=\frac{(1-d^h)}{(1-d)}$,

$$h=[\log_d(n(d-1)+1)].$$

The average number C of comparisons required to build and empty a d-ary heap will be dh comparisons per element. We can easily show that the partial derivative $\frac{\partial C}{\partial d}$ is positive, and therefore increasing d cannot reduce C. The average number of swaps, S, however, is $2h$ (independent of d), and there is a point when $\frac{\partial(C+S)}{\partial d}$ is zero just below $d=4$, getting closer to 4 as $n\to\infty$. Therefore, the best value of d is 4.

There are some more optimizations that we should consider. The first concerns caching since traversing the lower twigs of a branch will likely result in one page fault per level. We cannot solve the problem entirely, but we can ameliorate it by using a B-heap that arranges for more adjacent elements branch wise to be adjacent array wise. This can be accomplished by defining the parent/child index functions to vary throughout the heap. We don't have the space here to delve further into this idea.

We now come to a problem that arises, particularly when we need to delete or change the priority of an element that is not at the root. The priority queue does not support such operations. We will require such support for some of the graph algorithms that we will study later. For this, we will need a way to identify elements by index because, without an index, we would have to perform a linear search to find the location of an arbitrary element within the heap. We can accomplish this by adding two additional arrays to our design. (For more details of this design, see for example *IndexMinPQ.java* at https://github.com/kevin-wayne/algs4.)

One of the applications that requires the index is Dijkstra's shortest paths algorithm, in which changing the priority of a key is rather common compared with insert and remove. Actually, the operation that is most useful is increasing the priority: moving the element toward the root. For this and other applications, a lazy version of the binary heap called the Fibonacci heap is developed. (An excellent video that covers both the standard binary heap and the Fibonacci heap can be found at www.youtube.com/watch?v=6JxvKfSV9Ns&feature=youtu.be.)

Summary

A priority queue (PQ), implemented using a binary (or *d*-ary) heap, is an abstract data type that is perfectly suited to a situation when elements should be extracted from the queue in priority order and when some elements may have such a low priority that they never enter the queue at all. However, because a heap is only semi-ordered (in one direction only), it would not be a suitable choice for a database index or any other situation when we need elements to be ordered and to remain ordered after random insertions and deletions. For that use case, we need a binary search tree or, preferably, a balanced search tree such as a red-black tree.

Nevertheless, as has been mentioned already, the binary heap can be used as the basis of a sorting algorithm: heapsort. We will treat this in more detail in the next chapter.

Binary Search Tree

The binary heap is an ingenious—and compact—way to enqueue elements and then to dequeue them according to their priority. But if you wanted to traverse the binary heap in order, you wouldn't be able to do that for the simple reason that it is not perfectly ordered. Recall that it is only semi-ordered. If we're willing to make the switch to an explicit (noncompact) data structure, we can store keys—together with any associated values—in a *binary search tree (BST)*: a binary tree that has an invariant imposed on the structure:

SYMMETRIC ORDER

If we consider any node *x* in the tree and whose key is *k*, all the keys in the left subtree (i.e., the subtree whose root is the left child of *x*) are less than k. Similarly, all the keys in the right subtree of *x* are more than *k*. We assume that the keys are distinct.

This invariant provides the necessary signposts (the nodes) to traverse the tree quickly in order to find a key and its associated value, if any. Without the invariant, the structure of the tree would serve no purpose. It would take as long to find a key as it would to traverse a linked list of keys.

Search and Insertion

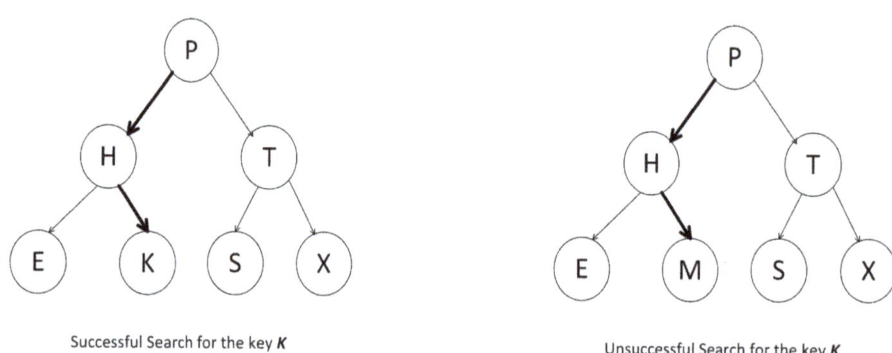

FIGURE 6.6. Successful search. FIGURE 6.7. Unsuccessful search/insertion.

Searching is easy in a binary search tree: The method **get(k)** applied to any node—recall that any node is itself the root of a (sub) tree—will return the associated value if **k=node.key**; otherwise, it will apply the **get** method to the left subtree if **k<node.key**, or to the right subtree if **k>node.key**.

For updating the binary search tree, we use the method **put(k,v)**, which is also very easy: We search for where the **k** *would* be if it was present and create a new **node(k,v)** at that place. If we in fact find a node whose key is **k**, we simply update its value to **v**. The tricky operation is deletion.

Because the binary search tree halves its scope at each node, starting with the root whose scope is the entire tree, it is easy to see that the number of nodes that must be traversed (the same as the number of comparisons) in order to find a particular key should be at most $\lceil \log_2(n+1) \rceil$, where n is the total number of keys in the tree. Just think about a binary search tree with $n = 2^h - 1$, where h is the "height" (or depth) of the tree. There is a key (node) at every possible position in each of h levels. We count the height as one when there is only the root node. This is the *best case*; it will only be true if the tree is perfectly balanced. And that is the problem with the binary search tree: Because it is a rigid (fully constrained) structure, the shape of the tree is entirely dependent on the order in which keys are inserted. Figures 6.8–6.10 are three binary trees with the same keys.

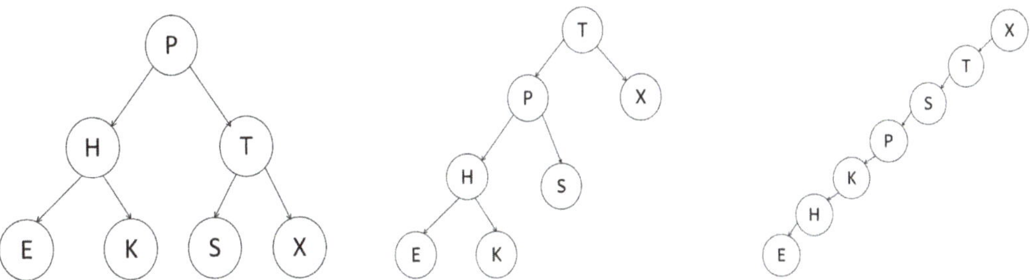

FIGURE 6.8 Balanced. FIGURE 6.9. Average case. FIGURE 6.10. Linear case.

We've seen that the best case is logarithmic, $\log_2 n$, to be precise when the root of each subtree is the median of the subtree, thus ensuring perfect balance. Further, we can show that the average case is also logarithmic, although a bit worse—in fact, where the keys are inserted in random order, we expect the number of comparisons to be $\sim 2 \ln n$. However, in the worst case, where the keys are inserted in order, the number of comparisons will be n (yikes!). This situation will be identical to putting the keys in a linked list. There is a perfect analogy between roots (of subtrees) and pivots in quicksort, which we will look at in more detail in the next chapter.

Traversal

Suppose that we need to visit every element in the tree in its proper order. The standard way to do that is to use a depth-first search (we will examine depth-first and breadth-first searches in more detail in Chapter 9). DFS has the advantage that the system stack will keep track of the "breadcrumbs" we need for navigating through the tree. However, if we want to do something with the keys, we will need to provide an auxiliary data structure such as a queue in which to store those keys. If we want to reverse the sense of the traversal, we would use a stack. How can we be sure to capture the keys in their correct order?

When we encounter a particular node, we must process its left subtree (the smaller keys) first, then the key of the node itself, and then the right subtree. Because we process the key in between processing the left and right subtrees, we call this an **in-order traversal**. Processing the key as soon as we reach the node would be a pre-order traversal; handling the key last of all, before leaving the node, would be a post-order traversal.

A traversal of all keys must take time proportional to the number of keys, at least.

Order Statistics

As well as insert and search, there are other properties of a BST that we would like to access in logarithmic time. The simplest examples are the minimum and maximum elements. We can easily find the minimum element simply by always taking the left subtree until there is no subtree. In that case, the key in the node we are looking at must be the minimum key. Similarly, for the maximum—always take the right subtree. However many levels we must descend to find these values, it will be at most $\log n$.

More generally, how can we find the key whose rank is *m* (meaning that there are *m* smaller keys)? This operation is called **`select(m)`** and is the inverse of the closely related operation **`rank(k)`** where we ask how many keys exist that are smaller than *k*. To solve this, we could perform an in-order traversal, counting the keys until we equal or pass the value of *k*. But that would take linear time!

To achieve logarithmic time, we must memoize the sizes of all subtrees by caching the value in each node. Additionally, if we allow rank to accept keys that are not in the BST, we will need to implement a floor and ceiling operation, too.

The logic for **`rank(node, k)`** is as follows:

```
int cf = k.compareTo(node.key)
int smaller = node.left.size;
if (cf == 0) return smaller;
else if (cf < 0) return rank(node.left, k);
else return 1 + smaller + rank(node.right, k);
```

EXERCISE

Implement the code for **`select(m)`**. Test by checking that $select(0)$ is the minimum element and $select\left(n-1\right)$ is the maximum element.

Deletion

It is easy to delete a leaf of the tree (a node with no children): You simply remove the pointer to the leaf (replace it with *null*). And it is almost as easy to delete a node (*x*) that has just one child (*y*)—replace the pointer to *x* in the parent node with *y*. However, it is not so easy to delete a node with two children.

A lazy solution is easy: Mark each deleted node with a "tombstone" marker but leave the node in place for navigation purposes. Insertion of a previously deleted node simply involves removing the tombstone. This strategy works as long as the number of such deletions is relatively small. But eventually—unless you rebuild the tree from time to time, the number of tombstones begins to impact the performance significantly.

Is there an efficient eager solution to deletion? For this, we use a technique called Hibbard deletion. But we do so with care.

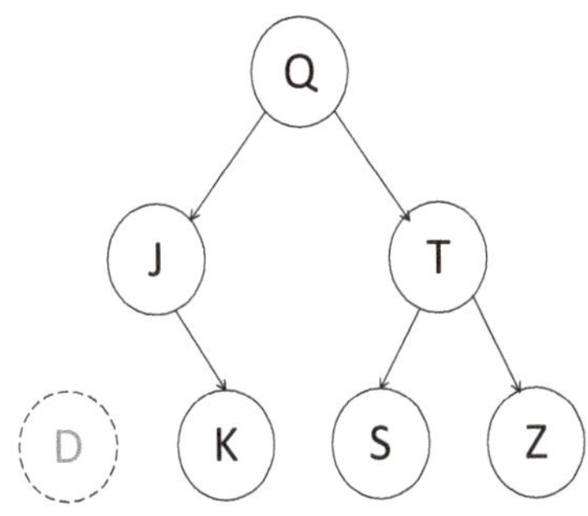

After removal of childless element *D* from the tree in Figure 6.8

FIGURE 6.11. Delete leaf node.

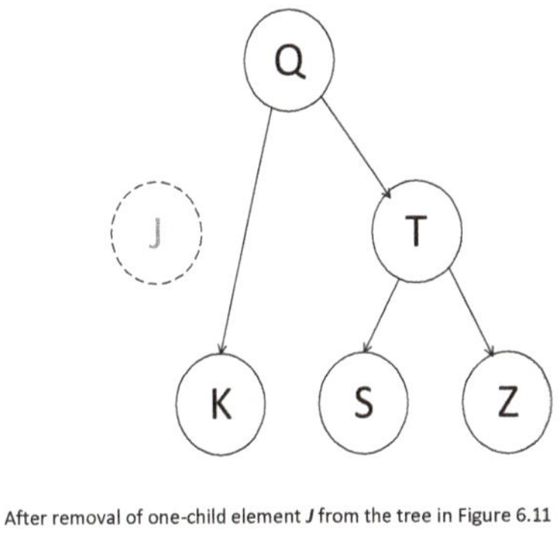

After removal of one-child element *J* from the tree in Figure 6.11

FIGURE 6.12. Delete node with one child.

Hibbard Deletion

When the node (*q*) to be deleted has two children, we must arrange for its successor —or predecessor—to take its place. Assuming that we choose the successor (*s*), we can find it as the minimum node of *q*'s right subtree. By definition of the minimum, *s* has no left subtree and so will have room to accommodate *q*'s left subtree when *s* is promoted into the place vacated by *q*. Since *q* and *s* must be adjacent key wise, we can achieve this substitution without fear of violating symmetric order. The right subtree of *s* will of course continue unchanged. See Figures 6.13 and 6.14 that demonstrate this idea.

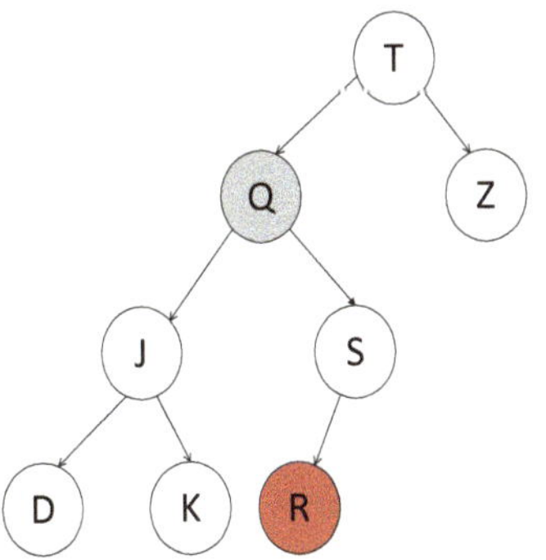

FIGURE 6.13. Hibbard deletion: Before.

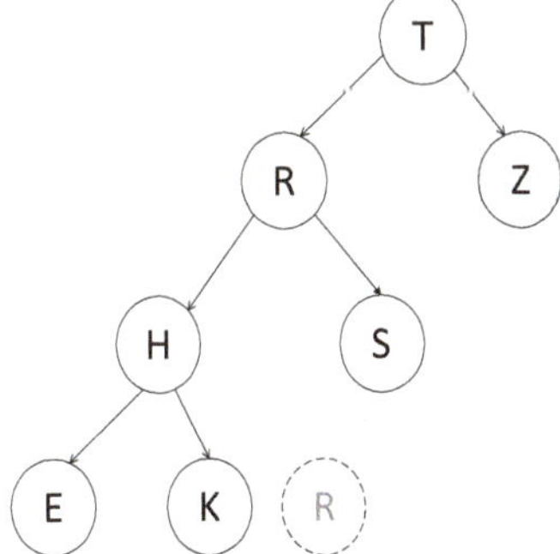

FIGURE 6.14. Hibbard deletion: After.

Unfortunately, repeated use of this method leads to significantly imbalanced trees. Did you notice any violations of the arbitrary substitution principle? You should. In the description (and figures), we used the successor when we could have used the predecessor. There was no justification for always using the successor. ASP violations should be noted and examined for any possible improvements. In this case, we can choose the algorithm that is predecessor-based or successor-based at random. Or we can keep track of the sizes of the left and right subtrees and base the decision on that. Either way, we keep the trees somewhat more balanced.

Balanced Search Tree

The problems that we noted with BSTs (potentially unbalanced trees as a result of unfavorable order of key insertion and problems with deletion) can both be solved by a data structure called a *balanced search tree*. What's the fundamental problem with a BST, though? Rigidity. If mechanical objects are too rigid, they tend to fracture when they experience extra stresses. Do you worry when you look at the wings of your plane and you notice that they are flexing? You shouldn't. If they weren't flexing when they should, they would be in danger of snapping off. It's the same with buildings and earthquakes: Too much rigidity leads to building collapse.

Flexibility

Flexibility is perhaps the hardest to understand of all the performance-enhancing techniques discussed in this book. There is no fixed formula to use to magically fix a rigid structure (or algorithm). But when it applies, it can reduce a worst-case linear performance to an amortized logarithmic performance.

With the binary search tree, we added an extra degree of freedom when we added an extra link to a node. Then we removed a degree of freedom when we added the symmetric order constraint. The rigidity of the structure means that it cannot comfortably deal with the case of unfavorable insertion order.

Let's think through some possible solutions. Our goal is to ensure that all branches of the tree have a similar length. The same length would be ideal. If we need to maintain the length of all branches the same, it implies that we cannot add nodes at the leaves.

Note that we haven't done anything to ease the rigidity of a BST. Earlier, we added a degree of freedom by putting two child pointers in a node (not just one as in a linked list). How about another? But not just another pointer, which would make the structure too flexible—and lose symmetric order. We add a pointer *and* a key. But wouldn't that simply be a (rigid) ternary tree? No! Because we can choose whether to have two or three pointers according to the requirements for balancing the tree. In fact, the idea of adding a key to the root of a subtree to keep that subtree of uniform depth can now be achieved by adding an extra key and pointer.

Having two keys (and therefore three subtrees) is directly analogous to the variant of quicksort called dual-pivot quicksort (see Chapter 7), whereby the classic quicksort algorithm is enhanced by choosing an additional pivot (two total) and, thus, an additional partition (three total). The effect is that, if a random pivot (or key) fails to divide a collection evenly, thus leaving a large partition (or subtree), there is still one other random pivot/key that should successfully divide that partition/subtree and avoid linear tree depth. It is similar in aircraft design, which relies heavily on redundancy to avoid being left without control of the aircraft. Such a tree is called a "2-3 tree." We will skip the details and go straight to a more practical, but analogous, mechanism called the "red-black tree."

Red-Black Tree

For a binary search tree of n keys, where each subtree is rooted by its median, we can achieve perfect balance with each branch of length $h \sim lg\, n$. To be precise, such a tree, when full, has $n = 2^h - 1$ keys, so a binary tree with one key has just one branch (the pointer to the root itself), and thus $h = 1$. If we extend the height (depth) of such a tree only when it is full, we might be able to maintain balance if the additional key becomes the parent of the existing root of the tree, because then all branches will be extended by one at the same time, and thus the tree will remain balanced.

Although this is a good idea, it is impossible for a binary search tree because, in a complete BST, each nonleaf node must have exactly two children. We can achieve this root-growing idea, somewhat surprisingly, by careful management of the nodes of a binary search tree. We do this by allowing some links between nodes to be treated specially—as magic links that we do not consider to be adding extra depth. To distinguish these links graphically, we color them red.

As mentioned, our goal for a balanced BST is to have all branches with a length of $lg\,n$ wherever possible. But, at all costs, we must never allow a branch to have length anywhere close to *n*. However, a branch with length $2\,lg\,n$ would be quite acceptable. Thus, we can achieve this by introducing an invariant to forbid two red links to be adjacent. However, the magic red link is only part of the story. We also allow two red links to be adjacent *temporarily*. This provides the flexibility we need to keep the tree balanced.

The "Rules"

The idea for the red-black tree (RBT), was first proposed in 1972 and they are used in many ADTs such as the Java *TreeSet* or *TreeMap*. To maintain the scheme described, there must be a set of "rules" and a set of procedures to be followed when the rules are (temporarily) violated in a particular way. First, here are the applicable invariants that apply in the steady state, i.e., when we are not inserting or deleting key-value pairs:

- **Symmetric order** (same as for a binary search tree): For any non-leaf node, the left subtree contains only keys that are not larger than the key of the node; the right subtree contains only keys that are not smaller than the key of the node.
- **Perfectly balanced tree:** Every path from the root to a leaf node (node with null subtree links) has the same number of regular (black) links.
- **Limiting branch length:** No node can have two red links attached to it. By limiting the incidence of red links to alternate links (i.e., every other one), we can ensure that no branch is longer than twice the length of any other.
- **Arbitrary choice:** Red links are left leaning and downward (all links are directed downward in all variants of a BST). It would be perfectly appropriate to state that red links lean right. But a choice has to be made, and our choice will be left.

Transitions

We should recall here that the invariants described apply when the structure is at rest, or not in transition. However, internally, an operation might violate one of the last three invariants (but never the first), provided that it is resolved before passing control back to the caller. During a transition, some configurations are only temporarily valid. Here are the transitions:

- **New node:** Every new node is attached via a *red* link, following the rules of symmetric order, of course. As usual, for a search tree, new nodes will always be leaf nodes. Because of the perfectly balanced tree rule, such a node will arise on the lowest level. Sometimes this operation will trigger the next type of transition.
- **Right-leaning red link:** If a red link leans down to the right, we must rotate it counterclockwise (also known in the literature as rotate left). Note that the link from the right-most node to its right subtree and the link from the left-most node to its left subtree are not changed in any way. But the left subtree pointer of the right node becomes the right subtree pointer of the left node. Sometimes this operation will trigger the next type of transition.
- **Two consecutive red links:** If two left links are adjacent, we must rotate the upper one clockwise (also known in the literature as rotate right). Sometimes this operation will trigger the next type of transition.
- **Two red children:** If both child links are red, we perform a "color flip." This changes the child links to black and the parent pointer from black to red. Note that this transformation may trigger one of the previous conditions.

A sequence of transformations, as described, will terminate either because none of the conditions is met or because the parent node is the root. The color of the pointer to the root itself is of no consequence. However, this is the moment when an additional level in the tree is introduced: what were two adjacent *red* links are now two adjacent *black* links. This is the mechanism by which the red-black tree maintains a maximum depth of twice the black depth. Figure 6.15 shows all these transformations in process.

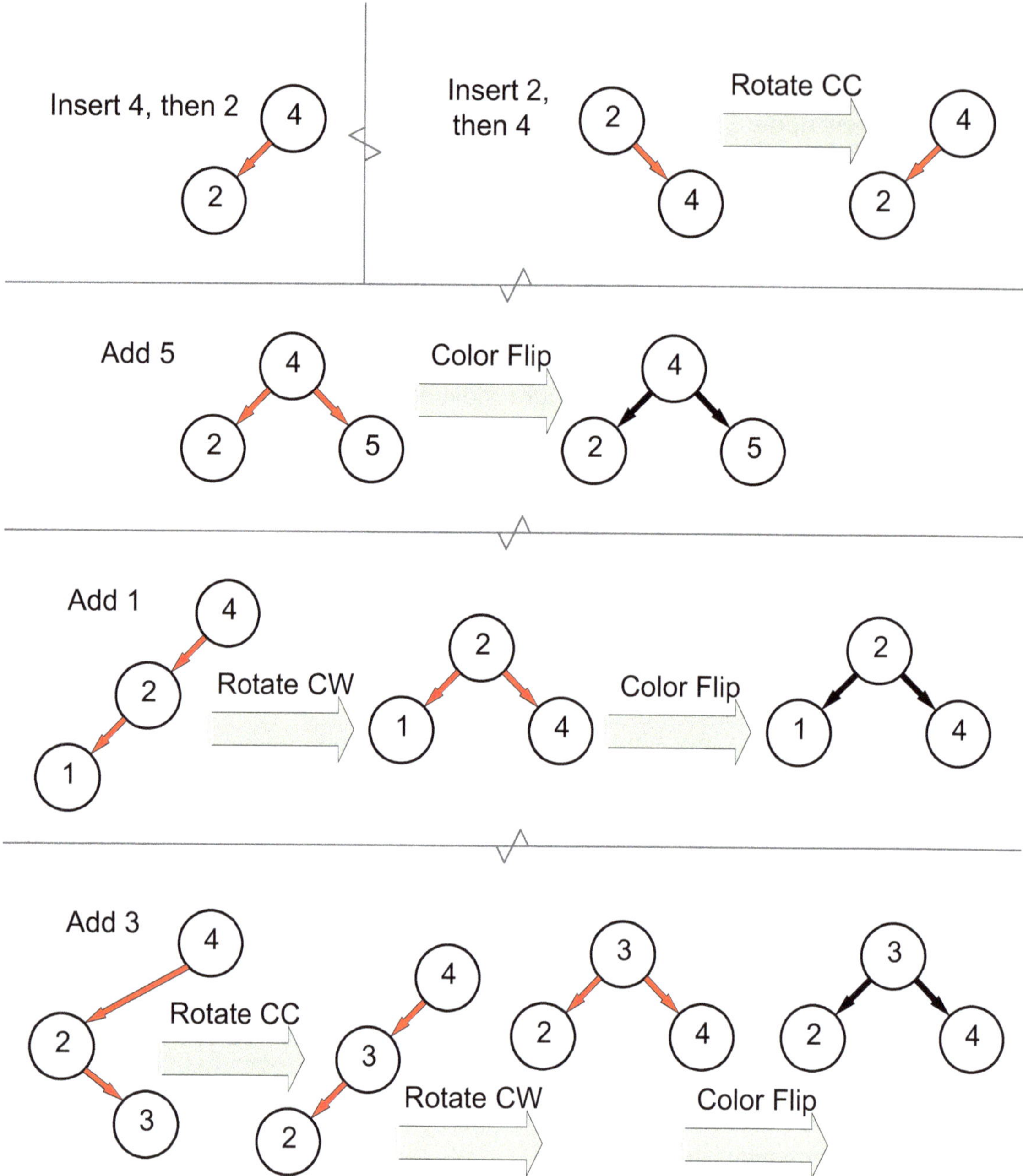

FIGURE 6.15. RBT transitions.

How many keys can an RBT of depth h accommodate? When there are no red links, it is the same as a BST. As mentioned previously, a perfectly balanced BST has exactly $n = 2^h - 1$ keys. What if the RBT has every one of the permissible red links? With only the root and one red left link ($h = 1$), we have room for two keys. If we add one additional black link at each of the three null links, so three additional red links, we have room for eight keys. The formula for the number of keys when full with all permissible red links is $n = 3^h - 1$. We can accommodate other values of n between these extremes due to the flexibility of the structure in having (or not having) red links. Thus, for a given value of n, the actual depth (counting all links) is limited by

$$\lceil \log_2(n+1) \rceil \leq h \leq 2\lceil \log_3(n+1) \rceil.$$

The ranges overlap considerably. For example, if $n = 7$, there are two possible configurations: all black links with $h = 3$ or three red links with $h = 4$. Add one key and there are two choices: Four red links (the max) with $h = 4$, or add just one red link to the all-black $h = 3$ configuration, thus giving $h = 4$.

B-Tree

The B-tree is a balanced tree that is used whenever it is advantageous to read a large block of information at once when following a link in the tree. This is typically the case with database tables and filing systems, particularly when stored on spindle disks. This is because it takes several milliseconds to get in position to read from a disk but, once there, a large block of data can be read very quickly.

A B-tree of order m can store up to $m - 1$ keys and m pointers. When constructing a B-tree, it is typically required that each node (block) be at least half full. This means that the minimum depth of a tree with n keys is $\log_m n$ and the maximum depth is $2\log_m n$. If m is 4,096 (typical), the maximum depth to store 2^{30} (1 billion) keys would be $2 \cdot \frac{30}{12}$: 5. If the root block is always in memory (as is usual), any key can be found in just four disk accesses.

2-3 Tree

The 2-3 is essentially a special case of a B-tree where $m = 3$. Some texts explain the 2-3 tree first and only then discuss the RBT. However, since the 2-3 tree is not typically implemented as an abstract data type, it is only mentioned here.

HISTORY NOTE

The 2-3 tree was first described by Hopcroft in 1970 (Aho, 1974). In that same year, the B-tree was invented (Bayer & McCreight, 1970). Bayer then went on to propose the RBT in 1972 (Bayer, 1972).

Conclusion

If the order of elements is important—for example, because you want to search for elements using binary search—you should plan to use an ordered data structure throughout. The ordered data structures that we have covered in this chapter are all, with the exception of the ordered array, which is a theoretical rather than practical data structure, some variation on a tree. Perhaps the least tree-like is the binary heap, but that is only because it is a tree embedded in an array. You should try to avoid using nonordered data structures if you plan to visit the elements in their ordered sequence at any time, as this only adds to the required work.

Takeaways

Following is a list of the main ideas to take away from this chapter:

- Keeping a collection in order is expensive, particularly an eagerly ordered collection.
- Flexibility works better than rigidity.

Chapter Review Questions

Directions: Refer to what you learned in this chapter to respond to the questions and prompts:

1. Is it really worth the effort to keep these ADTs in order? How about using a hash table?
2. Do you think that Java should provide an ordered array in its collections library? Why or why not?

References

Aho, A. V., Hopcraft, J. E., & Ullman, J. D. (1974). *The Design and Analysis of Computer Algorithms* (1st ed.). Addison Wesley.

Bayer R. (1972). Oriented balanced trees and equivalence relations. *Information Processing Letters*, *1*(6), 226–228. https://doi.org/10.1016/0020-0190(72)90016-6

Bayer, R., & McCreight, E. (1970). Organization and maintenance of large ordered indices. In *Proceedings of the 1970 ACM SIGFIDET Workshop on Data Description, Access and Control* (pp. 107–141). ACM. https://doi.org/10.1145/1734663.1734671

CHAPTER

7

Sorting

Creating Order Out of Comparison

Introduction to the Chapter

In Chapter 6, we defined an abstract data type called *OrderedArray*, which can potentially keep track of more information about the state of the elements of the array. However, we have so far not described how we would impose order on an ordered array. Whether we consider an ordered array to be a fully fledged abstract data type—or not—we must be able to sort arrays so that we can use binary search or present data in a form suitable for humans. Fundamentally, there are two quite different ways to sort an array (or list): by comparing pairs of elements and by counting. We look at the first strategy in this chapter; the second strategy will be examined in Chapter 8.

Learning Objectives

In this chapter students will learn about the following:

1. Total order
2. The principal techniques for creating order by comparing elements of an array
3. Insertion sort, bubble sort, selection sort, Shellsort, merge sort, quicksort, Timsort, heapsort

Key Terms

- **Comparison:** Compare two objects, *a* and *b*, to infer which of the following is true: $a < b$, $a = b$, $a > b$
- **Key:** A function of an object (that may be the identity function) that we use as the basis of a comparison or classification
- **Stable sort:** A sorting method whereby any two elements that compare as equal retain their original relative positions
- **Swap:** An exchange of two elements of an array that fixes one or more inversions
- **Inversion:** A situation when a pair of elements, not necessarily adjacent, is out of order
- **Adaptive:** An adaptive algorithm is one where the amount of work done is less when the input is similar to the desired output. For example, an adaptive sort is one where a partially ordered array requires less work than a randomly ordered array.

Creating Order Out of Comparison

Sorting

"What is the best sorting algorithm?" By now, you should be sufficiently conversant with the concepts of abstract data types to know that the best ADT for one sorting problem may not be the same as the best ADT for a different sorting problem. If an interviewer or colleague asks you this same question, you will only be able to answer after getting answers to your own series of questions. Your first question should be "How many elements do you need to sort?" Then you should follow up with such questions as these:

- *What types of objects will you be sorting?* This is particularly important because, knowing the relative costs of **comparison**, **swap**/copy may be significant.
- *Do you need to perform the sort in place?* If memory is scarce, you will probably want to use a single array; alternatively, you may have sufficient space to sort elements using an auxiliary array. Even if memory is plentiful, it takes extra time to access memory when it's not in the cache.

- *Do you need a stable sort?* For multikey sorts when subsequent sorts may run into duplicate keys, you may want to avoid disturbing the order created from previous sorts.
- *How likely is it that the elements will be partially or completely ordered before you start?* If this is likely—for example you add new elements to a previously ordered set—you want to choose an **adaptive** sort that can minimize the number of operations in this case.
- *Are the elements stored in an array or a list?* Array-sorting algorithms tend to be much more efficient than the list-sorting alternatives. It may be quickest to convert a list to an array (and back afterward) to get the best performance.

Order

Strictly speaking, what we generally refer to as "sorting" should more properly be called **ordering**. The true meaning of sorting relates to placing elements into *classes*. For instance, a postal service *sorts* letters and packages according to the city of their destination. We will find that this true sorting mechanism has a significant application in multikey sorting (see Chapter 8). But, for the sake of consistency with all the other texts out there, we will refer to *ordering* as *sorting*.

Technically, sorting can be thought of as a search problem whereby we test every candidate solution to determine if it meets our requirements and stop when we find a valid solution (by applying a "decision problem" to each). A naïve solution would entail, for each of the $N!$ possible permutations, comparing every pair of neighboring elements to see if they are "in order." This "brute force" method is essentially the technique behind the infamous Bogosort (Wikipedia, 2024). Its runtime grows exponentially with the size of the input (don't try this at home).

Let's consider what it means to say that two elements are in order. What's an element? It's some kind of *thing*—an object—that supports the notion of ordering. If these objects represent numbers, we have an implicitly defined order, provided that those numbers are scalars (each having only one value). Complex numbers, vectors, matrices, and so forth aren't readily orderable. There are no debates about the order of the (scalar) "counting" numbers because they're used for, well, counting. If you have five apples and I have four apples, you win—five is greater than four. Rational numbers can also be easily compared in this way.

Comparison: Total Order

Given a domain of objects (e.g., the English words), if *all* pairs of objects can be strictly ordered ($x < y$ or $x > y$), we can say that the domain defines a (strict) *total order*. If we allow that some pairs of elements compare as equals, we have a (nonstrict) total order. A total order is a binary relation $\leq$ on some set *X*, which satisfies the following for all *a*, *b*, and *c* in *X*:

- (Reflexive) $a \leq a$.
- (Transitive) If $a \leq b$ and $b \leq c$ then $a \leq c$.
- (Antisymmetric) If $a \leq b$ and $b \leq a$ then $a = b$.
- (Total) $a \leq b$ or $b \leq a$.

According to our earlier description of sorting, we should be able to sort objects from a domain with (strict) total order. But what about objects that don't have a strict total order? If they have a nonstrict total order, we can still sort, but we will have to be able to deal with equality because in general there will be duplicates.

What about classes of objects that don't have a total order? How would we order colors, for example? Maybe we could order them according to the frequency of the light—that would give us a nice number that we could use. The snag is that light is generally a mix of frequencies. If we still want to sort colors, we're going to need to introduce the concept of a **key**, for example the number from a color chart for paints.

Keys

To impose an order on two objects, we need a *key* (generalized to include any intrinsic order). The key represents a property (or function of properties) that can be compared using a *comparison*. A key for sorting is, therefore, defined and used much like a *feature* in machine learning whereby we expect the feature to be a *predictor* for classification purposes. For sorting, a key is the *discriminator* between two objects that defines their order. In the case of numbers, or any other type of object with an implicit ordering, the key is the object itself—only *one* **comparison** is required to order two such objects. However, other objects will need multiple, keys that are generally independent (like features in ML). A class of objects with multiple keys may be able to be sorted using one composite key corresponding to a strict total order. Alternatively, the objects might be ordered by applying successive sorts, each with a different key.

For example, people with two or three (or more) names might be ordered by sorting according to the least significant key first (for people in the United States, this might be the middle name or initial), then sort according to the given name, and then according to the family name. In this multistage sort, we require that each sort should be stable. We will cover multikey sorts in much more detail in Chapter 8. However, even an individual component of a name is itself a string of characters—i.e., it is a composite key: the first character, followed by the second, and so on (some languages define names in the reverse order to English names).

Natural language characters, which make up such a string, can be ordered, of course. But which language? That's going to make quite a difference. In the (traditional, pre-1994) Spanish word *order*, for example, "c" and "ch" were considered different letters, lexicographically. Even today "ñ" is collated after "n." If we have a collation scheme that defines the order of letters for a particular language, we can order words in that language.

Let's define *comparable* as a property of an object such that we can order it against another object *by comparing their keys*. And we're going to require such a key to have at least a nonstrict total order. When we compare the keys x and y, there will be one of three possible outcomes: $x<y$, $x=y$, or $x>y$. We will be able to navigate through our search space using the result. Note that if we want a Boolean result (for a decision problem), we need to combine these three results into two, for example *less*: $x<y$, where *not less* implies $x \geq y$.

Comparison in Java

Java has two different mechanisms for comparing values, each defined by an interface:

- *Comparable<T>*: This interface defines a method suitable for intrinsic comparisons, whereby any element of a class that implements *Comparable* can be compared with any other such instance:
  - `int compareTo(T t)`
- *Comparator<T>*: This interface defines a method suitable for explicit comparisons, for example where *T* may have several fields, which can logically be compared in several different sequences:
  - `int compare(T t1, T t2)`

In each case the result is negative if *this* (or *t1*) is less than *t* (or *t2*). If they are equal, the result is zero. Otherwise, the result is positive.

Counting Sorts

If we have a relatively high incidence of equal keys, comparison sorting will spend a great deal of time that's essentially wasted—there is no news in two keys being equal—because we will never swap in such a case. But sorting strings of digits or alphabetical characters is something humans have been doing for a very long time. The technique required to put groups of objects in order, whereby each group has the same key, is no more complex than the ability to count. Surprisingly, perhaps, the oldest way of sorting is also the most efficient, at least for these types of string objects (i.e., objects with multiple keys) and can generally be accomplished in time proportional to the total number of characters (i.e., linear). We will cover such sorts in more detail in the next chapter.

Comparison Sorts

When keys are (mostly) discrete (different), counting sorts are not the most efficient way of sorting because they still depend on the ability to order each group with the same key. For now, we will concentrate on the most familiar kind of sort: the comparison sort.

Perhaps the most significant property of comparison sorts is that they can be performed in place. Counting sorts *cannot* be implemented in place and even some comparison sorts, like merge sort, and its variant Timsort, are not in-place sorts either. While the ability to sort in place was most significant in the early days of computers when memory was scarce, even today, using additional memory necessarily adds time to an algorithm.

As noted, comparisons involve *pairs* of elements. How many pairs are in a collection of length *n*? It's the number of ways of choosing two objects from *n* objects, traditionally written $\binom{n}{2}$, one of the binomial coefficients. Its value is $\frac{n(n-1)}{2}$, which we can easily derive as follows: We have *n* possible ways of choosing the first element, but only $n-1$ ways remaining for choosing the second element. As far as invoking the comparison operator on a pair is concerned, it doesn't matter what order the elements are in (although the result cares). Therefore, we divide the number of permutations by two.

But that means there are $O(n^2)$ pairs! That would mean the algorithm runs in quadratic time! As we saw in Chapter 2, quadratic algorithms do not scale well.

Still, if n is small, and/or we have a fast computer, we can stop worrying too much about the total time. Let's see where this idea leads.

A comparison that is part of an in-place sort will, if the pair is **inverted**, be followed by an exchange (swap).

Adaptive Sorts

Supposing we were given an array to be sorted that happened to be in order (or even close to being in order) before we started. We would hope that our algorithm only does the necessary work to remove the inversions. The first two sorting algorithms we will look at have this desirable property.

Bubble Sort

Perhaps the most obvious sorting method is bubble sort (in pseudo-code) whereby we assume that the first element is at the left and the last element is at the right:

```
set w to point to the (nonexistent) neighbor of the last element
while true {
    set x to refer to the "first" element of the collection
    while x has neighbor y and y is not w
            conditionally swap x with y, and set x equal to y
    if the loop completed without swapping anything
            break
    set w to refer to the most recent value of x
}
```

Both loops have early exit possibilities. The inner loop exits when y reaches w. In other words, w represents the boundary between the elements on the left, which may be out of order, and the elements on the right, which are in final order. The outer loop exits whenever the inner loop doesn't swap anything. If the collection was already sorted, all we need to do is one pass through the collection. But, if the smallest element of the collection happened to be in the last place, we would have to run the outer loop a total of $n-1$ times because the last element must find its way to the first place one position at a time. The average ending point for the inner loop is half-way through the collection, so the number of compares we do in the worst case is $\binom{n}{2}$ (i.e., all pairs). Here is a graphical depiction of the process for a short array: the first pass is on the left, the second pass is on the right:

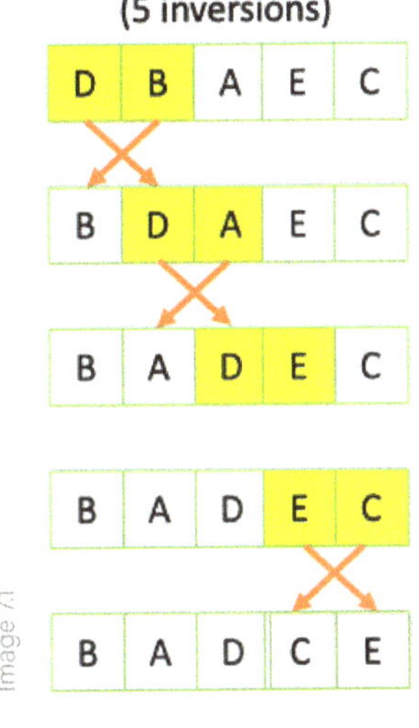

Image 7.1

The best case (when the collection happens to be sorted already) is $n-1$ compares; the worst case is $\frac{n(n-1)}{2}$ compares (all pairs); and the average case is, in practice, only slightly better than the worst case.

The fact that *w* (the gray element) always divides the unsorted partition from the sorted partition is an example of a "loop invariant" because it's valid at the same point in every iteration of the outer loop.

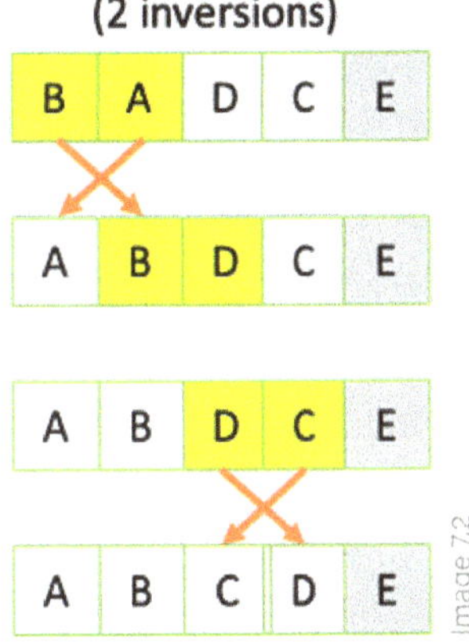

Image 7.2

Bubble sort has almost no redeeming virtues as a practical sorting method. Even Senator Barack Obama knew that bubble sort was the "wrong way to go" in 2007.

WATCH AT: https://www.youtube.com/watch?v=1nnj7r1wC-D4&t=408s

Bubble sort is nevertheless instructive. And it does have one feature that cannot be claimed by most other popular sorting methods. Did you notice that we referred to the input as a *collection* of elements—without specifying whether it was an array or a list? Most sorting algorithms work efficiently on arrays because they must do one or other of the following:

- compare/swap non neighboring elements
- traverse the collection right-to-left instead of left-to-right

These operations are quite awkward in a typical linked list when defined from left to right. In the pseudo-code, you can see that bubble sort will work for either an array or a linked list.

Swaps

To *swap* two elements is to *exchange* their values, something very efficient for an array, especially if the elements are close to each other. "Exchange" is of course more formal, but "swap" (pronounced as "swop") is just so much shorter and clearer. Now, it's time to introduce a term for the idea of a conditional swap. Let's call it a *coswap*, which you can think of either as a conditional swap, or compare-and-maybe swap. We already used it (but with its full name) in bubble sort.

An algorithm that is clever enough to do less work when the result has already been partially achieved is called *adaptive*. You might wonder why anyone would want to sort a collection that has already been sorted. To help discuss that, we need to introduce another term: *inversion*. An inversion is simply when any two elements of a collection are not in their correct (desired) order. The maximum possible number of inversions in a collection of size n is of course the number of distinct pairs, $\frac{n(n-1)}{2}$. As we've already noted, that occurs when the collection is in *reverse* order. Note that the term "inversion" applies to both neighboring elements and non-neighboring elements. When a collection is already sorted, it has zero inversions.

If the minimum number of inversions is zero and the maximum number is $\binom{n}{2}$, what's the average number? If a collection is in random order, any pair has a 50% chance of being inverted. Thus, the average number of inversions (for a random collection) is $\frac{n(n-1)}{4}$.

When the number of inversions in a collection of n elements is proportional to its length (rather than length squared), we consider that collection to be *partially ordered*. Why would that ever happen? And how would we know about it?

Let's say you are a birdwatcher. Every day you go out and note in your journal the names of the birds that you see. When you get home, you add those new names to your (ordered) lifetime list. Let's say you've already seen 100 birds. And today you saw eight more. How many inversions do you have, potentially? Today's list might have about 14, according to the formula. But each of those eight new birds might also be inverted with respect to the birds already in the list: that's 400 inversions, on average, for a total of 414. Assuming that the existing list is much longer than today's list, we can almost discount the smaller term and just think about the larger term, whose value is linear with respect to the length of the original list.

If the (complete) 108-element list was in random order, we'd expect about 2,900 inversions. But, as we know that is not the case, we have an example of a partially ordered list and will benefit from the use of an **adaptive** sort method.

This might seem like an unusual application. But database indexes get updated like this all the time. A transaction occurs that adds a few records to a table, and the index must be updated. Surely you want to use an adaptive algorithm that's linear in the size of the existing table rather than quadratic or linearithmic.

It's worth making a clear distinction between stable and unstable **swaps**. One way to do that is to write the neighbor swap method with just one index (it only needs one) and perhaps the word "stable" in the name. Finally, recall from the previous chapter, the concept of "half-swaps," which we can use whenever we need to insert an element and push several others aside.

Insertion Sort

A sorting method such as bubble sort is called an elementary sort, because, in general, it works by coswapping *elements*. But there's another very important elementary sort that is familiar to most people, especially bridge (or hearts) players. You are dealt 13 cards, and most players like to sort them into suits, and perhaps sort them according to rank within the suits. See Figure 7.1.

FIGURE 7.1. Unordered bridge hand.

The technique used by bridge (or whist) players is simply to scan the hand and look for a card that's out of place. Then they insert it into its proper place. The computer algorithm that mimics this is called insertion sort.

FIGURE 7.2. Ordered bridge hand.

Insertion sort is an improvement over bubble sort for random inputs because, in general, both the inner and outer loops are run, on average, $n/2$ times. By contrast, only the inner loop of bubble sort takes $n/2$ iterations; the outer loop requires $n-1$ iterations (unless the array is partially ordered). Insertion sort maintains two partitions: on the left is ordered; on the right is unseen. The transitional element at each iteration (i.e., the left-most element of the unseen partition) is inserted into the ordered part by doing a coswap with its left-hand neighbor, then (if swapped) with the next neighbor, and so on.

Each pass of the outer loop performs either zero or one comparisons more than the number of swaps. The difference comes from what terminates the inner loop: coming to the end of the elements (zero extra comparisons) or stopping because the moving element is in its proper place (one extra comparison). Therefore, in terms of the original number of inversions X, the number of comparisons for insertion sort is $\Omega(X+O(n-1))$ and $\Omega(n-1)$. As you will recall, $X=\frac{1}{4}n(n-1)$ when the input is random. Here is the pseudo-code:

```
for i from  1 up to and including n-1 {
   set j to the value of i
   while j > 0 & conditional-stable-swap j continue
}
```

Here, the method *conditional-stable-swap(j)* conditionally swaps the elements with indices j-1 and j and returns a Boolean indicating whether the swap occurred. It's a stable swap because it swaps neighbors, which is why we only need to specify one index. If the two neighboring elements are not inverted (including the possibility that they have the same key), they do not change places. And, if they are swapped, neither element moves relative to any other element.

Stable Sorting

Thus far, our (conditional) swaps have always involved neighboring elements. This type of swap has an important property. Suppose that we have two neighboring elements that have equal keys. We wouldn't ever actually swap them since they're not inverted. That means that, if those elements are already ordered according to a different key, that original ordering will not be disturbed.

For example, when grading students from different sections, a learning management system (LMS) orders all students alphabetically. But suppose you want them to be grouped into sections; you would order by the *section* key. You still want them alphabetically within each section, so you must use a **stable sort**. Spreadsheets know that you want to do this kind of thing, so spreadsheet sorts always are stable. And, because they use neighbor swaps, both bubble sort and insertion sort are stable, as well as adaptive.

What is it about non-neighbor swaps that cause instability? Imagine three elements, and two keys (an alphabetical key and a numeric key; see Figure 7.3).

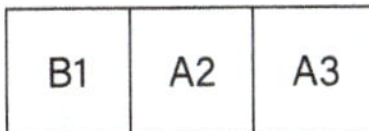

FIGURE 7.3. Before non-neighbor swap.

They have been previously ordered by the numeric key and now you are sorting alphabetically using an unstable sort (allows non-neighbor swaps). When we compare the first and last elements, we see that they are out of order so we must swap them. This results in:

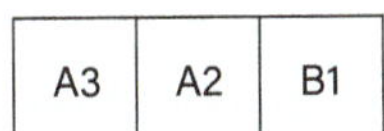

FIGURE 7.4. After Non-neighbor swap.

But now, A3 and A2 are no longer ordered numerically.

Nonadaptive Sorts

Next, we will look at some sorting algorithms that don't possess the adaptive property.

Selection Sort

Why would we ever use a non-neighbor swap? For efficiency. Neighbor swaps always fix exactly one inversion. That's why, if we start with the expected (quadratic) number of inversions in a random array, we must use a quadratic number of coswaps to sort it. That's usually a bad idea.

On the other hand, non-neighbor swaps can fix multiple inversions. Consider the three elements discussed in the previous section. And further imagine that the final ordering is what we wanted (reverse numerical followed by alphabetical). Then the original layout was in reverse order and had the expected $\frac{3*2}{2}$ (three) inversions: B1/A2, B1/A3, and A2/A3. The final layout is in order (zero inversions). Yet, we performed only one swap. Therefore, that swap was able to fix three inversions. In general, if an array of length n is in reverse order and we swap the outer two elements, we fix $2n-3$ inversions.

Now, let's imagine a different problem (one that does not often arise in software). It's trivially easy to compare two elements but hard to swap two elements. For example, a delivery truck randomly deposits 10 packages on pallets (skids) in a line on the warehouse floor. Your manager asks you to position them in the same line according to their barcodes. The packages are far too heavy for you to move, so you need a forklift. You also have a scanner that can easily tell you which of two packages comes first. Naturally, to do this as efficiently as possible, you must minimize the number of swaps while not being overly concerned with the number of comparisons.

Selection sort is the algorithm you need. You will have to pass over the elements of the array exactly nine ($N-1$) times. Each of these passes ends with a single swap operation. A pass involves finding the minimum (by barcode) of the elements that are still out of order, those packages on the right of a (blue) marker that we place between the packages on the left, which are in their final order, and those on the right that are still out of order. To begin, we place this blue marker to the left of the left-most package. Then, each pass—using only our scanner and a second (green) marker placed in front of the package to the right of the blue marker—requires comparing the value of the barcode of the (green-marker) package with each package to its right. When we find a package with a "smaller" barcode, we move the green marker to it. We then get into the forklift and swap the element immediately to the right of the blue marker with the package identified by the green marker. We conclude that pass by moving the blue marker one place to its right.

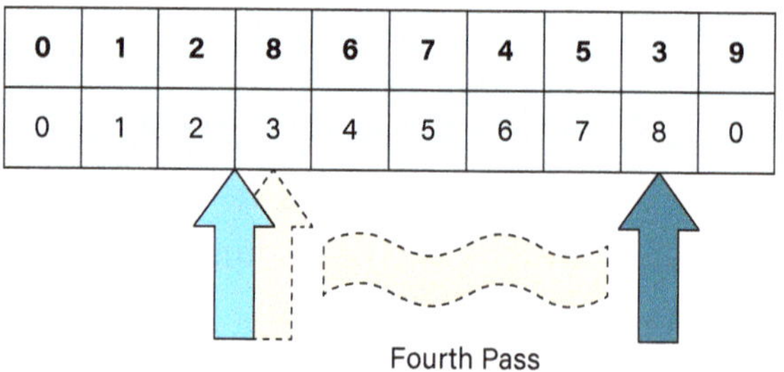

FIGURE 7.5. Selection sort.

In our example, once we've completed nine passes, there's only one package left, which must already be in its proper place. Clearly, successive passes do fewer comparisons. Thus, we perform, in general for n objects, $\frac{1}{2}n\ (n-1)$ comparisons and $n-1$ swaps. Because the swaps we do are not neighbor swaps, selection sort is not stable. But there is no better algorithm for this type of situation, as comparison is cheap, but swapping is expensive. Indeed, we can say that whenever $\frac{s}{c} > \frac{n}{n-4}$, where s is the time to swap, c is the time to compare, and the input is n randomly ordered elements where $n>4$, we should choose selection sort over insertion sort.

There's one more relevant observation to make. Both insertion sort and selection sort *reduce* the problem by dividing their input into two partitions: one representing the result (on the left) and one representing work still to be done (on the right). Each pass moves the boundary between the two partitions one place to the right. But in the case of selection sort, the "work" (finding the minimum remaining element) is done first, and then the repartitioning is affected. In the case of insertion sort, the next unknown element (from the right partition) is added to the left partition. Only then is the work—finding its proper place—carried out.

Optimal Sorting

For any problem, we should try to determine the minimum number of operations that are required (the best case for the problem). Then we seek an optimal solution. Revisiting our discussion of entropy in Chapter 2, let's start with the observation that there are $n!$ (i.e., n factorial) possible permutations of n elements, of which only one is ordered. Suppose that we could randomly pick a pair of elements and compare them. According to whether they are inverted (or not), we can partition our set of candidate solutions into two: One set (the "good" set) includes the pair in order; the other does not. Now, we perform another random comparison and divide the good set into two as before. What is the minimum number of such comparisons we must perform to end up with a set containing *only* the ordered permutation? The answer is $\log_2 n!$. But what is this number? According to Stirling's approximation, it is around $n\ (\log_2 \frac{n}{e})$. Note that $\log_2 n$ is usually notated as $lg\,n$. Keep in mind that this is the theoretical minimum *possible* number of comparisons, if we make an ideal choice for each comparison. Since we are usually concerned only with the rate of growth, we normally drop the (linear) term involving e and just use $n\,lg\,n$. Therefore, we can say that the problem of comparison sorting an array of n elements requires at least $n\,lg\,n$ comparisons (i.e., $\Omega(n\,lg\,n)$). Any sorting algorithm whose order of growth is $O(n\,lg\,n)$ is therefore considered *optimal*.

Suppose we simply perform $N\,lg\,N$ coswap operations on random pairs as our first attempt at an optimal solution. Approximately half of these will result in action, and half will not. But, after each operation, we divide the solution space into the good half and the bad half. The effect of this sort is to derive a partially ordered array. At the conclusion, we must apply insertion sort to fix any remaining inversions in linear time. In practice, because each pair tested is as likely to be inverted as not, the algorithm can be improved somewhat by performing $2N\lg N$ coswaps.

The "random sort" described doesn't do a very good job in practice because the pairs are not intelligently chosen (there will be repeated comparisons and other comparisons that don't contribute information). Note that random sort is not stable because it does non-neighbor swaps. It does sort in place, though. However, it's not a good practical sorting method, so don't look for it in your favorite sorting library. Variations on this idea are sometimes called "monkey sort."

Merge Sort

Can we find a good optimal solution, one that also requires something very close to the minimum number of comparisons? Indeed, we can—by using the technique of "wishful thinking," or recursion, also known as DnC (see Chapter 1).

First, we divide the input array of length *n* (this method only works well with arrays) into two partitions as evenly as possible. Next, we sort each partition recursively, resulting in two sorted sub-arrays. But what we want is the entire array sorted. For this, we must "merge" the two partitions. Unfortunately, try as you might, you cannot perform this merge operation in place. You will need another temporary array of length *n* in which to store the whole sorted array. Then this temporary array, known as the auxiliary array, must be copied back into the original array. The extra memory required slows the algorithm down but is unavoidable using this elegant sorting method, called merge sort.

```
procedure mergesort(xs) ■ sort the array xs
    mergesort(xs,0,xs.length) ■ sort the 0:xs.length partition
of xs (all of it)
procedure mergesort(xs,from,to) ■ sort the from:to partition
of array xs
    mid ← from+(to−from)/2 ■ the mid-point of the
partition
    mergesort(xs,from,mid) ■ recursively sort the left-hand
partition
    mergesort(xs,mid,to) ■ recursively sort the right-hand
partition
    merge(xs,from,mid,to) ■ merge the two sorted partitions
```

Note that the *to* parameter is chosen to represent the index of the first element that we *do not* sort. This is in keeping with a 0-based indexing scheme, and it simplifies the code. Note also that we haven't said anything about any auxiliary array. Logically, this is private to the merge method (not shown here).

However, we can use the same auxiliary array for the entire merge sort process, and we can also avoid one of the copy operations described by exchanging array pointers at every level of recursion and making the auxiliary array a clone when it is first allocated. Nevertheless, the use of the auxiliary array does slow merge sort down noticeably, simply because we must access twice as much memory as for other sorting algorithms. Recall (from Chapter 2) that the number of hits (net array accesses) with the number of lookups (dereferencing heap objects), and bearing in mind the total memory required yields a good predictor of the time it will take for an algorithm to run.

How many comparisons are required? At each level, the algorithm must do between $\frac{n}{2}$ and $n-1$ comparisons. We only need to do half the comparisons if the elements are already ordered. The number of levels, of course, is $lg\,N$. So, merge sort is indeed an optimal sorting algorithm, as we would expect from applying the Master theorem (for a video, see https://youtu.be/2H0GKdrIowU?si=8n-5BHVuT_u6b9_o).

There are some other worthwhile optimizations, in addition to the trick of avoiding extra copies mentioned. The first of these arises from an interesting, perhaps surprising, observation. $n\,lg\,n$ grows more slowly than $\frac{1}{4}n^2$ of course. But if you compare their values where $n<16$ (i.e., one of the points where $n=4\lg n$), you will notice that insertion sort will do fewer compares than merge sort (in the random case). And, because it will not have to create extra stack frame entries for the recursion, it will do it more efficiently too. At some threshold in the region of 16, it makes sense for merge sort to invoke insertion sort, instead of recursing into merge sort. Benchmarking with Java (see *SortBenchmark* in the repository) suggests that the cutoff should be 20. Java used a cutoff of 7 when merge sort was the standard object sorter.

There is another optimization that makes sense if you think that the input array may be partially ordered. Consider the situation when the last element of the left-hand partition is smaller than the first element of the right-hand partition. In this case, we won't need to do any further comparisons—we simply copy all the elements to the destination. It's an example of taking out insurance. The premium is the extra test that you perform for every pair of partitions, which, in many cases, will not benefit you. But, when it does pay off, it saves $\frac{m}{2}-1$ comparisons (net), where *m* is the total number of elements in the two partitions. One further observation regarding merge sort is that we don't do any swapping. All reordering is performed via copying. An analysis of the required numbers of comparisons (k) reveals that

- $k = O(n\,h - 2^h + 1)$
- $k = \Omega(\frac{nh}{2})$ (when the array is sorted)
- $k = \Omega(2^h - 1)$ (when the array is sorted, and the insurance test is used)

where $h = \lceil \lg n \rceil$.

Of course, when n is a power of two, we can instead write

- $k = O(n \lg n - n + 1)$
- $k = \Omega(\frac{n \lg n}{2})$ (when the array is sorted)
- $k = \Omega(n - 1)$ (when the array is sorted, and the insurance test is used)

HISTORICAL NOTE

Merge sort was introduced in 1945 by John von Neumann for the EDVAC project. Von Neumann had to implement the recursive aspects of the method himself, resulting in 23 hand-written pages of code! The only alternatives for general comparison-based sorting were the "elementary" sorts, viz. insertion sort, bubble sort, and selection sort. Von Neumann was generally considered by everyone who knew him as the smartest person they knew.

Quicksort

Does that optimization where we perform the "insurance" comparison in merge sort suggest anything to you? What if we could somehow arrange for that condition to always hold true? We could skip the merge (and therefore the auxiliary array) entirely! But aren't we at the mercy of the elements as presented? What if—before performing the recursion—we swapped any element in the left-hand partition that belonged in the right-hand partition with an element that was similarly mislocated in the right-hand partition? Good idea, but we would need to know the value of the median element. And to determine that for each partition would be far too much work to be efficient. On the other hand, perhaps we could simply guess the median, provided we don't require each partition to be the same size (as was the case in merge sort). Now, we could arrange the elements appropriately.

There's another snag, however. The median element will almost certainly not be in its proper place *before* sorting, so we need to do our swapping based on where we expect our guessed median to end up. Because this element will be used for determining which elements are out of place—too "heavy" or too "light" for their actual position—we call this pseudo-median element the *pivot*. The advantage of this method is that, once all swapping has occurred, and the pivot has been moved to its proper place, we will have a situation like Figure 7.6, with two partitions surrounding the value of the pivot, *v*:

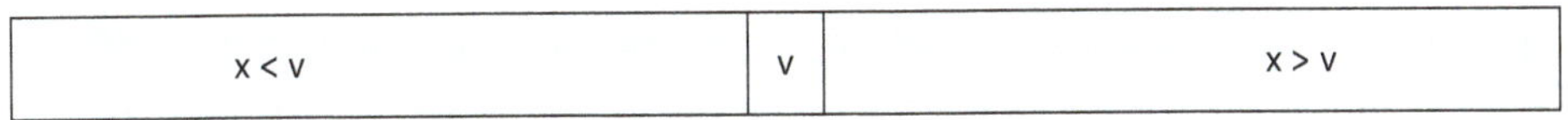

FIGURE 7.6. Quicksort partitioning.

Now, we recursively sort the left-hand partition, then the right-hand partition, and, when we're finished, no merging needs to take place. Not only does this eliminate the need for any more comparisons, but it also eliminates copying. Therefore, we no longer need that auxiliary array! This sorting method operates *in place* and is called "quicksort."

HISTORICAL NOTE

Quicksort was developed in 1960 by Tony Hoare, although he couldn't implement it right away because no languages of the time provided recursion (Algol 60 was the savior). I don't know if he thought about it the way I have described it, but it was a brilliant improvement to sorting at the time. The best alternatives for general comparison-based sorting were Shell sort, approximately $O(N^{\frac{3}{2}})$, and merge sort, linearithmic in comparisons but using twice the memory needed by the elements themselves. This may not sound like a big deal today, but if your memory was only 4,000 words, it was a huge limitation.

There is, however, one more issue to address. When we partitioned for merge sort, we partitioned the array as equally as possible. Can we still operate our recursive algorithm even though the partition sizes may not be the same? Yes, it will work just fine. However, the (exact) equal partitioning did result in the algorithm requiring just $n\lg n$ comparisons. Suppose that our guess for the median is so bad that we simply randomly choose any element as the pivot. We show that the number of comparisons required will be $2n\ln n$, which is approximately 39% more than for merge sort.

Randomly choosing the pivot has an even more serious potential problem. It is possible that each time we choose the pivot, we pick the smallest element (or the largest). This will result in two partitions: one of zero size, the other of size $n-1$. This will take n levels of recursion to successfully sort the array. That implies, since each level will on average need to do $\frac{n}{2}$ comparisons, a total number of comparisons equal to $\frac{1}{2}n^2$ (i.e., no improvement over bubble sort or selection sort). Therefore, it's important to answer $O(n^2)$ when asked "What is the worst-case complexity for quicksort?" But realistically, the danger is far-fetched. There are several ways to avoid the problem in practice. The first, and perhaps least effective, method is to shuffle the array before starting quicksort or, equivalently, to pick a random element at each level of recursion (but the number of random elements used thus is linearithmic, not linear as in the initial shuffle). Either of these methods will reduce the odds of truly quadratic performance to about 1 in n^n.

A better method is to guess the median by, for example, taking the median of three elements, typically the first, last, and middle elements. It requires only two or three comparisons to determine the median of three. Again, the likelihood of quadratic performance is vanishingly remote.

The state-of-the-art approach is to take a leaf from the book of engineering redundancy. Just as an aircraft has multiple hydraulic systems, for example, quicksort can benefit from having multiple pivots. If it's unlikely that a single pivot will cause quadratic behavior, it's even less likely when two or more pivots are employed. It has been standard practice in recent years (e.g., in Java) to use Yaroslavskiy's 2011 "dual-pivot quicksort."

HISTORICAL NOTE

Even when precautions were taken to avoid quadratic performance, quicksort was very slow when certain patterns were present in the input data. And it did not perform well when there were many duplicate elements (indeed, there were even a few incorrect implementations in the public domain, especially when duplicates were present). Various improvements were introduced over the years, including three-way quicksort and dual-pivot quicksort.

Two other aspects of quicksort should be noted. Because the swap operations that perform the partitioning use general, non-neighbor swaps, quicksort is not stable. And, of course, quicksort is not adaptive. Even if we don't shuffle, we must look at each element to see if it should be swapped.

As noted regarding insertion and selection sorts, the order in which we perform the recursion and the work can be significant. In merge sort, we recurse into the two partitions first, then merge (the work). In quicksort, we start with the rearrangement of elements (the work), then recurse into the partitions defined by the pivot. Note that it's traditional when discussing quicksort to call the rearrangement process "partitioning," but here we try to use the term "partition" uniformly to mean simply dividing the array into parts.

Merge Sort versus Quicksort

The foregoing discussions of merge sort and quicksort have left out some important practical aspects. For example, quicksort typically performs more comparisons than merge sort yet is generally faster. This is a good illustration of the fact that the number of instructions isn't the whole story. The time spent waiting for memory is usually more important. Merge sort must deal with twice the memory. As a gross oversimplification, the time spent by merge sort waiting for cache pages to be refreshed is likely to be double the time spent by quicksort. For other, more subtle, differences, dual-pivot quicksort spends less time waiting for memory (i.e., is more cache friendly) than original quicksort.

You might have noticed that quicksort uses non-neighbor swaps (so is not stable) but that merge sort doesn't do any swapping at all. It *copies* elements. However, when we have two equal keys in the two different partitions, we can ensure that merge sort is stable simply by always choosing the element from the left-hand partition.

There's another significant difference between merge sort and quicksort that has to do with the complexity of individual comparisons. If we are comparing scalar values (e.g., integers, floating point values) directly, the time for a compare will necessarily be less than when a pointer must be followed to one (or more) scalar values. This is particularly because the destination of that pointer is likely to require a cache page refresh. In the Java world, we call these two types of information primitives and objects, respectively. Because objects are always more expensive to compare, we want to minimize the number of comparisons—and thus we should use merge sort. But, for primitives, the fast comparisons allow us to use quicksort. And this is reflected in the default sorting methods that Java provides for objects and primitives.

One more factor that yields a small improvement in quicksort's favor is that all the comparisons in merge sort are array element to array element (and sometimes these may be far from each other), whereas, in quicksort, the comparisons are array element to the pivot (stored as a variable and located, typically, in a register—a very fast memory location).

To get a good estimate of the time required for a sorting algorithm, we should consider both hits and lookups. We define a lookup as dereferencing an object. Since objects are typically stored on the heap, a lookup is quite likely to cause a cache page fault. (Note that in Java, primitives don't require a lookup.) Actually, it could be worse: An object might contain more than one value that has to be looked up and compared. My own research has shown that the time taken for a hit or a lookup is, very approximately, 4 or 5 nano-seconds. This is reasonably accurate for all comparison sorts. It's not, however, a good predictor for the sorts we will cover in the next chapter.

Timsort

There's another optimization we could try for merge sort. Instead of using recursion, how about converting it to an iterative method? This is possible, even though merge sort, with two partitions to recurse on, would not normally be *tail-recursive*. Nevertheless, because merge sort does not produce a *result* (instead, it mutates the given array), it is able to be iterated—the so-called "bottom-up" merge sort.

Unfortunately, the straightforward bottom-up merge sort takes slightly longer than the top-down version. However, if the input array is likely to be partially ordered, it is possible to speed the process by looking for arbitrarily sized "natural" runs of elements in order. Similarly to its top-down cousin, merge sort, Timsort does not merge small runs, devolving to insertion sort instead. Thus, if a run is too short, it will be expanded using insertion sort until a threshold length has been achieved.

A further significant optimization in Timsort is that runs are merged intelligently. Typically, runs can be merged by using binary search to find where the first/last elements of a run will end up in the merged run. This knowledge determines which of the elements must be copied into auxiliary storage. Usually, that number is significantly smaller than *n*.

HISTORICAL NOTE

Peter McIlroy introduced some of these ideas for merge sort in his 1993 paper "Optimistic Sorting and Information Theoretic Complexity." When Python was looking for a sort algorithm, Tim Peters made further optimizations (2002) and Timsort was born. Today, Timsort is also the default sort method for *objects* in Java and various other languages.

Heapsort

Let's take another look at *selection sort*. The thing that makes it so slow is looping over the remaining elements to find the smallest element. But in the previous chapter, we learned about the binary heap, which is designed to optimize this very process. What would happen if we started by loading the elements into a binary heap? We could run a modified version of selection sort. We would delete the minimum n times and would have our sorted array. The time complexity of this modified selection sort would be $O(n\,lg\,n)$, while its memory complexity would be $O(n)$, accounting for the space required by the binary heap.

Because the sink/swim operations (the swaps) in the binary heap are not neighbor swaps, our sort method would not be stable. It has the same time and space complexity as merge sort but is not stable. What use could it be?

But wait: The binary heap is itself an array. Could we perhaps avoid creating a new array for the binary heap? Let's try pretending that the input array is a maximum binary heap. If the array happened to be in reverse order, it would satisfy the "heap order" invariant. But, in the usual situation, it would not. However, we already know how to fix a heap that is not in heap order: We apply the sink operations. Starting with the last sub-heap of two or more elements (which is exactly halfway through the array), and working in reverse toward the root, we sink each sub-heap as appropriate. By the time we have operated on the entire heap, it will be in heap order. The properties of this sorting algorithm, which we will call *heapsort*, are $O(n\ lg\ n)$ comparisons, with $O(1)$ memory; not stable and not adaptive.

Incidentally, because the elements are not being inserted one by one into the binary heap (but are already present at the start), the number of comparisons required for this phase of the algorithm is $O(n)$ rather than $O(n\ lg\ n)$. However, the number of swaps remains $O(n\ lg\ n)$.

Once the binary heap has been thus constructed, the next step is to perform the delete-max operation for each of the n elements. The difference is that the result of each delete-max is not passed to a caller but is given back to the ownership of the original array: We swap the last element of the binary heap with the root element, perform the sink down of the new root, and simply decrement the count, thus yielding that element back to the original array. In this way, the largest element (the original root) ends up in the last place of the array, and so on.

What's the point? We already have an algorithm that is (on average) $\sim(n\,lg\,n)$, unstable, and in place. It's called quicksort. And, it has a smaller coefficient than heapsort. But, if you recall, quicksort has a worst-case growth of $O(n^2)$. Heapsort has a natural use case whenever quadratic performance cannot be tolerated, for example, in the kernel of the Unix operating system.

Shell Sort

In the section on optimal sorting, we tried the idea of "random sort" as a preprocessor to insertion sort. The idea was to eliminate almost all inversions before the final pass of insertion sort. Any algorithm that can remove most inversions would be a suitable preprocessor (see the next chapter for more preprocessor designs). How about using insertion sort itself on sub-arrays of the array? The problem we run into is that even though we might partition the array, neighbor swaps can fix only one inversion at a time.

But, suppose that, instead of the usual type of partitioning, we divide the elements by *striding* through the array. Let's say that we want h such partitions. Partition 0 (colored light blue in Figure 7.7, where $h = 3$ and $n = 16$) must therefore be made up of elements at indices $0, h, 2h, 3h$, and so on up to $\frac{n}{h}h$. Partition 1 (yellow) would include indices $1, h+1, 2h+1, 3h+1$, and so on. Partition 2 (medium blue) would consist of the remaining elements. In general, the partitions won't all be the same length. Here, there are six light blues, and five each of medium blue and yellow.

FIGURE 7.7. Shellsort partitioning.

Let's consider an inversion between (light blue) elements at indices 0 and h. If we fix that inversion by swapping those elements, it's possible that we could fix as many as $2h-1$ inversions in the original array. In practice, when averaged over the partitions, the number of fixes per swap will be more modest. However, if the average number of fixes per swap is greater than one, this method can do an efficient job of preprocessing the array, albeit in an unstable manner.

The way each pass of this algorithm, known as Shellsort (Shell, 1959), works is that there are h independent insertion sorts—one for each of the partitions. The light blue sort will require, on average, $7\frac{1}{2}$ coswaps, the yellow and medium blue partitions will require an average of 5 coswaps each. At the close of the pass, each of the partitions will itself have zero inversions, yet approximately one third of the initial number of inversions in the array will remain. This is because we have not yet compared any of the light blue elements with yellow or medium blue elements.

How should we go about choosing h (also known as the "gap")? One simple method is to divide n by three and then divide by three again for the next pass. The final pass will have $h=1$, which is of course plain insertion sort. Successive gaps should be relatively prime; otherwise, we will repeatedly compare the same pair of elements.

The analysis of Shellsort is very complex and beyond the scope of this book. And there are many proposed gap sequences. One of the best is the Sedgewick (1986) scheme: 1, 5, 19, 41, 109, ... (see https://oeis.org/A033622). Many of the simpler gap sequences result in worst-case growth of $O(n^{\frac{3}{2}})$. However, Sedgewick's sequence grows at $O(n^{\frac{4}{3}})$ and the Pratt sequence $O(\log^2 n)$. No good expression exists in general for the average growth rate.

When the input array is already ordered, each pass will do $\sim n$ compares. Thus, the total number of compares is pn, where p is the number of passes. For the division-by-three scheme, $p \sim \log_3 n$.

HISTORICAL NOTE

Shellsort is mostly of historical interest today. But when D. H. Shell published it in 1959, the only alternatives were insertion sort and merge sort among the comparison sorts. Recall that, at the time, merge sort's almost fatal flaw was that it required double the memory—something in very short supply in those days. Shellsort is still sometimes found in firmware or other situations when the size of the actual code really matters and when n tends to be relatively small.

Conclusion

Comparison sorts for random inputs are always $\Omega(n \log n)$ in comparisons, and $\Omega(1)$ in (additional) memory usage, but a solution can't have both at the same time. The best combination is with heapsort, when the additional memory usage is $\Omega(\log n)$ due to the need to place information on the stack. However, in practice, dual-pivot quicksort is the algorithm of choice when comparing simple values such as *int* or *double* (because we don't mind doing a few more comparisons when comparing is cheap). When comparing more complex values (objects) that need fetching from the heap and may involve more than one comparison, Timsort is the preferred algorithm even though it requires $O(n)$ additional memory.

Takeaways

Following is a list of the main ideas to take away from this chapter:

- When sorting a small data set, say fewer than 1,000 elements, it probably will not matter which sorting algorithm you use. However, if you have more elements, it behooves you to consider which is the most efficient algorithm.
- Adding an auxiliary array will approximately double the number of cache page faults invoked by your algorithm.
- Swapping and copying operations are always fast. Comparison operations may be much slower depending on the type of objects being sorted.
- In practice, most sorting is performed on partially ordered datasets. Consider that when choosing an algorithm.

Chapter Review Questions

Directions: Refer to what you learned in this chapter to respond to the questions and prompts:

1. Does it really matter if we have to allocate an auxiliary array?
2. Why do you think we spend so much time learning about sorting? Is it really that important?
3. There are several fundamental operations required in sorting: comparison, classification, counting, copying, and swapping. Do these all take the same amount of microprocessor time? Which of these operations require following a pointer into the heap?
4. How important is it to recognize that dual-pivot quicksort has a worst-case complexity of $O(n^2)$? Is it a practical issue or a theoretical issue?

References

Sedgewick R. (1986). A new upper bound for Shellsort. *Journal of Algorithms*, 7(2), 159–173. https://doi.org/10.1016/0196-6774(86)90001-5

Shell, D. H. (1959). A high-speed sorting procedure. *Communications of the ACM*, *2*(7), 30–32. https://doi.org/10.1145/368370.368387

Wikipedia. (2024, September 25). *Bogosort*. https://en.wikipedia.org/wiki/Bogosort

Credits

Fig. 7.2a: Dmitry Fomin, "3 of Diamonds," https://commons.wikimedia.org/wiki/File:English_pattern_3_of_diamonds.svg, 2017.

Fig. 7.2b: Dmitry Fomin, "Queen of Spades," https://commons.wikimedia.org/wiki/File:English_pattern_queen_of_spades.svg, 2017.

Fig. 7.2c: Dmitry Fomin, "4 of Hearts," https://commons.wikimedia.org/wiki/File:English_pattern_4_of_hearts.svg, 2017.

Fig. 7.2d: Dmitry Fomin, "6 of Diamonds," https://commons.wikimedia.org/wiki/File:English_pattern_6_of_diamonds.svg, 2017.

Fig. 7.2e: Dmitry Fomin, "4 of Clubs," https://commons.wikimedia.org/wiki/File:English_pattern_4_of_clubs.svg, 2017.

Fig. 7.2f: Dmitry Fomin, "7 of Diamonds," https://commons.wikimedia.org/wiki/File:English_pattern_7_of_diamonds.svg, 2017.

Fig. 7.2g: Dmitry Fomin, "5 of Spades," https://commons.wikimedia.org/wiki/File:English_pattern_5_of_spades.svg, 2017.

Fig. 7.2h: Dmitry Fomin, "Jack of Hearts," https://commons.wikimedia.org/wiki/File:English_pattern_jack_of_hearts.svg, 2017.

Fig. 7.2i: Dmitry Fomin, "King of Spades," https://commons.wikimedia.org/wiki/File:English_pattern_king_of_spades.svg, 2017.

Fig. 7.2j: Dmitry Fomin, "9 of Hearts," https://commons.wikimedia.org/wiki/File:English_pattern_9_of_hearts.svg, 2017.

Fig. 7.2k: Dmitry Fomin, "10 of Clubs," https://commons.wikimedia.org/wiki/File:English_pattern_10_of_clubs.svg, 2017.

Fig. 7.2l: Dmitry Fomin, "Ace of Diamonds," https://commons.wikimedia.org/wiki/File:English_pattern_ace_of_diamonds.svg, 2017.

Fig. 7.2m: Dmitry Fomin, "8 of Clubs," https://commons.wikimedia.org/wiki/File:English_pattern_8_of_clubs.svg, 2017.

Fig. 7.3a: Dmitry Fomin, "3 of Diamonds," https://commons.wikimedia.org/wiki/File:English_pattern_3_of_diamonds.svg, 2017.

Fig. 7.3b: Dmitry Fomin, "Queen of Spades," https://commons.wikimedia.org/wiki/File:English_pattern_queen_of_spades.svg, 2017.

Fig. 7.3c: Dmitry Fomin, "4 of Hearts," https://commons.wikimedia.org/wiki/File:English_pattern_4_of_hearts.svg, 2017.

Fig. 7.3d: Dmitry Fomin, "6 of Diamonds," https://commons.wikimedia.org/wiki/File:English_pattern_6_of_diamonds.svg, 2017.

Fig. 7.3e: Dmitry Fomin, "4 of Clubs," https://commons.wikimedia.org/wiki/File:English_pattern_4_of_clubs.svg, 2017.

Fig. 7.3f: Dmitry Fomin, "7 of Diamonds," https://commons.wikimedia.org/wiki/File:English_pattern_7_of_diamonds.svg, 2017.

Fig. 7.3g: Dmitry Fomin, "5 of Spades," https://commons.wikimedia.org/wiki/File:English_pattern_5_of_spades.svg, 2017.

Fig. 7.3h: Dmitry Fomin, "Jack of Hearts," https://commons.wikimedia.org/wiki/File:English_pattern_jack_of_hearts.svg, 2017.

Fig. 7.3i: Dmitry Fomin, "King of Spades," https://commons.wikimedia.org/wiki/File:English_pattern_king_of_spades.svg, 2017.

Fig. 7.3j: Dmitry Fomin, "9 of Hearts," https://commons.wikimedia.org/wiki/File:English_pattern_9_of_hearts.svg, 2017.

Fig. 7.3k: Dmitry Fomin, "10 of Clubs," https://commons.wikimedia.org/wiki/File:English_pattern_10_of_clubs.svg, 2017.

Fig. 7.3l: Dmitry Fomin, "Ace of Diamonds," https://commons.wikimedia.org/wiki/File:English_pattern_ace_of_diamonds.svg, 2017.

Fig. 7.3m: Dmitry Fomin, "8 of Clubs," https://commons.wikimedia.org/wiki/File:English_pattern_8_of_clubs.svg, 2017.

CHAPTER

8

Order

Introduction to the Chapter

In Chapter 7, we discussed the principal comparison-based sorts in the context of creating order from comparisons. Although we didn't use the term *hybrid sort* at the time, it's clear that the idea of hybrid sorting—when we utilize different algorithms and/or different keys, is already well established. For example, we noted that we can speed up merge sort by using insertion sort whenever we have a small array to sort. Then, we showed how we can combine the concepts of selection sort and a binary heap to give us heap sort. Most of the methods described in this chapter will also be hybrid sorts.

We will look at other ways of determining order, including classification sorts (i.e., counting sorts, string sorts, radix sorts). These are essentially both hybrid sorts and multikey sorts. We'll also look at some other hybrid sorts.

Multikey sorts are required when an object has several properties, each typically extending over a limited domain. A string has multiple properties (one for every character), so string sorting should be amenable to these multikey methods. After strings, the most obvious example is names. Although new names are being created all the time, the majority of names, in the English-speaking world at least, are chosen from an existing set. This means that, when sorting, we will inevitably encounter duplicates. Traditional ordering for English names is to sort first by first name and then by last name, thus making the last name the most significant. The final phase is required to utilize a stable sort. This requirement eliminates such candidates as quicksort, heap sort, and so on. Finally, we will look at two other order-related topics: selecting an element with a particular rank and shuffling—destroying order.

Learning Objectives

In this chapter students will learn about the following:

1. Other ways of imposing order on an array of objects besides comparison
2. Counting sorts (also known as radix or "string" sorts)
3. Selecting an element of rank *k* from an array
4. How to shuffle properly
5. Comparisons of sort times

Key Terms

- **Classification:** A method of dividing a population into classes according to some property
- **Multikey ordering:** A method of sorting based on a sequence of sorts, each based on a different key
- **Counting sort:** A method of ordering objects based on counting to determine the ultimate position of an object
- **Radix or string sort:** A method of sorting that uses counting sorts to partition a collection of objects according to which character/digit appears in a particular position
- **Hybrid method:** A type of reduction for solving a problem that uses more than one technique, as opposed to, for example, DnC when the techniques used at each level of recursion are the same

Classification Sorts

Classification

We discussed the optimization possible due to **classification** in Chapter 4. It's how filing systems have worked forever. We can use the same principle to divide a collection into classes, which, because they are so much smaller than the entire collection, can be sorted much more efficiently. We start with bucket sort.

Bucket Sort

Just as we improved the efficiency of searching by grouping elements into "files," we can do this with sorting. Suppose we have r partitions (one per class), called "buckets." Given a suitable classifier for populating the buckets, the classification process itself can be accomplished in linear time. And with a total of n elements and a more-or-less uniform classification, we will end up with buckets of size $k = \frac{n}{r}$. If k is small, it will be efficient to use insertion sort to order each bucket. For random input, there should be about $\frac{rk^2}{4} = \frac{n^2}{4r}$ inversions and therefore approximately the same number of comparisons. This compares with the $n \lg n$ required if we sorted the entire array by merge sort. These will be approximately equal if $k = 4 \lg n$. For example, if $n = 1{,}000$, then $r \geq 25$ with k at most 40. And if $n = 1{,}000{,}000$, then $r \geq 12{,}500$ with $k \leq 80$. We don't have to sort on the same key (or algorithm) between classes as within classes. The goal of this version of bucket sort is to keep each bucket at around 16 elements, that is the point at which $\lg n = \frac{n}{4}$, when merge sort and insertion sort will have approximately equivalent performance.

The snag is that, whereas merge sort requires only that we can determine which of two elements is "larger," bucket sort requires a classification scheme (the "classifier") that can distinguish between a fairly large number of classes more or less uniformly. Furthermore, all elements in one class must be larger than all those from the previous class. For a few hundred names, we could reasonably divide them according to their initial letter. But for much larger collections, we require much more complex—and less intuitive—classifiers. That's the reason bucket sort is not used much in practice. If the elements were strings, could we recursively refine the classes by selecting successive letters from elements? That's what MSD radix sort does.

Analysis

Did you notice that our sort was accomplished in the usual three steps?

1. Divide the problem into r sub-problems using a classifier.
2. Sort the elements of each bucket using an appropriate sort algorithm.
3. Position each bucket in the appropriate order so that the entire collection is sorted.

Note that the additional memory required is $O(n)$ because we must (temporarily) store the buckets.

In general, step 3 requires $\Omega(logr)$ comparisons to order the buckets, but since *r* is usually small compared to *n*, this step will be fast. In the case of a simple classifier such as the decimal digits 0–9 or the alphabetical characters A–Z, we can order the buckets in constant time.

There are four important conclusions to be drawn from this analysis:

- For a simple classifier, step 3 amounts to only counting the number of elements in each bucket (class).
- Step 2 can utilize different sort algorithms according to size:
  - insertion sort for small buckets (classes)
  - recursively call bucket sort, perhaps with a different classifier
- The sequence of steps 2 and 3 can be reversed: Position the elements according to the counts and then sort the entire array. In this case, the sort algorithm used must be adaptive so that its processing time is linear in the total number of inversions plus the number of elements, viz., $4r(\lg N)^2$. Insertion sort and Timsort are good examples of such algorithms.
- If a recursive solution is used, the size of the problem is reduced by a factor of *r* at each level, which implies that the depth of recursion will be approximately $\log_r n$. Note that the actual value of *r* may differ at each level. For example, if the classes correspond to the English alphabet, we may not in practice find 26 at the top level and 26 at subsequent levels.

Note also that the classifier(s) and sort key are each independent and so are well suited to any type of sort that is a **multikey ordering**.

Counting Sorts

Keep in mind the previous analysis while we discuss **counting sorts** from a more traditional viewpoint. Counting sorts are perhaps the oldest way of sorting (organizing) things. It's essentially the way that filing systems work. Classifiers (e.g., the initial character of the last name) will result in different numbers of elements for each class. To file efficiently, we need to estimate the amount of space to reserve for each initial. And to do that, we need to count.

LSD Radix Sort

Suppose you want to index your friends by their 11-digit international phone number. Let's start with the least significant digit (0–9). We put all the 0s together, all the

1s, and so on up to the 9s. But we're going to need a place to put them that has equal length as our input. What if the first one we need to copy (starting at the top or left of our list) is a 2? We'll need to know how many 0s and 1s there are and put our 2 in the next slot. How do we know where that would be? We count them at the start. We'll need some storage to put the 10-count values too (actually, 11 spaces—one more). It should be clear that we're using the phone number as the key—but the objects are going to be in the form of key-value pairs (phone number, name). Obviously, when we copy from the input to the temporary storage (and back), we need to copy the whole object (k-v pair), not just the key.

If we're careful never to change the order of numbers with equal keys (we always copy them from the first uncopied number into the first available slot for that digit), we have what's called a "stable" sort. A stable sort means that we don't disturb any existing order for equal key values (see "Stable Sorting" in Chapter 7). We do this for each of the w digits ($w = 11$ for phone numbers) to eventually get a sorted list of phone numbers and friends. We call this method LSD (least significant digit) **radix** sort, and the radix (r) in this case is 10.

How long will it take? If we have n friends, we must do n counting operations and 2n copying operations. Each copy involves the original array and the auxiliary array and thus requires two hits. We must also determine the cumulative counts, once for each digit. If each string has w digits, the total amount of work performed is $\sim w(5n + 2r)$. Assuming that $r \ll n$, we can consider this $\sim 5wn$.

5w is a constant, so the amount of work is linear with respect to the number of friends. Doesn't everyone say that sorting can't be done in linear time? Well, yes, but that applies to *comparison-based* sorting. Counting sorts like LSD radix sort *are* linear. They are useful when each object is made up of a string of values, each of which is one of r possible values (r could be as few as two but has no upper limit). For this reason, they're often referred to as *string sorts*.

```
public void sort(String[] xs, int from, int to) {
    // Preliminary filtering and determining the longest
string.
    int maxLength = … ;
    for (int d = maxLength; d > 0; d--)
        sortByChar(xs, d - 1, from, to);
}
private void sortByChar(String[] xs, int charPosition, int
from, int to) {
```

```
    // Do sorting for 7-bit ASCII.
    int ASCII_RANGE = 128;
    int[] count = new int[ASCII_RANGE + 1];
    for (int i = from; i < to; i++) {
        int c = charAsciiVal(xs[i], charPosition);
        if (c >= 0 && c <= count.length) count[c + 1]++;
        else throw new SortException("count index " + c +
" out of range");
    }
    // Accumulate counts, i.e., transform counts to indices.
    for (int r = 1; r < ASCII_RANGE + 1; r++)
        count[r] += count[r - 1];
    // Distribute: essentially a copy block with an extra
function.
    String[] result = new String[xs.length];
    distributeBlock(xs, from, to, result, x -> count
[charAsciiVal(x, charPosition)]++);
    // Copy back.
    copyBlock(result, 0, xs, from, to - from);
}
```

For the complete code, see LSDStringSort in the repository. Those identifiers in bold are declared elsewhere and do what their names suggest. The *distributeBlock* method applies the given function (the "lambda" in this code) to each string *x* in the block, yielding an (*int*) array index that determines where in *result* the string should be placed.

They say that there's no such thing as a free lunch! To some extent, that's true here. The coefficient 5*w* may be comparable to lg *n* if *w* is more than just a few. For example, suppose we have 1,000 strings to sort, and each has 10 digits like a social security number (SSN); merge sort will require 40,000 array accesses (hits) while LSD radix sort will require about the same number (50,000) of hits. Each will require the same additional memory. However, increasing *n* tends to favor LSD radix sort as its growth is purely linear.

MSD Radix Sort

The LSD method works well when the strings have equal length (or are mostly equal and can be padded to equal length). The SSN example is a perfect use case for LSD radix sort. However, we should be able to start at the *most* significant digit and work recursively toward the least significant. That way, we can easily deal with unequal strings as long as there is a terminating character (or a known length). As soon as we encounter a bucket with a small number of elements, we can stop the recursion and invoke insertion sort.

Here is code for a general algorithm that depends on a Unicode codepoint mapper function. This takes a codepoint (an *int*) and returns an *int* corresponding to the "class," the character in the desired alphabet. Codepoints that don't map to the alphabet are assigned to the "zero" (null) character. An example alphabet is the (extended) ASCII set of 256 characters. Don't use this exact algorithm when you expect non-ASCII characters.

```
public void sortMSD(String[] xs, int from, int to, int d) {
    int n = to - from;
    if (n < cutoff) sorter.sort(xs, d, from, to);
    else {
        // Allocate auxiliary memory.
        String[] aux = new String[n];
        // Allocate count memory.
        int[] count = new int[mapper.range + 1];
        // Compute frequency counts.
        for (int i = from; i < to; i++)
            count[mapper.map(charAt(xs[i], d)) + 1]++;
        // Accumulate counts.
        for (int r = 0; r < mapper.range; r++)
            count[r + 1] += count[r];
        // Distribute.
        distributeBlock(xs, from, to, aux, x -> count
[mapper.map(charAt(x, d))]++);
        // Copy back.
        copyBlock(aux, 0, xs, from, n);
        // Recursively sort on the next character position
in each String.
        for (int r = 0; r < mapper.range; r++)
                sortMSD(xs, from + count[r], from + count
[r + 1], d + 1);
```

For the complete code, see MSDStringSort in the repository. The identifiers and steps are essentially the same as for LSD except that we cycle through the strings from first to last character and that we loop via recursion rather than iteration. When the partition of elements is smaller than cutoff, we use a different adaptive sorter. Typically, we use insertion sort.

The downside of MSD radix sort, at least for the basic version shown here, is that each node of the solution tree (one node at the root, r nodes at the second level, r^2 nodes at the third, etc.) requires memory of size r to store the counts. If we ignore the cutoff mechanism, the number of nodes is limited by $m = O(n)$, implying that you might need as much as nr additional memory! That would be a huge amount of additional memory, although the cutoff mechanism will limit it to something like $O(\frac{nr}{c})$, where c is the cutoff value. Additionally, each level requires an additional memory of n elements, but the number of levels is so small—$O(\log_r n)$—that it's not very significant. There are several variations of the method designed to reduce the amount of additional memory, including "3-way radix quicksort," but we will not go into details here.

The Optimum Sorting Method

Any multikey sort with

- a very large number n of elements (typically, millions) and
- a relatively small number r of classifiers forming the first key

will benefit from using at least one classification (counting) sort for the first key. The number of hits (array accesses) will be $\sim 5n$, and the extra memory will be hn, where h is the depth of recursion. It should be pointed out that classification also requires a lookup (just one per element, of course).

For the second key, we have a choice of recursively applying a counting sort (as in MSD sort) or switching to a linearithmic sort (or insertion sort if the remaining number of elements is sufficiently small). Assuming that we switch to a linearithmic sort, which should we choose? We already have an auxiliary array allocated, so perhaps we should use merge sort. However, the problem with merge sort isn't the allocation of the extra memory itself. It's the fact that when we access an element of the array, it's only half as likely to be in the cache. Thus, we will choose quicksort.

There will be r invocations of quicksort, each averaging $\frac{n}{r}$ elements. The total number of hits + lookups for (dual-pivot) quicksort will therefore be $\sim 6n \ln\frac{n}{r}$, counting 3 hits/lookups for the inner loop. The grand total will therefore be

$\sim 6n\ln(e+\frac{n}{r})$, instead of $\sim 6n\ln n$. An alternative scheme is to invoke the MSD algorithm recursively until the array size is smaller than a cutoff value, then switch to quicksort. A cutoff of 256 works well.

Hybrid Sorts

Husky Sort

We can take this idea of classification to its logical extreme. That's to say we "classify" the objects into the 18 quintillion different classes of a (Java) *long*. Most probably, each class will contain one or zero elements and, as usual with radix sorts, we will clean up any remaining inversions at the end using insertion sort—a linear process. For sorting the classes, we could use something like LSD, but there will be 64 passes, and it will be very inefficient ($\sim 320n$). Yet, for a random array of *long* values (primitives in Java), we already have an ideal fast sorting method: quicksort. Although linearithmic, the value of $\log n$ will be much smaller than 320.

Suppose that we must sort objects or strings that are costly to compare. An example of the latter is a Chinese name. The reason for the difficulty of comparison is that the Unicode order of Chinese characters is not the normal sorting order. To sort such characters, we first must convert the characters to pinyin, of which there are approximately 450—depending on the specific coding scheme—and then sort those according to the English spelling. I'm not making this up! Incidentally, the Unicode order may be somewhat related to the traditional ordering of Chinese characters, by radical and number of strokes.

As a general rule, we want to move work from the linearithmic phase of a sort to a linear phase (the initialization or cleanup processes). We can, during a linear pass over the names, convert each to a sequence of pinyin characters. This represents a manageable alphabet: 512 elements (9 bits) can handle pinyin in addition to various other "foreign" characters such as English letters. We can simply use MSD radix sort for this use case.

Another alternative—the "extreme" idea mentioned—is to encode the whole name into a *long* (64 bits is sufficient for as many as seven characters—more than necessary). With a little modification, we can then use quicksort to sort since it is extremely fast for Java primitives like *long*. And, these days, 64 bits is the typical word length of most processors. The modification is in the *swap* (exchange) method: We must swap not only the encoded *long* values, but also the corresponding original names. The final phase of the sort is to use insertion sort to remove any remaining inversions. This would not arise for Chinese names but might occur if we used the same idea for sorting English words (or names). We need at least five bits for each English letter, and that means we can only distinguish accurately 12-character words or names. We can skip the final pass if we know for certain that there were no objects that could not be uniquely encoded.

I developed this method of sorting (Hillyard, Liaozheng, Vineeth) in 2018 as an exercise for my Husky (Northeastern University) students in optimizing sorts by using **hybrid** methods. It is in practice an extremely fast way of sorting Chinese names.

HISTORICAL NOTE

Introsort (Musser, 1997) is another hybrid sorting algorithm that starts out using quicksort. If it finds that the recursion depth is getting out of hand ($> 2\,lg\,n$), it switches to using heap sort. Both cut over to insertion sort when a partition gets small. In a considerable amount of testing Introsort with random inputs, I have never, ever hit the threshold that invokes heap sort! Its main purpose of course is to guard against what might happen with partially ordered inputs.

Selection

Another aspect of order that we have not yet covered is the ability to select the kth largest (or smallest) element of an array. This section covers mechanisms to perform such a task efficiently.

Imagine that you have been asked to find the largest element of an array. You can do this in linear time with just two variables:

- a current largest value that will be updated any time a larger value is found
- an index that cycles through all valid indices of the array

How about looking for the second largest element? This is slightly more complex. We will need the following:

- a current largest value that will be updated any time a larger value is found
- a current second largest value that will be updated any time a larger value is found
- two indices:
  - one that cycles through all valid indices of the array
  - another that cycles through the two current values

You can still perform this in linear time, but each time a new element is found, it potentially must be compared with both the largest values. If it's smaller than the second largest, we can ignore it. But if it's larger than the second largest, we must check to see if it's also larger than the largest. In that case, we swap two values. In the worst case, we will take twice as long to accomplish this as for the largest-only case.

What if we want the kth largest element? We still need the two indexes, but the current largest values must be represented by a (sorted) array of length *k*. Ignoring the indexes, the extra memory we need is proportional to k, and the worst-case complexity is proportional to $n \log k$ (we can find the correct index for the k-length array using binary search). If we are looking for the median, the complexity is $O(n \log n)$, which is acceptable but no better than the following really easy method.

As noted in Chapter 1, we can reduce this problem (that of the median) to

- sort the array: $O(n \log n)$
- select the element at the midpoint: $O(1)$

Of course, $n \log n$ is acceptable. But it should bother you that this method results in a fully ordered array even though we don't care about the order of the other $n-1$ elements. We've done more work than necessary. How can we optimize this problem?

Quickselect

Let's revert to the more general problem of finding the kth largest element. And we will generalize it some more and say that we want to find the element with *rank k*, where rank refers to the number of larger (or smaller) elements. And, by convention, we consider values of *k* such that $0 \le k \le n-1$, where the 0 value (rather than the 1 value) is the largest (or smallest) of the array.

If the array was already sorted, we would simply return the element at index *k*. What can we do with an array in random order? We could start by partitioning the array into two partitions: elements smaller than some pivot value (*v*) and elements larger than *v*. We know how to do this in linear time because we used the same technique for quicksort. Now, we compare *k* to the index *p* of the pivot (recall that *p* is the returned value from the partitioning process). If $k < p$, we discard the right-hand partition (assuming conventional ordering) and repeat the process. If $k > p$, we discard the left-hand partition, and so on. Otherwise, if $k = p$, the result (the value of the kth element) is *v*, and we are finished.

What is the complexity of this method, which we call *quickselect*? If we were magically able to choose the median value as the pivot for each iteration, the array would be partitioned into two equal parts. The number of iterations would be h where $h = \lg n$. But the work performed by each iteration (remember, this is linear) is *halved* at each iteration. If we started with, say, 2^h elements and required all iterations to find the kth element, we would need $2^h + 2^{h-1} + 2^{h-2} + \ldots 2^2 + 2^1 + 2^0 = 127 = 2^{h+1} - 1$ comparisons. In other words, the total comparisons would be $\sim 2n$.

In practice, as with quicksort, we cannot guarantee that the pivot will be the median, and we will need a similar analysis as for quicksort, when we consider the number of comparisons required if the pivot happens to be in each of the n possible positions. The value of k also affects the number of comparisons. Without derivation, the number of comparisons is

$$C_{n,k} = 2n + 2k \ln\frac{n}{k} + 2(n-k)\ln\frac{n}{n-k}$$

Here are some examples:

- the smallest/largest: $C_{n,0} = 2n$ (twice as much work as the naïve method)
- the median: $C_{n,\frac{n}{2}} = 2n(1 + \ln 2) \sim 3.39n$

Like quicksort, quickselect is susceptible to bad pivots when the data is partially ordered and the same schemes may be used to lessen the danger of quadratic performance. Median-of-three can be used to choose the pivot (at a cost). And, naturally, there is an *Introselect* method that corresponds to Introsort.

Shuffling

Whereas sorting is eliminating entropy from a random, or partially ordered, data set, shuffling is the opposite: the injection of entropy. There is a simple technique for shuffling that reduces to these steps:

1. Add a property to the elements to be shuffled such that this property has completely random values.
2. Sort the elements using the random property as the key.

The only snags with this technique are as follows:

- The time complexity is $O(n \log n)$ because we have to do a full sort.
- The space complexity is $O(n)$ because we need to add an extra property to each element.

Is it possible to shuffle in linear time and constant space? There is a method for shuffling called the modified Fisher–Yates algorithm. In the original algorithm, elements were successively extracted from a set. The modified algorithm shuffles in place. Essentially, the original idea is simplicity itself: Choose at random any of the remaining elements.

Where should we get the required entropy, or randomness? How about using a pseudo-random number generator? The problem with this is that, once the seed has been chosen, the other elements are preordained. It is only the lack of knowledge on the part of the observer that makes the sequence appear random. What about the seed itself? Java uses the current time in milliseconds as the seed. In theory, this is a 64-bit value, but how random is it really in practice? If you know the current date, there are really only 86,400,000 different possible values. And, if the granularity of the time is more like 10 milliseconds (fairly common), we only have about 23 bits of randomness, assuming that the program could start up at any time of the day. It's even worse if your program starts up according to a schedule!

If it matters, a better source of entropy is the */dev/random* device on a unix-type machine (there is something similar on Windows computers). For something critical, a hardware random number generator is required.

HISTORICAL NOTE

The original Fisher–Yates shuffle was first described in 1938. Both Fisher and Yates were brilliant statisticians. Fisher, in particular, is said to have essentially created the modern field of statistics. He also was the most significant contributor to the ideas of neo-Darwinism or the modern synthesis, which combined the natural selection of Darwin with the genetics of Mendel. The modified (computer) version was developed by Richard Durstenfeld in 1964 and popularized by Donald Knuth as "algorithm P." Thus, it is also frequently referred to as the Knuth shuffle. Neither Durstenfeld nor Knuth apparently knew about Fisher and Yates.

It's important to get the modified algorithm exactly right. Minor bugs can generate permutations that look fine but are in fact nonuniform in terms of probability.

Here is the algorithm in pseudo-code (see Java *Collections.shuffle* for the real code), using a PRNG called *random*:

```
for (int i=size; i>1; i--)
    swap(list, i-1, random.nextInt(i));
```

Note that the *nextInt(n)* method of *Random* returns a number in the range $0 \to n-1$ (inclusive).

Conclusion

Which of these sorting algorithms is really the fastest? Is it worth bothering with, for example, MSD radix sort? Yes, the latter sort is consistently faster than other sorts for sorting English strings. Table 8.1 compares running times (milliseconds) with Timsort, merge sort, and quicksort for English words with various problem sizes (run on Macbook Pro with Apple M1 and 16GB memory):

TABLE 8.1 Sorting Times for Various Algorithms (Milliseconds)

ALGORITHM	1k	4k	16k	64k	256k	1M	4M	16M	64M
MSD string sort (ext. ASCII with 256 cutoff)	0.16	0.69	3.1	13.8	51.5	180	716	2,547	7,553
Timsort	0.24	1.13	6.3	34.1	141.1	699	2,908	12,993	42,517
Merge sort (no copy)	0.14	0.85	3.5	17.0	74.1	319	1,373	6,160	26,016
Quicksort (classic)	0.13	0.68	3.3	16.3	70.0	284	1,131	4,611	18,597

Only when used for problems of size 4k or smaller is MSD not the fastest algorithm. Note that these are for random inputs, which is somewhat unusual for words or names. When there is some partial ordering, Timsort will become significantly faster, and Quicksort will be less favored (maybe use Introsort instead).

You may have been wondering if insertion sort is really faster than merge sort or quicksort for small arrays? See Table 8.2 for where the times are in microseconds.

TABLE 8.2

ALGORITHM	8	16	32	64	128	256	512
LSD w = 20	3.0	4.4	7.5	13.5	25.1	48.5	95.4
Merge Sort with no copy or cutoff	1.5	3.2	6.8	14.9	30.5	64.4	143.3
Quicksort with no cutoff	0.3	0.7	1.8	4.5	10.9	25.4	58.9
Insertion sort	0.2	0.7	2.4	9.0	33.5	123.8	496.2

Notice that even non-optimized insertion sort is fastest for any array size below about 16 (as expected). Clearly, the merge sort and quicksort shown here do not cut over to insertion sort, but rather recurse down to an array of size one. In real life, they would be as fast as insertion sort because of the cutoff.

Takeaways

Following is a list of the main ideas to take away from this chapter:

- Comparison sorting is not the only way to sort objects, provided that there is a meaningful classification, where the number of classes is much smaller than the number of elements.
- Using classification and counting, we can reduce the complexity of sorting from $O(n \log n)$ to $O(n)$. However, for small data sets, the linearithmic comparison sorts tend to be faster.
- Insertion sort is faster than any other sort for arrays with fewer than 16 elements.
- Quickselect can be performed in linear time, which is always going to be faster than sorting and selecting the appropriate element.
- Shuffling can and should be done in linear time.

Chapter Review Questions

Directions: Refer to what you learned in this chapter to respond to the questions and prompts:

1. How can you use one of the sorting techniques described in this chapter to count the number of inversions in an array in $O(n \log n)$? Hint: Use one of the two $O(n \log n)$ algorithms—but one will be easier to use than the other.
2. Can you improve upon the MSD radix sort described in the chapter by managing the memory used more efficiently?
3. When is LSD Radix sort most efficient? When is Insertion sort most efficient?

Reference

Hillyard, R., Liaozheng, Y., & Sai, R. (2020). Huskysort. *ArXiv (Cornell University)*. https://doi.org/10.48550/arxiv.2012.00866

CHAPTER

9

Graphs

The Ultimate Abstract Data Type

Introduction to the Chapter

The most general type of abstract data type is a *graph*. At its heart, a graph is simply a way of representing a set of objects (also known as nodes or vertices) and any connections between those objects. Because a graph is so general, there are many different kinds of graphs, each formed by constraining some property of the most general graph type. We will be looking at various common types of graphs in this chapter.

Learning Objectives

In this chapter students will learn about the following:

1. Graphs: ADTs with few rules and unlimited complexity
2. How to traverse a graph in depth-first or breadth-first order
3. The differences between trees, DAGs, and graphs
4. Representations for edges including undirected-, directed-, and no-edge
5. The ideal representation of the connections in a graph

Key Terms

The following important terms will be introduced in this chapter:

- **Vertex:** A node (intersection) in a graph (plural: vertices); a vertex typically has an attribute (describes all aspects of node); an endpoint of any number of edges (including zero)
- **Edge:** A connection (relationship) between exactly two vertices (not necessarily different); an edge typically has an attribute (describes all aspects of the relationship)
- **Graph:** A set of vertices, connected pairwise by a set of edges
- **Directed Acyclic Graph (DAG):** A directed graph with no cycles
- **Tree:** An undirected acyclic graph or a DAG constrained such that nodes have at most one parent
- **Visitor:** A programming pattern wherein the function to be applied to an object when it's encountered is passed into the procedure for visiting such objects. Its advantage is that navigation and processing are decoupled.

Graphs: The Ultimate Abstract Data Type

There is no abstract data type more powerful, flexible, or complex than a **graph**. Graphs are the natural extension (by removing constraints) of lists and trees. Of course, with great power comes great responsibility, and we need to have a good understanding of what goes on under the hood of a graph ADT lest we invoke an operation that is needlessly expensive. Before getting into details, you should be aware that there are many graph libraries or database systems out there that have ready-made implementations of the ADTs that we will study. Yet, as we've seen before, there is nothing quite like implementing something to really understand it.

If the objects and relationships you wish to represent are amorphous, fluid over time, or lightly constrained (if at all), you probably need a graph. Graphs are the most flexible data structure and the most powerful in terms of their ability to represent large interrelated data sets. The size of graphs can be staggering. The Facebook graph has 2.96×10^9 (three billion) users (vertices) worldwide (Q3 2022) who are active at least monthly. These people are connected by, on average, 338 friendships (edges), which gives a total of 500 billion edges. Note that friendships on Facebook are symmetric, or undirected. That's why there aren't 1 trillion edges.

Such a graph is, however, extremely sparse. It should be obvious that the dominant measure of complexity, even for sparse graphs, is that of the edges. On the other hand, the attributes of one edge typically contain a small amount of information compared with the attributes of a vertex. The total information content of edges versus vertices might be more evenly divided. The definition of a graph is not the same as when you learned about graphs in high school. Those should properly be called *function graphs*.

So far, you know about many ADTs, including linked lists (each node has one pointer) and trees (each node may have more than one pointer). Each of these structures has the implicit constraint that each node has exactly one parent (prior) node. We will see that in the world of graphs, we must relax this constraint.

Definitions

Graphs

Disjoint Sets (Edgeless Graphs)

The most general type of graph can be represented as $\mathcal{S}(\mathcal{N},\mathcal{C})$, where $\mathcal{N}$ is a set of nodes or objects and where $\mathcal{C}$ is a set of *connected components* or *connected sets*, each made up of a subset of $\mathcal{N}$. This type of graph is known as a *disjoint-set* or *"union-find" data structure*. Many texts do not consider it as a graph at all, yet it is closely related to graphs—and is used in at least one important graph algorithm (Kruskal's). Therefore, we cover it—but only in Chapter 10, which serves as a case study that attempts to wrap up many of the ideas presented in this book.

There is no concept of an edge in a disjoint set. The set $\mathcal{N}$ is partitioned into a collection (the set $\mathcal{C}$) of disjoint subsets. If two nodes belong to the same connected component, say $\mathcal{C}_i$, we say that those nodes are connected. Otherwise, they are not connected. Thus, the disjoint set offers us no information about *how* the two nodes are connected—only that they are or are not. Another way to regard a disjoint set is as an edgeless (or "no-edge") graph. We will now look at the more traditional type of (edge-based) graph, which will be further divided into undirected and directed graphs.

Edge-Based Graphs

A *graph* $\mathcal{G}(\mathcal{V},\mathcal{E})$ or, more briefly, $\mathcal{G}$, is made up of a set $\mathcal{V}$ of *vertices* (singular: **vertex**), also known as nodes or even as objects, connected pair wise by a set $\mathcal{E}$ of **edges**. We retain the general idea of a connected component, but in a graph, it is not represented explicitly, as it would be in a disjoint set. The connectedness of vertices in a graph are determined by seeking a *path* from one vertex to the other. Throughout this chapter, we will use m to stand for $|\mathcal{V}|$, the cardinality (size) of $\mathcal{V}$, and n to stand for $|\mathcal{E}|$, the size of $\mathcal{E}$. Incidentally, $n \geq m$ for all graphs that are not trees. This definition tells us that a particular vertex may have any number of edges meeting at it, including zero. It also tells us the more useful fact that every edge connects exactly *two* vertices (which may sometimes even be the same vertex).

We define a *path* in a graph as a subset of $\mathcal{E}$, which connects two vertices *v*, and w, such that we start at *v*, follow the subset of connected edges, passing by other vertices along the way, until we reach *w*. If we can do this in such a way that *v* and *w* are the same vertex, we call such a path a *cycle*. There is no requirement in a graph for a vertex to be connected to any other vertex. This is why we need to specify the sets $\mathcal{V}$ and $\mathcal{E}$ independently.

In an object-oriented representation of a graph, we do not necessarily need an explicit edge type. That will be necessary only if an edge has properties. But if an edge is just a connection between two vertices, we can represent such a "logical" edge simply as a *vertex pair*.

Thus far, we haven't said anything about the direction that we can travel along an edge. For graphs in general, we consider edges to have a specific direction of travel for the time being (something like a one-way street). We say that such an edge is *directed*. Later, we will see how we can relax this constraint and allow edges to be traversed in either direction (an *undirected* edge). Most graph algorithms operate on directed as well as undirected graphs. Exceptions will be noted in the appropriate place.

If a vertex has *k* edges leaving it, we say it has an *out-degree* (or simply *degree*) of *k*. On the other hand, if a vertex has *k* edges entering it, we say it has *in-degree* of *k*. If there is an edge e that leaves vertex *v* and connects it to vertex *w*, we say that *w is adjacent to* v and that *e is adjacent to v*. A *subgraph* $\mathcal{G}'$ of graph $\mathcal{G}$ is composed of a set $\mathcal{V}'$, which is a subset of $\mathcal{V}$, together with a set $\mathcal{E}'$, which is a subset of $\mathcal{E}$.

Types of Edges

It is customary to classify graphs according to the nature of its edges. To some extent, we must do that here too. Yet, there is so much commonality between the different edge types, structurally speaking, that it makes sense to treat the use cases (applications) of graphs at a higher level than their edge types. Whenever it is appropriate, we will discuss the difference according to the edge types.

There are two primary edge types that can be represented—and traversed—in essentially the same way. These are *undirected* and *directed* edges. If you can travel along an edge in one direction only, it's a *directed edge*. This kind of edge comprises a *start* vertex (the source node) and an *end* vertex (the destination node). Similarly, a *directed path* can be traversed in only one direction; a *directed cycle* can be traversed in only one direction, although in this case, each pair of vertices that lies on a directed cycle is connected because, whichever vertex you start at, you will be able to reach the other by a shorter or longer route.

Directed versus Undirected Graphs

A graph that includes one or more directed edges is a *directed graph*. A directed graph $\mathcal{G}$ has a "transpose" operator that reverses the direction of each edge, resulting in the graph $\mathcal{G}^R$.

HISTORY NOTE

Imagine the process on the day that rejoiced in the name Högertrafikomläggningen (September 3, 1967) when the entire road network of Sweden, considered as a directed graph, was reversed!

If, however, you can travel in either direction along an (undirected) edge, you have an undirected graph. As we will see, some graph ADTs are better suited for one of these types of graphs, but, generally speaking, if you can operate on a directed graph, you can operate on an undirected graph. This is true because one valid model of an undirected graph is $\mathcal{G} \cup \mathcal{G}^R$, where $\mathcal{G}$ is a directed graph. In other words, an undirected graph is simply the union of a directed graph and its transpose. On the other hand, some ADTs work only for undirected graphs because they require the ability to travel along an edge in either direction. An example of this type of ADT is the minimum spanning tree.

How should we represent these two types of graphs in the adjacency model (*A*)? The model is ideally suited to a directed graph because, for every vertex *v*, we can easily obtain each adjacent vertex w. In other words, there must be a (directed) edge that starts at *v* and ends at *w*. How can we represent an undirected graph? By, literally, storing $\mathcal{G} \cup \mathcal{G}^{R,}$ where $\mathcal{G}$ is a directed graph with all the same pairs of vertices connected as in the undirected graph. The result of this is that the adjacency set for *v* must include *w*, and the adjacency set for *w* must include *v*. As far as the **construction of a graph** is concerned, from a list of its edges, we must be aware if an edge *vw* is to be considered undirected so that we can update both adjacency lists.

However, as far as **graph traversal** is concerned (depth-first or breadth-first search), the algorithm does not know if the graph is directed or undirected. It simply follows the adjacent edges/vertices as appropriate. If we are presented with a graph of unknown provenance, we are always safe in treating it as a directed graph, because that's how our model is designed. If we need to treat it as an undirected graph, for example to determine the minimum spanning tree, we must treat each edge as being reversible. Thus, an undirected graph is a special case of a directed graph—not the other way around. In what follows, we will refer to the adjacency model representation of a graph as its *adjacency map*.

Connectivity

We define an undirected graph as connected if, for all pairs of vertices of the graph, there is a connecting path. If a graph $\mathcal{G}$ is not connected, there will be more than one (connected) component, each of which is a subgraph of $\mathcal{G}$ and whose vertices and edges are subsets of $\mathcal{V}$ and $\mathcal{E}$, respectively. If there is only one edge (or vertex) that connects two components, such that its removal would result in an unconnected graph, we call that a biconnected graph.

The definition of a connected directed graph is not nearly so simple. If the union of a directed graph $\mathcal{G}$ with its transpose $\mathcal{G}^R$ is a connected (undirected) graph, we say that $\mathcal{G}$ is *weakly* connected. Otherwise, for any subgraph $\mathcal{G}'$ of $\mathcal{G}$ (which of course may be $\mathcal{G}$ itself), if every pair of its vertices is on a directed cycle, we say that $\mathcal{G}'$ is *strongly* connected.

Directed Acyclic Graphs

A **directed acyclic graph (DAG)** is, as the name implies, a directed graph without cycles. Because all edges point generally in the same direction (if there *was* a cycle that would not be the case), a DAG can be rendered in order (known as *topological* order), where all edges point in the same general direction. A DAG may be a subgraph of a directed graph where all nonaligned edges have been eliminated. However, note that while a DAG explicitly excludes cycles, there can nevertheless be more than one path from one vertex to another vertex. Therefore, a DAG is not necessarily a directed tree. DAGs are especially useful when time is involved (scheduling) given that the arrow of time points in only one direction (and edges of DAGs also point generally in one direction). This is also true of software dependency which is unidirectional like time.

Trees

Like a DAG, a **tree** cannot have cycles. But whereas the term DAG is well defined, the terminology of trees can be quite confusing, especially since we already know all about search trees like the red-black tree. But the trees we've met before are represented as trees and moreover are *directed* trees, each with a *root*. The more general type of graph—represented by an adjacency map—that has the properties of a tree should be assumed to be a graph when considering whether to keep track of visited nodes.

Directed Trees

A directed tree is simply a directed acyclic graph with the additional constraint that no node can have multiple parents. Since it is acyclic, it satisfies the noncyclic property of trees in general. Following this definition, it must have a point of entry (i.e., the *root*). Such a tree has a special name: an *arborescence*. It is the type of tree that we have previously studied, for example, the red-black tree. However, note that the term arborescence is rarely, if ever, used in practice—we do not talk of a red-black arborescence, for instance. Two vertices of a directed tree have at most one path connecting them. A particular type of directed tree that is of special interest is a connectivity tree: a spanning tree.

Undirected Trees

An undirected tree $\mathcal{T}(\mathcal{E}')$ is a connected subgraph of an undirected graph $\mathcal{G}(\mathcal{V}, \mathcal{E})$ in which there is *no cycle*. Note that we can represent a tree by its edges alone. This follows from the fact that there are no disconnected vertices in a tree. Indeed, for any tree, $m = n + 1$. Adding any new edge to a tree, without adding a new vertex, must form a cycle, and therefore the result is not a tree. Removing any edge from a tree renders it a (disconnected) *forest*. As a consequence of a tree's noncyclic nature, any two vertices of a tree have exactly one path connecting them. It is possible to define many distinct trees within a graph, whether that graph is connected or unconnected. We naturally call such a set of disconnected trees a *forest*.

Spanning Trees

One particular type of undirected tree is of special interest. Given a connected, undirected graph $\mathcal{G}(\mathcal{V}, \mathcal{E})$, it is possible to define a *spanning tree* $\mathcal{T}(\mathcal{E}')$—where $\mathcal{E}'$ is a subset of $\mathcal{E}$—such that the vertices of $\mathcal{T}$ comprise the entire set $\mathcal{V}$. That's to say that every vertex of the original graph $\mathcal{G}$ is present in $\mathcal{T}$. The cardinality of $\mathcal{E}'$ must therefore be $m - 1$, where m is $|\mathcal{V}|$ as before. In general, there will be many such spanning trees. Later, we will discuss in detail how to find the *minimum* spanning tree, given some edge property that can be minimized.

Graph Representations

Choosing an appropriate representation (data structure) for a graph might make or break our ability to implement graph ADTs. Because every graph application involves traversing a subset of the graph, at the very least, the representation should be chosen to minimize the work required in graph traversal. It is obvious that a traversal must follow a path through the graph. We already defined path as a sequence of edges connecting one vertex to another. This in turn implies that, at each vertex, we need to find the *adjacent* vertices. Therefore, we need a method to yield, for any given vertex, a set (or multiset) of adjacent vertices or edges; it amounts to the same thing. For the following model descriptions, we will represent the same graph (see Figure 9.1).

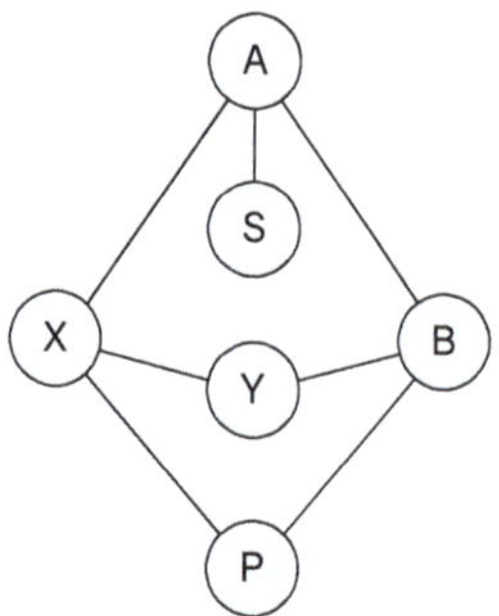

FIGURE 9.1. Sample graph.

Model E

The most obvious representation, since each edge joins exactly two vertices, is a list of edges. Let's call this model E. This model is particularly convenient for *defining* graphs. But is it the best representation for the purpose of traversing a graph? How much effort will be required to get the list of adjacent edges/vertices to any particular vertex *v*? We need to scan the entire edge list, looking for edges involving *v*. That's going to take *n* operations, where *n* is the number of edges. If traversing each of *n* edges took time proportional to *n*, we would have a model that required quadratic time to traverse it. That's unacceptable as we know that quadratic solutions do not scale.

When we met quadratic solutions before, we generally tried to reduce the time complexity to be linearithmic. How might we do that here? Suppose that the time required to find the adjacent edges to a vertex was logarithmic. That would do it. Do we have any quantity that's log*m*? We'll come back to this again in the section on graph complexity.

TABLE 9.1 Model E

A	X
B	Y
P	B
S	A
X	P
Y	X
A	B

Model V

We should briefly consider another possible representation: a connection matrix of vertices versus vertices. To find the adjacent vertices for a vertex v, we would have to scan the row or column corresponding to v. As with model E, we would end up taking quadratic time to traverse the graph. Furthermore, this representation would also require quadratic space!

TABLE 9.2 Model V

	A	**B**	**P**	**S**	**X**	**Y**
A		X		X	X	
B	X		X			X
P		X			X	
S	X					
X	X		X			X
Y		X			X	

Model A

Let's propose a data structure such that, for any particular vertex *v*, we maintain a set of adjacent edges/vertices. The size of this set (i.e., the out-degree) would be a relatively small number compared with the number of edges. Let's call this model A. What would be the number of operations required to find the adjacent edges/vertices of *v*? It would simply be the out-degree of *v*—unlike models E and V—significantly less than linear.

Assume that we will use this representation for now. One detail needs to be determined. Should we use a linked list, an array, set, or some other structure for the adjacent edges/vertices? An array would not be so convenient for adding an edge to a vertex. A list would be ideal—except for one little detail: A list has an intrinsic order arising from the position of the elements. What should the order of the adjacent edges be? One of the aspects of a graph not mentioned is that there is no reason to follow one edge from a vertex before any other edge. Whichever edge you follow first, the graph remains the same. A set would seem logical because it has no intrinsic ordering. Yet, when dealing with edges having no attributes, there may be more than one way to get from one vertex to another. Therefore, we use the concept of a *multiset* (also known as a *bag*) to store the adjacent edges/vertices because, like a set, a bag is unordered.

TABLE 9.3 Model A

A	SBX
B	YAP
P	XB
S	A
X	PAY
Y	XB

We have described this model in terms of a set of vertices (it should be a set because we do not want any duplicates), each with a bag of either adjacent edges or vertices. But which should it be? In general, we should choose edges because an edge will always lead us to another vertex. However, if the edges of our graph do not have attributes, we can use the vertex pair. In this case, we can fill the bag with the adjacent *vertices*, with no need to store or define any edges. Henceforth, however, we will always assume that an adjacency bag contains *edges*, even though these edges might be virtual (i.e., vertex pairs). This representation should be used for almost all graphs. It is particularly well suited to traversing, via depth-first search, relatively sparse graphs based on edges with attributes.

Graph Complexity

Consider again a list of length m. We can do most operations in linear time as there is only one way to traverse it: Start at the head and follow the pointers until you reach the end. If we are allowed to change the order of the nodes (set up a different set of connections between them), there would be $m!$ possible lists.

But imagine a graph with m vertices. There are $2^{\binom{m}{2}} = 2^{m^2}$ different ways just to connect (or not connect) the vertices. That's because each of the $\binom{m}{2}$ pairs may be connected by an edge—or not. For now, we will ignore the possibility of more than one edge connecting a pair of vertices.

How do these large numbers compare? We can rewrite the number of possible lists (i.e., $m! \sim 2^{m \lg m}$). And the number of possible graphs is 2^{m^2}. Clearly, the number of possible graphs will typically be orders of magnitude greater. Let's take m = 4, a very small list or graph. The number of possible lists is 24. The number of possible graphs is 65,536.

We need to put some bounds on the complexity of graphs if we are going to be able to manage them in polynomial time. Fortunately, most graphs are, in practice, *sparse* graphs. What do we mean by this? No expression defines a sparse graph. However, there is a measure of connectedness we can use. We refer to the Erdös-Rényi-Gilbert model of random graphs. Without going into too much mathematical detail here, if p is the probability of an edge existing between any pair of vertices, we can say that if

$$p > \frac{\ln m}{m}$$

the graph is probably connected. But note also that pm is the mean degree ξ of the graph. Thus, we can say that any connected graph will have a mean degree of at least $\ln m$. A graph whose mean degree is exactly $\ln m$ is the most sparse graph that is probably connected. We have thus derived a minimum value for the mean degree of a connected, sparse graph. In other words, $\xi = \Omega(\ln m)$. Although this expression is the minimum value of ξ for a sparse graph, it may serve as a guideline. In practice, we always describe the complexity of graph algorithms in terms of m and n.

What constitutes a dense graph? The densest graph we can possibly have has $p = 1$, in which case $\xi = m$. We might further argue that any graph where $\xi = \Omega(\sqrt{m})$ can be considered dense. However, there is no uniformly accepted definition of a dense graph.

We have now established bounds on the value of ξ for a sparse graph, viz., $\xi = \Omega(\ln m) = O(\sqrt{m})$. Indirectly, we have set bounds on *n*, the number of edges since, for a directed graph, $n = \xi m$ and, for an undirected graph, $n = \frac{1}{2}\xi m$. Furthermore, an algorithm such as a depth-first search, which requires $m + n$ operations, can therefore be shown to have growth of $\Omega(m \ln m)$ for sparse graphs. As you may readily observe, this is linearithmic complexity, the same as for sorting an array of *m* elements using merge sort or something similar. Thus, we have established that, using our chosen representation for a graph (model *A*), we expect to be able to traverse such a graph in something like linearithmic time based on the number of its vertices. We will find that most of the more complex algorithms are not substantially worse than linearithmic.

By way of example, let's look at the graph of a fictional social network. There are 1 billion members, and each member "follows," on average, 100 other members (i.e., *m* = 1,000,000,000 and ξ = 100). Is this graph likely to be connected, according to the ERG model? We have $\ln m \sim 21$, so $\xi \sim 5 \ln m$. Thus, the graph is probably connected given that $5 > 1$. And, since 5 is a small constant (and not obviously proportional to *m*), we can treat this graph as sparse.

Graph Applications

Depth-First Search

As noted, our preferred graph representation (identified as model A) is ideal for depth-first search. We can write the algorithm recursively as

```
void dfs (Vertex vertex) {
    for (Edge edge : vertex.edges()) dfs(edge.other(vertex));
}
```

where, for a vertex, *edges()* yields the bag of adjacent edges.

In principle, this method is all we need, at least for trees. But it's a little too simplistic to be useful for graphs. The first objection that we note is that it doesn't actually *do* anything. We can fix that with the **visitor** pattern. We pass as a parameter an instance of *Visitor<Vertex>* such that we can invoke its *visit* method for each vertex as we encounter it. Thus, responsibility for doing something for a vertex is devolved to the application by the construction of an appropriate visitor. Even this is insufficiently general because sometimes we want to visit the vertex *before* calling *dfs* recursively, and there will be other times when the visit should come *after* the recursion. Therefore, we should provide two visitors, one for previsiting and one for postvisiting.

The second problem pertains to graphs. Whereas in a tree there is only one path (or none) from any vertex to any other, graphs in general allow multiple paths. Note that DAGs also allow multiple paths. It is possible, therefore, that when we visit, say, vertex *w*, we have already encountered *w*. If we simply follow our *dfs* method, we must fall into an infinite loop. To prevent that, we need to keep track of the vertices that have already been discovered. Our revised method is as follows:

```
void dfs (Vertex vertex, Visitor<Vertex> preVisitor,
Visitor<Vertex> postVisitor) {
    preVisitor.visit(vertex);
    setDiscovered(vertex);
    for (Edge edge : vertex.edges()) {
          Vertex w = edge.other(vertex);
          if (!isDiscovered(w) dfs(w);
    }
    postVisitor.visit(vertex);
}
```

As written, this method relies on side effects (both the discovery mechanism and the visitor pattern). Of course, a pure (functional) method can be written, but that's beyond the scope of this chapter.

dfs is eminently suited to recursion, relying on the compiler and run time to manage the recursion and its necessary breadcrumbs (i.e., the compiler provides the stack). However, *dfs* can also be written iteratively. In this case, you the programmer have to provide the necessary stack explicitly.

The essence of *dfs* is that it is guaranteed to visit every *connected* (or reachable) vertex in the graph from the given starting point. For a directed, rooted tree there is of course only one starting point: the root. But for any other type of graph, the choice of starting point may be quite significant. The visited vertices of a graph that is made up of multiple components (often called, confusingly, *connected components*) will depend very much on the starting vertex.

Note that our *dfs* algorithm is oblivious to whether the edges are directed or undirected. That is because the data structure that it follows is designed to be the same for directed and undirected graphs. The difference between these two types of graphs is in the construction of the data structure, not its traversal. (See the red-black tree in Chapter 6.) There is one detail that pertains to the edge type itself, and that is the method to yield the other end of the edge. In the case of a directed edge, it is unambiguous. However, if an edge is undirected, we need to know which end we're at now to get the other end. The algorithm as shown reflects this ambiguity for undirected edges. However, the code can very easily be simplified if we know that an edge is directed; there will be no need to pass in a *Vertex* parameter.

There is one further, and important, aspect to depth-first search. It is detail oriented, perhaps obsessively so, as it will blindly search out every vertex in the graph, which often is exactly what you need. However, this makes *dfs* unsuitable for some applications, such as web crawling when the graph to be traversed is essentially unbounded. Other applications, involving a goal or when measurement is involved, are better suited to the alternative traversal method: breadth-first search.

Because *dfs* simply follows the adjacency map of a graph, the algorithm is the same whether the edges are directed or undirected. And, because we must visit every edge and every vertex once, the complexity of *dfs* is $O(m+n)$.

Breadth-First Search

Breadth-first search (*bfs*) is typically used instead of *dfs* when some sort of measurement is involved, for example determining the shortest path from one vertex to another. This includes any search for a particular goal, such as a winning state of a game.

```
void bfs (Vertex start) {
    Queue<Vertex> queue = new Queue<>(start);
    while (queue.nonEmpty()) {
            Vertex v = queue.take();
            for (Edge edge : v.edges())
                    queue.give(edge.other(v));
    }
}
```

As before, this is the basic algorithm, which neither does anything useful nor checks for prediscovery. Furthermore, it doesn't check for any kind of goal, something frequently needed in *bfs* applications. We can accomplish something useful together with goal seeking by supplying an appropriate visitor. A variation on the algorithm that is frequently used when goal seeking is to calculate a heuristic for each of the candidate vertices and add them to the queue in the order of maximizing (or minimizing) the heuristic. This can significantly speed up goal seeking.

There is a useful invariant in the *bfs* algorithm: At any moment the vertices in the queue have distances (in terms of the edge count, or *hops*) at most one different. So, while the cohort of vertices at the same distance should properly be processed in random order, that randomness cannot affect the ordering beyond those specific vertices. In other words, vertices are guaranteed to be processed in the order of their distance (in hops) from the start.

Many graph applications, such as finding a path from one vertex to another, can be accomplished by either *dfs* or *bfs*. But here are examples of use cases for *bfs*:

- Route finding (i.e., calculating the shortest path)
- Goal-oriented traversal, for example choosing a move in a game (especially because the graph of all moves may be effectively infinite)
- Web crawling

For *bfs* evaluations that do not end with a goal (i.e., all vertices and all edges are visited), the complexity is the same as for dfs: $O(m+n)$.

Connectivity

Simple queries from the following list can easily be answered using either *dfs* or *bfs*:

- Are vertices *s* and *t* connected?
- (particularly for directed graphs) Can *t* be reached from *s*?
- Which vertices are connected (i.e., what are the *connected components*)?
- What is a path from *s* to *t*?
- What is a (directed) path from *s* to *t*?

One solution is to evaluate *dfs(s)* with a judiciously chosen visitor such that pairs $\{e,w\}$ are memoized where edge *e* is that which leads to vertex *w*. In what follows, we will refer to *e* as the *discoverer* of *w*. From these edges, we can form a directed tree that spans the connected component that includes *s* and represents possible (but not unique) paths from *s* to each other vertex in the component.

If the connected component does not include all the vertices of the graph, we repeat *dfs(t)*, where *t* is an undiscovered vertex. Once the entire graph has been spanned—which must happen eventually—we will have a list of connected components, each with a directed tree rooted at the starting vertex for that component.

Ordering

Can we arrange the graph such that all edges point in more or less the same direction? In this case, we can identify an ordering (called the "topological order") of the vertices starting with any "source" vertices (those without predecessors) and ending with any "sink" vertices (those without successors). It should be clear that this application can only apply to a DAG. But how can we tell if a graph representation is indeed a DAG? Recall that the adjacency map of the graph does not include any constant-time indication of what type of graph is represented.

Perhaps the simplest and most obvious way is to try to derive the topological order and, if we fail—either because it's a directed graph with cycles or it's an undirected graph—the graph must not be a DAG. Again, we use *dfs* with a suitable visitor—a postvisitor that places the vertices into a stack—to get the order. The resulting list, derived by successively popping from the stack, is known as the "reverse postfix" order.

STUDENT EXERCISE

How can you test that the original graph is a DAG? Hint: You'll need the reverse postfix order together with the list of (directed) edges.

Strong Connectivity

We covered the simple type of connectivity. *Strong connectivity* is the property of a directed graph whereby some sets of vertices are mutually connected: They lie on a cycle. Such a set is known as a *strongly connected component* (SCC). Strong connectivity doesn't apply to undirected graphs because the entire graph would be strongly connected and therefore not very interesting. To determine these SCCs, we need to find pairs of vertices that are connected in both $\mathcal{G}$ and $\mathcal{G}^R$. We can use a two-pass version of *dfs* for this purpose: Kosaraju's algorithm.

Recall that we can detect any connected components using *dfs* by starting, in sequence, at arbitrarily chosen unvisited vertices. If we run *dfs* on both $\mathcal{G}$ and $\mathcal{G}^R$, we will get a set of connected components either way. But if we continue to choose the starting vertices at random, we may further subdivide connected components in a way that is not helpful. Kosaraju's algorithm ensures that the components align properly by using the topological order of vertices from $\mathcal{G}^R$ to start each component traversal in $\mathcal{G}$. This rather elegant scheme therefore results in identifying the strongly connected components of a directed graph. What if there are no strongly connected components (each vertex is its own SCC)? Then we must have started with a DAG—no cycles and therefore no SCCs.

Look at Figure 9.2. As expected, within each SCC (only one in this graph), there are edges going in all directions (because an SCC contains at least one directed cycle). But if you look at the edges between SCCs, all the edges align in the same direction. Therefore, the SCCs can be topologically ordered.

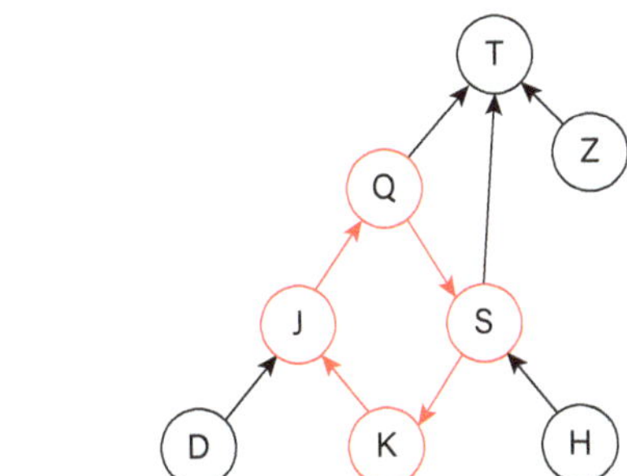

Directed Graph with Strong Component: JKQS (marked in red)

FIGURE 9.2. Strong connectivity.

STUDENT EXERCISE

Verify that the topological order of $\mathcal{G}^R$ that we derived in the first phase of Kosaraju's algorithm contains the first vertex of each SCC, in order.

Minimum Spanning Trees

A spanning tree is a subset of the edges of an undirected graph such that all vertices are visited ("spanned"). Because it is a tree, it will be connected, and there can be no cycles. For any graph that is not itself a tree, there will be many possible spanning trees.

We saw how easy it was using *dfs* to create a spanning forest of trees—one for each connected component. For the purposes of a spanning tree, the direction of the edges is not significant, so we can treat each edge as undirected—the same as for the original graph.

There's nothing that interesting about the set of all possible spanning trees. But a spanning tree that minimizes some property of the edges, assuming the edges have such a property, may be interesting. We call this the minimum spanning tree (MST).

Suppose, for example, that a university plans to build tunnels to connect every building on campus. Tunneling is very expensive, so they would probably want to minimize the total length of the tunnels while still including every building. A graph of *m* buildings (the vertices), connected by candidate tunnels (the edges) would form a dense graph $\mathcal{C}$. By determining the minimum spanning tree $\mathcal{M}$ of $\mathcal{C}$, where the edge property to be minimized is the cost to dig the tunnel (or perhaps just its length), we can design a tunnel system that will be the least expensive to build while still connecting every building to the system. Some routes might be much longer than walking. We might propose additional tunnels for shortcuts. But such a graph would no longer be a tree as it would necessarily include cycles.

How should we determine the MST? While constructing the MST, we will in general have a set of edges $\mathcal{T}$ (not necessarily connected) to which we must add one or more edges until $\mathcal{T}$ has $m-1$ connected edges without any cycles. Candidate edges are (a) from the graph $\mathcal{C}$; (b) not in $\mathcal{T}$; (c) without an endpoint already in $\mathcal{T}$; (d) the least cost edge available. We will describe two such algorithms: Kruskal's and Prim's.

As an example for my Northeastern students, I created this fanciful tunnel design, using Kruskal's algorithm, to connect all the buildings on the campus. Any of the MST algorithms will do, of course.

WEB LINK: https://www.google.com/maps/d/viewer?ll=42.340443821047074%2C-71.08815849999996&z=16&mid=1l18DCx827hvqaif5sndVLoqd6CxdOPIU

Kruskal's Algorithm

We start by putting all candidate edges into a priority queue *O*(*n log n*). Then we place the vertices into a disjoint set. We will discuss disjoint sets in the final chapter, but the purpose of a DS is to determine if two vertices are connected in *O*(*log m*) time. We will see that we can do significantly better than logarithmic time. $\mathcal{T}$ is empty.

For each edge to be added $\Omega(m) \& O(n)$, we remove the lowest cost edge from the PQ $O(\log n)$ and check if a cycle would be formed if we used it. If so, we discard it and get the next edge. This is why we may end up taking more than m elements from the PQ. Once we have added $m-1$ edges, we must have the MST.

Kruskal's algorithm is reasonably fast and simple to understand. It has two minor drawbacks: (a) During construction, $\mathcal{T}$ might not be connected; (b) it runs in $O(n \log n)$ time when we would prefer $O(n \log m)$.

Prim's Algorithm

Prim's algorithm dispenses with the disjoint set and maintains a connected $\mathcal{T}$ while storing only a subset of all possible edges. $\mathcal{T}$ starts as a single (arbitrary) vertex from $\mathcal{C}$ and the priority queue begins empty.

Each of $m-1$ iterations operate as follows:

1. Identifying, by traversing the adjacency map of $\mathcal{T}$, all edges with exactly one end in $\mathcal{T}$. These edges are the candidates that are then inserted into the PQ. At the time of insertion, they cannot possibly cause a cycle.
2. The minimum-cost edge e is removed from the PQ (it won't necessarily be one of the edges recently added in step 1) and added to $\mathcal{T}$, along with its outer vertex v.
3. Any edge adjacent to v that is already in the PQ should be deleted. However, note that the implementation of the priority queue described earlier does not support an arbitrary deletion operation. In practice, we can (lazily) mark the edge as ineligible.

Such is the lazy version of *prim*. From the description, it appears it might run in $O(n \log m)$ time, but, in practice, it is $O(n \log n)$.

There is an eager version that makes use of an enhanced, vertex-based, priority queue. We will leave its details to the code repository. Its complexity is $O(n + m \log m)$. From our discussion of graph complexity earlier, we know that n is likely to be of a similar order of magnitude to $m \log m$.

Shortest Paths

The problem of finding the shortest path (SP) from vertex s to vertex t in graph $\mathcal{G}$ involves summing the costs (in time, distance, fuel, etc.) of individual edges that lie on possible paths and minimizing their total. We have implicitly summed costs before (minimum spanning tree, especially Prim's algorithm), and we have accumulated the count of edges before (breadth-first search). It shouldn't be too surprising that the solution has attributes of each of those two algorithms.

Could depth-first search work better? *s* and *t* might be close together in the context of $\mathcal{G}$, in which case *dfs* might perform a lot of unnecessary work looking at long, fruitless paths. And, generally, *bfs* is better for goal-seeking traversal like SP.

Dijkstra's Algorithm

The algorithm that we derive first is called Dijkstra's algorithm after computer scientist Edsger Dijkstra (1930–2002). When we looked at *bfs*, we noted that the order of processing vertices was strictly determined by the number of hops from the start. But, for SP, that property will be meaningless because we want to process the vertices in terms of their actual distance (or cost) from the start. We can cater to this by using a priority queue instead of a queue. Thus, whenever we take a vertex *v* from the queue for processing, it will always be closer to *s* than any other unprocessed vertex. Now, for each edge *e* adjacent to *v*, we process its other vertex *w*.

HISTORY NOTE

Dijkstra was one of the most influential and innovative computer scientists of the 20th century. He received the Turing Award in 1972 for his contributions to "structural programming," for example his work on the Algol 60 compiler, one of the first languages to implement recursion.

As we did in *bfs*, we can track the total distance of *w* from *s* simply by adding the cost *c* of edge *e* to the cost of reaching *v*. What if *c* is negative? That would imply that *w* ought to have been visited before *v*. That would introduce inconsistencies in the algorithm. Therefore, it's required—for *dijkstra*—that all edge costs are non-negative. This is quite acceptable for navigation purposes because—in our (known) universe—there is always a positive cost to move from one location to another.

Thus, we emerge with a spanning tree, and we know the total distance from *s* of every vertex of interest. Note that we have implicitly assumed that any vertex in $\mathcal{G}$ might appear on the shortest path to *t*. Or we might be interested in keeping a cache of all shortest paths from *s* in $\mathcal{G}$. When *t* is an arbitrarily chosen vertex of $\mathcal{G}$, we probably want to limit the scope of the algorithm to a subgraph $\mathcal{G}'$. To determine this subgraph will be the job of another algorithm, the A* algorithm, not covered here.

Did you notice a problem with the statement about the spanning tree that results from *dijkstra*? It would have been accurate for a directed tree. But for a graph? When we considered vertex *w*, we did not allow for the fact that we might have previously encountered *w* and found its total distance from *s*. What if the two totals are different, as generally they will be? If the distance at the second encounter is greater (or the same), we will be happy with *w*'s distance value. But suppose that we found a shortcut? A path with lower total cost? We need to take account of this by reducing *w*'s distance value and by changing the value of *w*'s discoverer. We call that process *relaxation*.

As simple as this sounds, this introduces a complication in the priority queue. Consider that *w* will have previously been added to the PQ. But relaxation causes its priority to be increased; it may need to be promoted in the PQ. Our implementation of the priority queue (Chapter 6) does not support this operation. Indeed, it doesn't support any operation that refers to an item in the queue other than at the root. We can solve this by

- indexing the elements in a priority queue
- enabling swim/sink operations on specific elements

As usual, we can estimate the complexity by considering what happens in the algorithm. We must visit every edge once; therefore, we have a term $O(n)$. The other complexity is in the priority queue: Each vertex must at some point be inserted and removed from the PQ. Thus, its complexity will be characterized by $O(m \log m)$. The total complexity is therefore the same as for *prim*: $O(n + m \log m)$.

Recall how we continually extend a spanning tree in *prim* by choosing the lowest cost edge from among the eligible edges adjacent to the existing tree. We do something similar in both *dfs* and *bfs*, although in those cases we don't require edges to have any kind of property. We begin with a tree that consists only of the starting point, and then, one at a time, we add edges to the existing tree. In the case of *dfs*, we choose the most recent edge, whereas for *bfs* we choose the least recent edge. In *dijkstra*, we follow a similar approach but choose the closest point to the start.

Because these four algorithms are based primarily on the traversal of the adjacency map, they should work equally well for both directed and undirected graphs. Only *prim* is restricted to undirected graphs. That's because when we consider the eligibility of an edge to extend the tree, it could potentially form a cycle in either direction. In any case, a minimum spanning tree is defined for an undirected graph. *Dijkstra* is normally considered an algorithm for directed graphs because navigation is directional. If you follow an undirected edge *ab* from *a* to *b* and back, that will require double the cost of *ab*—not zero cost.

Acyclic Algorithm

What if we have a DAG? Could we find the shortest paths in less time? Yes, we can use the topological order to simplify calculating the SP. The algorithm is essentially the same as *dijkstra*, including the relaxation of edges, but without the complexity of the priority queue. The worst-case time is, therefore, $O(m+n)$. For some graphs, this will be a slight improvement over *dijkstra*. However, one other advantage is that, because of the guaranteed order of visiting vertices, we are no longer concerned if some of the edges have a negative cost. That enables a more general class of scheduling problems to be solved.

Bellman-Ford Algorithm

By constraining the type of graph while relaxing the type of edge costs, the acyclic algorithm can improve SP performance for some graphs. Bellman-Ford goes in the opposite direction: The types of subject graphs are relaxed at the same time as relaxing edge costs, but all at the expense of (typically) much worse performance.

Recall bubble sort (Chapter 7) applied to an array (or list) of length *n*. The algorithm undergoes a series of $n-1$ passes through the data, each requiring $n-1$ conditional swaps. What saves bubble sort from being an abjectly terrible algorithm is that, if a pass is completed without doing any swaps, the algorithm terminates. Bellman-Ford uses a similar mechanism.

Starting from *s*, the algorithm proceeds as for *dijkstra* and *acyclic*. But because there are no restrictions on individual costs, it's possible that a vertex *w*, adjacent to vertex *v*, is closer to *s* than *v*. Indeed, relaxation means that any vertex can move closer to *s*. The consequence is that we are obliged to start over again—and again—relaxing each of the edges. If there are no relaxations in a pass, the algorithm can terminate because every distance value must now be correct.

Because, in general, a path through the graph can have a maximum value of $m-1$ edges, it may be necessary to undergo $m-1$ passes, each of which visits *n* edges. Thus, the worst-case performance of the *bf* is $O(mn)$, or quadratic. Various improvements can be applied that can reduce the average number of edge visits overall, but they cannot improve the worst-case scenario.

There is one pathological case that *bf* cannot correctly handle (SP is not defined in such a case, so no other algorithm can handle it either). That is the presence of a negative cycle. If there is such a cycle, it's obvious that a shorter path can always be found by taking the cycle again (*ad infinitum*). However, *bf* can discover this situation and will terminate appropriately.

Bellman-Ford is the most versatile SP algorithm and, consequently, can be used in many optimization scenarios. In particular, it is the fundamental engine behind dynamic programming (see Chapter 10).

Interesting Graph Problems

The Seven Bridges of Königsberg

Given an undirected graph, can you find a cycle that traverses each edge exactly once? For such a cycle to exist, each vertex must have one way in and another (different) way out. The vertex is also valid if it has any number of other edge pairs—each pair providing a way in and a way out. Therefore, each vertex must have even degree. If such a cycle exists, it is called a *Eulerian circuit* or *Euler tour*.

HISTORY NOTE

Leonhard Euler (1707–1783), the father of graph theory, was one of the greatest mathematicians of all time. Apart from graph theory and topology, Euler's other contributions involve complex analysis (Euler's identity), infinite series, number theory (primes, etc.), calculus, geometry, and structural engineering. There are at least 52 different numbers, theorems, formulas, and so forth named after him.

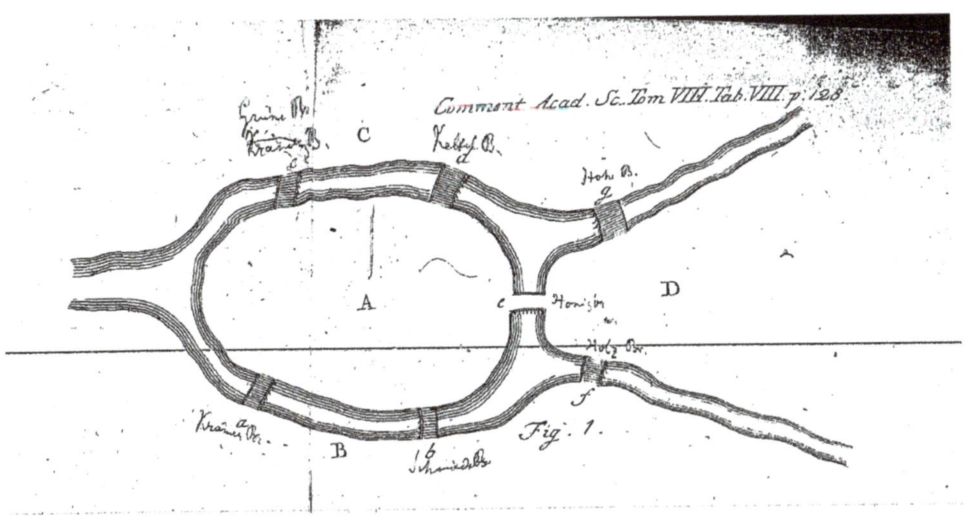

FIGURE 9.3. The seven bridges of Königsberg.

Euler was asked by the gentlemen of Königsberg in East Prussia—now called Kaliningrad and part of Russia—to determine if there was a circuit of the bridges such that you could start in one part of the city (A, B, C, or D in Figure 9.3) and return to the same point, having crossed each bridge exactly once.

STUDENT EXERCISE

Show that no Euler tour of the seven bridges of Königsberg is possible. Assuming that you have a graph for which a Euler tour *is* possible, how would you find it? What would be the complexity of the solution?

Hamilton Cycle

A similar problem can be devised: Find a circuit that visits every vertex exactly once. This is a difficult problem and is NP complete, as is its cousin, the traveling salesman problem. In the latter problem, we are not restricted to the existing edges of a graph—we must add our own edges between vertices in such a way as to minimize the total cost (distance) of traversing the added edges and returning to our starting point.

Subgraph Isomorphism

Another unexpectedly difficult problem in general is subgraph isomorphism. Given two graphs $\mathcal{G}$ and $\mathcal{H}$, are they isomorphic (i.e., topologically the same), ignoring any attributes of vertices or edges, and considering the order of visiting edges around a vertex to be completely arbitrary? In other words, are the adjacencies (the model A representation) equivalent? A more general problem is to ask if $\mathcal{G}$ is a subgraph of $\mathcal{H}$, or the other way around. If $\mathcal{G}$ and $\mathcal{H}$ are planar graphs, it is possible to determine isomorphism in linear time; otherwise, the problem is also NP complete.

Conclusion

Graphs are extremely versatile and support many applications. There are probably thousands of different use cases for graphs. Because graphs are generally sparse, the performance measures of the various algorithms are reasonably efficient. However, while many applications can be solved with simple traversal techniques, more complex problems require expertise for their development. If you need to solve a graph problem, you should therefore always look for an existing, well-tested solution.

Takeaways

Following is a list of the main ideas to take away from this chapter:

- The standard graph data structure is the adjacency map, which supports traversal in $O(m+n)$ time.
- The structure is the same for directed graphs and undirected graphs—the only difference is in the construction, not the traversal.
- *dfs* is the "go-to" algorithm as it handles most of the traversal applications of graphs.
- *bfs* should, however, be used when a goal, or the optimization of some measured quantity, is required.
- Four traversal algorithms (*dfs*, *bfs*, *prim*, and *dijkstra*) build spanning trees, edge by edge.
- *Prim* and *dijkstra* require a modified priority queue that can be indexed and support priority change.

Chapter Review Questions

Directions: Refer to what you learned in this chapter to respond to the questions and prompts:

1. What is the purpose of the Kosaraju-Sharir algorithm? What is its growth rate in terms of *m*, the number of vertices? What happens if you apply it to a directed acyclic graph?
2. What is the meaning of the "topological order" of a directed acyclic graph? What happens if the graph has a cycle?

Reference

Euler, L. (1741). Solutio problematis ad geometriam situs pertinentis. *Commentarii Academiae Scientiarum Petropolitanae*, 128–140. https://scholarlycommons.pacific.edu/euler-works/53/

Credit

Fig. 9.3: Leonhard Euler, "The Seven Bridges of Konigsberg," https://commons.wikimedia.org/wiki/File:Solutio_problematis_ad_geometriam_situs_pertinentis,_Fig._1_-_Cleaned_Up.png, 1736.

CHAPTER

10

Other Graph Topics

Introduction to the Chapter

There are two parts to this chapter, and they are related only inasmuch as they are applications of graph theory. The first part is a case study of what we learned earlier about complexity. The second part is an extension of graph theory to give us a different type of reduction technique: dynamic programming.

This chapter will draw on your understanding of the concept of reduction (Chapter 1), complexity (Chapter 2), and directed graphs (Chapter 9).

Learning Objectives

- Understand two important extensions of graph theory:
  - The connectivity of no-edge graphs to the Union-find problem
  - The concept of reduction whereby the sub-problems can be expressed in the form of a directed graph (dynamic programming)
- Determine how to optimize the union-find problem to a quasi-constant-time connectivity query

Key Terms

- **Disjoint set:** A set of sets, such that the intersection of any pair of sets is empty
- **Memoize:** Store a value in an addressable location (i.e., not the stack) for later reuse
- **Eager solution:** A solution that obeys all appropriate invariants
- **Lazy solution:** A solution that relaxes some invariants at certain stages of the solution to save what might be unnecessary operations

Part 1: Union-Find (Disjoint Sets)

The **disjoint sets** (union-find) abstract data type stores sets such that the intersection of any two sets is always empty (i.e. they are disjoint). This situation arises, for example, when a number (*n*) of singleton disjoint sets are, successively, unioned *m* times where $m < n$. In the union-find model, the singleton disjoint sets are "objects," corresponding to nodes (vertices) of a graph that does not support edges. If two nodes are connected, that is the sum total of all information about them. The data representation does not keep track in any way of how they are connected.

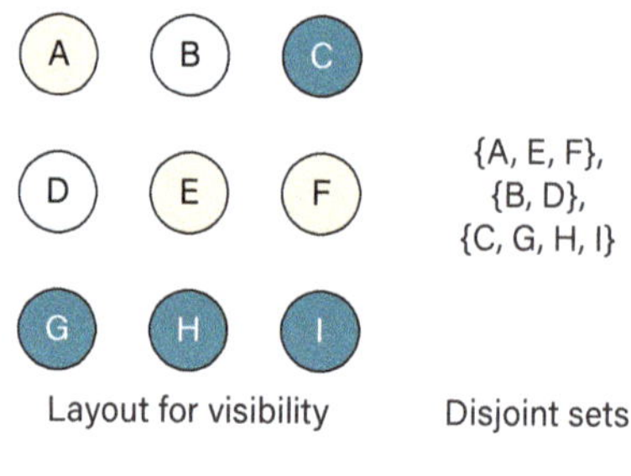

FIGURE 10.1. Disjoint sets.

Thus, we do not normally consider union-find as a graph structure, although it can be used in graph algorithms—as we saw in Kruskal's algorithm for the minimum spanning tree. The operations that the ADT must support are (a) *connect(p,q)* and (b) *isConnected(p,q)*, where *p* and *q* are objects. In the disjoint set model, these operations correspond to $union(\mathcal{P},\mathcal{Q})$ and $\mathcal{P} \equiv \mathcal{Q}$, where $\mathcal{P}$ is the set containing p and $\mathcal{Q}$ is the set containing q.

Given that n may be extremely large and that $m = O(n)$, how can we efficiently represent these disjoint sets? Everything that we have previously done in a graph has taken time, which is $\Omega(n\log n)$ and $O(n^{\frac{3}{2}})$, assuming that the graph is connected and sparse. (See the last chapter for the justification for these limits.) Is it possible to determine if two objects (vertices) are connected in something closer to linear time?

The Best Case

In the best of all solutions, there exists a constant-time function *set(x)* such that *set(x)* (uniquely) contains x and, further, that the complexity of the operation to union two sets is also constant time. In this case, the total time to build a disjoint set with n objects and m connections should be m. In other words, the problem appears to be $\Omega(m)$. In the union-find model, this *set(x)* function is known as *find(x)*.

Eager Solution

In the **eager solution**, we represent the object parentage by an array. This satisfies our constant-time function *set(x)* and, because the algorithm is eager, the data structure is always consistent and up-to-date so that we can make *isConnected* queries in the midst of *connect* operations. Because the *set(x)*, or *find(x)*, function is fast, this solution is called *quick find*.

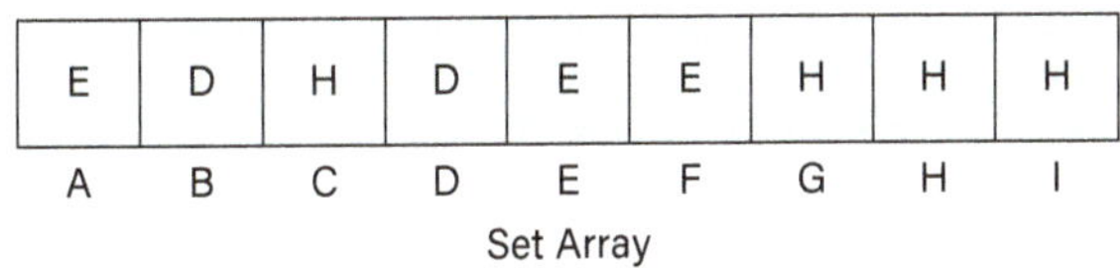

FIGURE 10.2. Eager representation (quick find).

In the figure, you can see that object A belongs to set $\mathcal{E}$, object B belongs to set $\mathcal{D}$, and so on. You can immediately sense some arbitrariness in this scheme (see Chapter 1). Why should the set called $\mathcal{E}$, containing member objects A, E, and F, be called $\mathcal{E}$? Why not $\mathcal{A}$ or $\mathcal{F}$? Does it matter?

Unfortunately, this solution cannot support *connect* (union) operations in anything close to constant time. Indeed, once we know the $\mathcal{P}$ and $\mathcal{Q}$ for objects p and q (in constant time), we must essentially find all members of $\mathcal{P}$ and reassign them to $\mathcal{Q}$ (or find the members of $\mathcal{Q}$ and reassign them to $\mathcal{P}$). With the data structure proposed, this will take linear time (i.e. $O(n)$). Thus, the total time to perform m unions will be $O(mn)$ or, more simply, $O(n^2)$. If n is 1 billion and one, and each operation can be completed in one nanosecond, it will take 32 years to complete one billion unions!

Lazy Solution

Perhaps it is not necessary to have an eager representation. Maybe we can save some work with a **lazy solution**. Instead of always directly knowing the value of *set(x)*, perhaps we could store the value of *parent(x)* and, if the resulting tree of parent-child relationships is not too deep, we would only have to follow a small number of parents before discovering the value of *set(x)*. Furthermore, we know that the maximum depth of such a tree would be $\log_2 n$, provided that the resulting tree is binary (or ternary, etc.). We are used to the idea of a tree minimizing the number of probes.

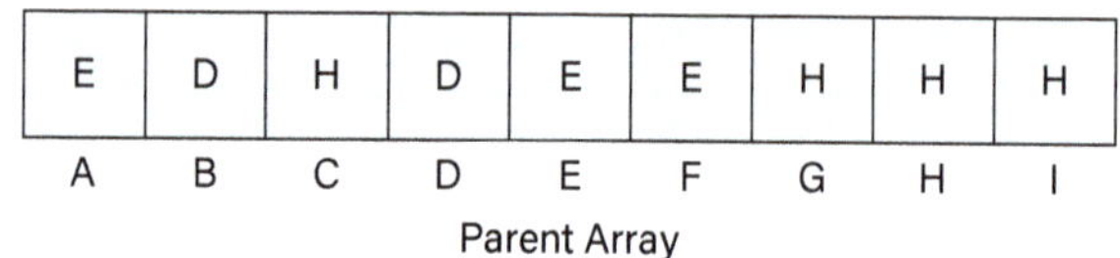

FIGURE 10.3. Lazy representation (quick union).

Because, having found the roots of each tree using the *set* method, *union* is a constant-time operation, we call this algorithm *quick-union*. But can we be sure that the resulting data structure would be a (binary) tree? What if some parents had only one child? Then the maximum depth would be n. Let's see how this might arise.

Let's look at some typical code:

```
union(p, q) -> void { parent(set(p)) = set(q) }
```

This looks straightforward. But, as written, this code violates the ASP. That's because joining $\mathcal{P}$ to $\mathcal{Q}$ will to result in a different representation than joining $\mathcal{Q}$ to $\mathcal{P}$. Are there any inferences that we can take from this? There are.

If the two operations are not identical, we should try to understand why not. Suppose the depth of $\mathcal{P}$ is k, and the depth of $\mathcal{Q}$ is $k-1$. If we join $\mathcal{P}$ to $\mathcal{Q}$, the resulting set will have a tree depth of $k+1$, whereas if we join $\mathcal{Q}$ to $\mathcal{P}$, the result will be a tree of depth of k. This difference is profound!

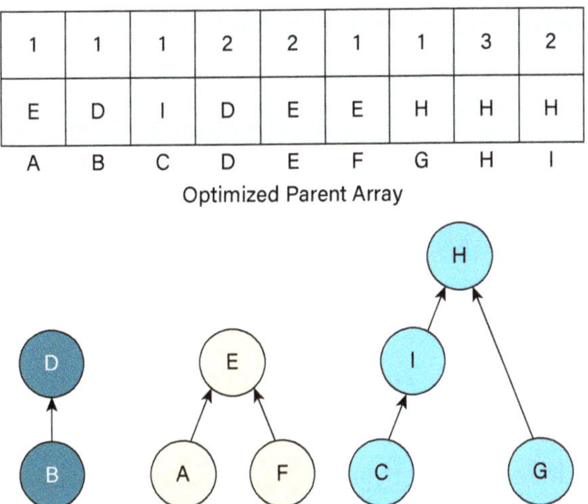

FIGURE 10.4. Optimized lazy representation (weighted quick union).

The solution to our ASP dilemma is to **memoize** the depth of each tree and use that information to determine which set should be joined to which set. Guessing is not good and potentially results in a depth of n. This fix for the inadequate *quick union* is generally called *weighted quick union*. We can prove that the depth of any tree will be $O(\log_2 n)$. It's equally effective to keep track of the size of each set (tree), and that is typically what is done for this abstract data type. Overall, using *weighted quick union*, will require $O(m \log_2 n)$ operations to build the data structure for n objects and m connects.

An Optimal Solution?

The theorctical best case was derived as $\Omega(m)$. We are not there yet. The depth of any tree is known to be $O(\log_2 n)$, but that is, clearly, the worst case corresponding to a binary tree. But in our hypothetical best-case solution, the depth of each tree is one. That's to say that, if the size of any tree is s, the root node is s-ary (i.e., s children). How can we promote objects from deep in the original binary tree such that they point directly to the root? By updating their parent to point to their grandparent. Every time we invoke the *set(x)* method, x will move one level closer to the root, as will x's parent, and so on. It is also possible, using a two-pass approach, to promote every element directly to its root, but this strategy doubles the number of operations and doesn't really improve overall efficiency.

In terms of the forest of trees shown in Figure 10.4, the one improvement that this method achieves is to switch the parent of C to be H directly, thus avoiding the intermediate step of I. In Table 10.1, the depths of I and H will change to 1 and 2, respectively.

If we need a label for this scheme, we can call it *path compression*. Thus, our best algorithm is *weighted quick union with path compression*. How good is it in practice? It's not optimal, but it's not far off. According to a paper by Robert Tarjan, one of the great graph algorithm exponents, the total number of operations $N(m,n)$ is

$$N(m,n) = O(m\alpha(n))$$

where $\alpha(n))$ is the inverse Ackerman function, which is known to grow extremely slowly. However, we will use a prior result by Hopcraft and Ullman that is a little easier to describe:

$$N(m,n) = O(n + m\,log*(n))$$

where $log*(n))$ is the iterated log function, which also grows very slowly. This function is defined recursively:

$$log*(x) = \{0\; if\; x \leq 1 | 1 + log*(\log x)\; if\; x > 1\}$$

In other words, for every time that we can successfully yield a positive value for the (recursive) log, we add one. We can derive the Table 10.1, where uses logs to the base 2 and ε is an infinitessimaly small number.

TABLE 10.1 Iterated Log Function

$\lfloor n \rfloor$	$\lceil n \rceil$	$log*(n)$
ε	$1 = 2^0$	0
$1 + \varepsilon$	$2 = 2^1$	1
$2 + \varepsilon$	$4 = 2^2$	2
$4 + \varepsilon$	$16 = 2^4$	3
$16 + \varepsilon$	$65536 = 2^{16}$	4
$65536 + \varepsilon$	$10^{19,728} = 2^{65536}$	5

If you're wondering if this function could ever exceed five, consider that our universe is estimated to hold around 10^{80} atoms. We can thus safely substitute the value 5 for $log*(n)$, regardless of n. Thus, $N(m,n)$ simplifies to $n+5m \sim 6n$, a linear function of n. Using this approach, we can theoretically handle 1 billion objects in 6 seconds, compared with 32 years as predicted for the quick-find algorithm.

Depth or Size?

In our discussion of weighted quick union, the representation used was the depth of each subtree. We could also have counted the number of objects in each subtree (i.e., its *size*). Does it matter which one we use? It doesn't matter as far as weighted quick union is concerned. But did you notice in our discussion of path compression how, when C was connected directly to H, we reduced the depth of subtrees I and H. It is slightly easier to do the appropriate updates when we use size instead of depth. Note that the size of H does not change under the path compression of object C.

Summary

We set out to solve the disjoint set (union-find) problem. We iteratively improved our solution until we found a quasi-linear algorithm.

Part 2: Dynamic Programming

Introduction

What is dynamic programming? And why is it in a chapter dealing with graphs? Dynamic programming is a fancy name for another type of reduction (i.e., a method of solving problems in terms of easier problems). We discussed the concept of reduction in some depth in Chapter 1, including, for example, how merge sort uses a style of reduction called DnC. However, in those other types of reduction, the order in which sub-problems must be solved is well-defined *a priori* (in advance). Because the branches of any tree (as in the case of DnC) are independent, there is no mystery about the sequence of operations. Recall that, for a directed tree, there is exactly one directed path (dependency) between two vertices or none.

Let's look at the reductions we've considered before, starting with a DnD example: selection sort. The final result of invoking selection sort on an array of n elements is based on the following reduction:

1. Divide the problem into two sub-problems:
    a. Find the smallest element.
    b. Sort the remaining $n-1$ elements.

2. Solve these two sub-problems:
   a. Determine the smallest element by scanning all elements in the problem and returning the smallest.
   b. Apply selection sort to the remaining $n-1$ elements recursively.
3. Concatenate these two solutions and we have the final solution.

In other words, the topology of the DnD reduction is linear—a list. We described the process recursively but, as we know, we can implement selection sort iteratively just as well.

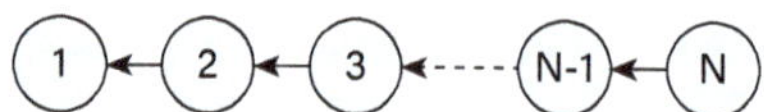

The solution for N is dependent on the solution for N-1 which is...

FIGURE 10.5. DnD.

Now let's consider an example of DnC: merge sort. Here, the reduction is as follows:

1. Divide the problem into two equal sub-problems:
   a. Get the left-hand partition in order.
   b. Get the right-hand partition in order.
2. Solve each of these two sub-problems by applying merge sort recursively.
3. Merge the two sorted partitions.

In this case, each branch is independent, and therefore it does not matter in which order we solve the two sub-problems (that's why step 2 doesn't specify the order). What we have is a solution *tree*.

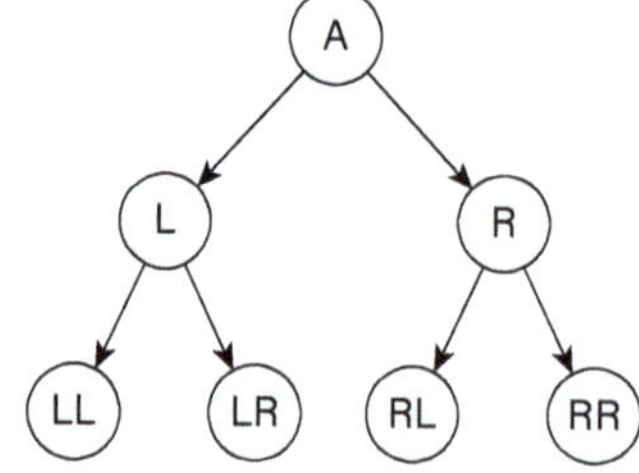

The task of sorting the array A is dependent on both L and R.
L is dependent on both LL and LR, similarly for R.
But L does not depend on RL or RR.

FIGURE 10.6. Merge-sort solution tree.

As we've just seen, the topology of a DnD reduction is list/array like (e.g. selection sort), while a DnC reduction is tree like (e.g., merge sort). What if the necessary reduction is not so neat and tidy? And what if the "branches" are not independent but are mutually dependent in some complex relationship? In other words, what if the sub-problems and sub-solutions form a graph? This is what dynamic programming is designed to solve.

Dynamic Programming

Reduction by Directed Graph

Dynamic programming (DP) is in principle quite simple. Like any other reduction, the simplest way of thinking about a DP solution is based on recursion. Fundamentally, it is solving a graph of sub-problems (the vertices of the graph) using depth-first search. Once the traversal is complete, we will therefore have a graph of sub-solutions. Like any other *dfs*-based traversal, if we've already visited a vertex (we have a sub-solution available), we simply reuse the result. We need a separate structure (list, hash table, etc.) for these results because we can't rely on the stack as we would for a tree. We call this technique of remembering sub-solutions *memoization*. The edges of the graph correspond to *dependencies*. Any one sub-problem is either trivial (a node that has no dependencies) or dependent (it depends on the solution to at least one other sub-problem).

To summarize, we have a directed graph of sub-problems and their dependencies that we can traverse to discover the solution to our original problem—that is the node (sub-problem) that directly or indirectly depends on all other nodes. We can align our edges in one of two ways: either the edge points from the dependent to the dependencies or from a dependency to its dependent. Because the latter direction represents the flow of information as we solve the problem, we're going to draw our arrows in that direction.

You're probably asking, "Surely, it's more complicated than that?" Well, there are a few aspects that can add some complication:

- Modeling the problem (i.e. determining the reduction graph): The sub-problems and their dependencies—this is usually the hardest part of using DP
- Ensuring that the sink node of the directed graph does in fact represent the original problem
- Deciding whether to solve the problem in a top-down (recursive) manner or bottom-up (iterative)
- If bottom-up, solving the sub-problems in their topological order

- Knowing what to do if there are cycles
- Recognizing that the manner by which sub-solutions are combined to solve the dependent sub-problem can vary widely, from simply taking the minimum (or maximum) value to applying a complex multivariate function

We could call the technique *directed-graph-based reduction*. However, logical as it may sound, this term is never used. Instead, we always use the term *dynamic programming*. An almost trivial reduction such as finding the median by sorting and taking the middle value would be represented as shown in Figure 10.7.

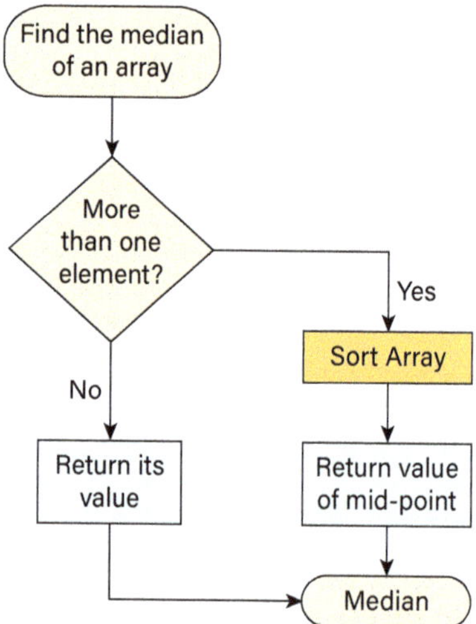

FIGURE 10.7. Simple reduction for the median problem.

While edges represent (static) dependencies, the optimal value of a sub-solution may nevertheless depend on the order of evaluating its dependencies. In the worst (most general) case, the value of a sub-solution may require evaluation many times. It is this aspect of the solution that gives rise to the term *dynamic* in dynamic programming. In the special case of a DAG, this dynamic aspect is missing because the graph can be traversed in topological order. An example of this is evaluating the Fibonacci series. However, the term "dynamic programming" is still used for such problems.

Reduction by Directed Acyclic Graph

How are we to traverse this directed graph? If it is a DAG, the traversal will be simple: We visit the nodes in their topological order. This is the basis of the so-called acyclic shortest paths method of traversal. Frequently, problems to be solved by dynamic programming will require the solution of a multistage-based problem. Such a graph is a special case of a DAG.

We already know how to find the topological order of a DAG—we use depth-first search and keep track of the vertices that have zero out-degree by putting them on a stack. This process is what relates the top-down solution (*dfs*) to a bottom-up solution (topological order).

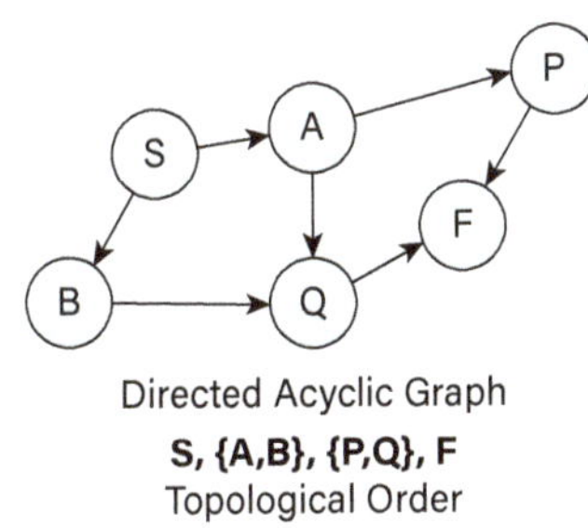

FIGURE 10.8. DAG and its topological order.

Reduction by Cyclic Directed Graph

What if our solution graph is not acyclic—or perhaps we don't know that it is acyclic? Then we cannot confidently solve the problem in topological order. It's possible that evaluating a sub-solution provides a more optimal solution to a sub-problem than we currently have chosen. We need to revisit that sub-problem just as we did for Dijkstra's shortest paths algorithm or the Bellman-Ford algorithm. However, in general, there is no simplifying assumption that we can make, as we did for *dijkstra*. Instead, we must employ the full *bf* algorithm. The *bf* algorithm solves the most general shortest paths problem—we can't make any simplifying assumptions about our graph—by dynamic programming.

HISTORY NOTE

Richard Bellman introduced the term "dynamic programming" in 1953, although at that time it was applied to much more specific optimization use cases from the fields of control theory and economics. The principles of optimality that were inherent in the method were described by the Bellman equation. He chose the term because he knew that anything in his organization that sounded like mathematics or research would likely be shot down. Five years later, he described what came to be known as the *bf* algorithm, although Ford had published the algorithm in 1956. Actually, the *bf* algorithm was first proposed by Shimbel in 1955. This is another example of Stigler's law at work.

Note that the shortest paths algorithms are special cases of dynamic programming whereby each sub-problem that must be optimized is the total cost over all edges that make up the sub-problem. For any edge, its total cost is the sum of its cost (weight) and the cost of the sub-solution corresponding to the other end of the edge. That is indeed the *bf* algorithm. But, as you will recall from Chapter 9, we can improve performance significantly if we know that the graph is acyclic (we use the *acyclic* algorithm) or that the costs (weights) are non-negative (we use *dijkstra*). Although you might often see DP problems that really are just shortest paths problems, the true power of the method is its much greater applicability in general.

Applying the Dynamic Programming Method

Fibonacci

While, in general, reduction involves three steps, DP is often described as having five steps. We will cover these steps in relation to the Fibonacci evaluation problem:

1. Define the sub-solutions (the vertices of the graph), in this case, each F_i (the value of the ith Fibonacci number) is a sub-solution.
2. Determine the sub-problems (the sub-graphs—with the graph in the figure representing the sub-problem of evaluating $F)_4$. The sub-problem (sub-graph) of finding F_3 is shown in the Figure 10.9. For the Fibonacci use case, any sub-problem is solved by adding the (dependency) solutions indicated by the sub-solution (vertex) at the other end of each edge in the corresponding sub-graph. That's to say, for example, the problem of evaluating F_4 is solved by adding the values of F_2 and F_3.

3. Decide which order we should evaluate: just in time (recursively when not known) in a top-down approach or proactively in an iterative manner (bottom up). In this case, we will choose top down.
4. Solve each sub-problem using the memoized value for each sub-solution dependency (if no value memoized, we evaluate and memoize it). Here, for example, $F_3 = F_2 + F_1$. Note that, for every sub-problem, we only ever need to recurse on one evaluation, not two because one value will have been memoized.
5. If necessary, transform the top-level solution (in this case, F_4) to suit the true problem. For Fibonacci, there is no transformation required: F_4 *is* the solution.

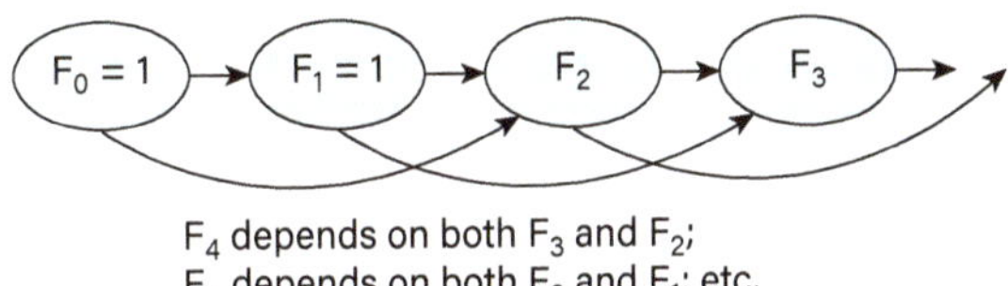

FIGURE 10.9. Determining Fibonacci F_4.

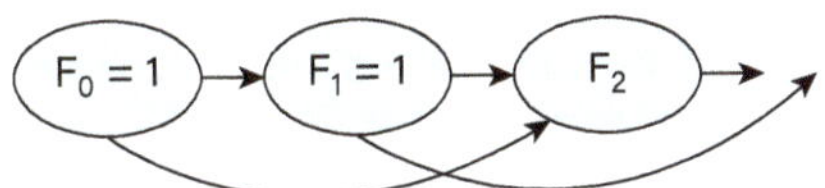

FIGURE 10.10. Determining Fibonacci F_3.

Coin Chooser

In this problem, you are to determine the fewest possible coins that have a given value, v. The denominations of the coins are c_i., where $0 \leq i < w$, where w is the number of different coin denominations. You have an unlimited number of each denomination. The problem is general, in that different nations have different coinage. But in the examples that you are likely to encounter, the denominations are presumed to be those of the United States: 1¢, 5¢, 10¢, 25¢, (i.e., $w = 4$). A brute-force approach would find every possible collection of coins that totaled v and then choose the one requiring the fewest coins. The number of candidate solutions would be exponential, something like $\sim v^w$. Applying the Bellman–Ford algorithm naïvely will result in $O(vw)$ steps.

We can improve a little on this solution by using a more focused dynamic programming approach. Let's work through the details:

- Each sub-problem is to find the minimum (optimal) number of coins $\mu(x)$ required to represent value x. If we base all our solutions on such optimal solutions, our overall solution must also be optimal (the principle of optimality).
- The solution we need for our original problem is represented by $\mu(v)$.
- We treat the problem as a normal (recursive) top-down problem.
- The dependencies of a sub-problem represent (optimal) collections of coins where one coin is missing.
- The resulting topology is a tree, so there is no complication due to cycles.

Let's write our recursive relationships for $\mu(x)$.
Base case: $\mu(0) = 0$
Recursive cases: $\mu(x) = \min_i \{ if\,(x > c_i)\, then\, \mu(x - c_i)\, else\, \varnothing \} + 1$

It is understood that the symbol $\varnothing$ represents "not a solution." This implies that there is one value of c_i that is 1; otherwise, the problem might not be solvable. Note also that, assuming all c_i values are positive, the sub-problems that are invoked recursively are smaller problems than the problem itself. This is an essential condition for any recursive reduction.

We will look at the "standard" example: $v = 87$ (you will see this example value quite often). Starting with 87, we want to get to zero as quickly as possible. We should probably start by choosing the biggest coin (25¢)—the same as we would do with a greedy algorithm. We have one coin and need the optimal solution for 62. In this way, we evaluate 37, 12, 2, and 1. The minimum number of coins is therefore six: 3 x 25¢, 1 x 10¢, 2 x 1¢. In addition to the (trivial) zero value, we will have evaluated six sub-solutions.

It seems that we simply solved the problem with a greedy algorithm (always choosing the locally optimal sub-solution). In fact, we did describe the greedy algorithm. The DP algorithm, as described, solves 87 sub-problems! How can that be an improvement over six?

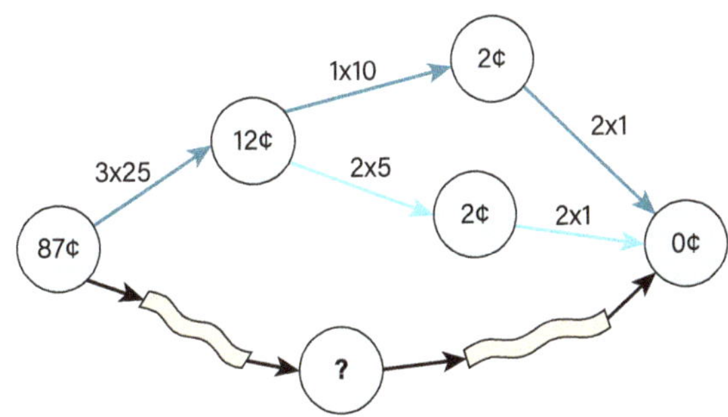

FIGURE 10.11. Coin changer.

The answer is that, while coin choice does provide a nice easy exemplar for dynamic programming, it's not an ideal use case. That's because DP does not assume such a simple optimizing function—it must evaluate all possible branches of the tree just in case it finds a really good solution on what appears to be a less favorable branch. Assuming that all coin denominations are available (and unlimited) at every turn, this won't happen. But DP is a general method that doesn't know that. Equally important is to recognize that the greedy approach won't always work, even though it may work well for certain problems, like the coin chooser. In our DP solution for coin choice, the time and space are both $\Theta(v)$.

We can generalize the coin problem to make it a little more interesting. Instead of an infinite number of coins of each denomination, we generalize our coins to valuable objects, perhaps several of each type. Furthermore, these more general "coins" have varying values and weights. Instead of counting objects, we place a limit on the total weight and try to maximize the total value.

Knapsack Problem

The 0-1 knapsack problem is an NP-complete problem that is amenable to a DP approach. You are planning a hike and deciding what items to carry from a (multi) set of items $\mathbb{P}$. In this version of the problem, the knapsack will stretch, but your back will not. You must impose a limit on the total weight W of the items carried. You can take an item or not—you cannot take two or more of the same item, but the items in $\mathbb{P}$ do not have to be unique. Naturally, you wish to maximize the total value of the items that you take. The problem is not very interesting for small $n = |\mathbb{P}|$, but a brute-force evaluation would require evaluating 2^n candidate solutions.

Each item p_i has two properties: its weight w_i and its value v_i. The total weight of all your packed items is $\sum w_i$, and the total value is $\sum v_i$, where i is iterated over the items actually in the knapsack.

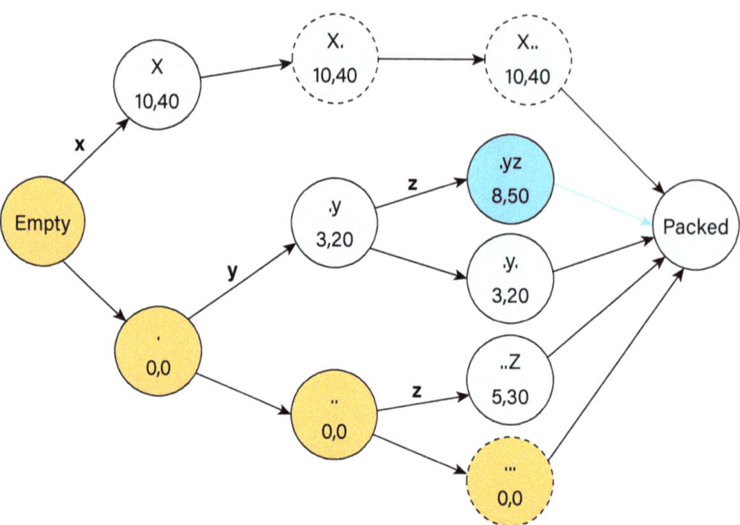

FIGURE 10.12. The 0-1 knapsack problem.

In the simple example of Figure 10.12, the maximum weight the knapsack can carry is 10. There are only three possible objects to take: *x* has weight 10 and value 40. Clearly, if we choose to pack *x*, there will be no room for anything else. Objects *y* and *z* have weights/values of 3/20 and 5/30, respectively. The optimal packing of this knapsack is with both *y* and *z*. The combined weight is only 8, but the total value is 50. Note that we could show the DAG without the *x*., *x*.., and ... states—they do not contribute meaningfully to the solution of the problem.

However, it's easier to think of this as a subsequence problem in that any subsequence of the given items is valid (not only prefixes or suffixes). However, subsequence problems tend to grow exponentially, and DP itself won't help. We need to model this problem in some other way.

Suppose that we consider a slightly different (sub) problem: If we limit the choice of items in the knapsack to the first *k* items of $\mathbb{P}$, we can consider the function

$$\mu(\kappa,\omega)$$

to represent the maximum value achievable where the knapsack choice is limited to the first κ elements of $\mathbb{P}$, and whose total weight does not exceed ω. The answer to our original problem is therefore $\mu(n,W)$.

We can write the following recursive relationships for μ:

Base case: where $\kappa < 1$: $\mu(\kappa,\omega) = 0$ for all ω.

Recursive cases:

- If $w_\kappa > \omega$, $\mu(\kappa,\omega) = \mu(\kappa-1,\omega)$
- Otherwise, $\mu(\kappa,\omega) = \max\{\mu(\kappa-1,\omega),\ \mu(\kappa-1,\omega-w_\kappa)+v_\kappa\}$

Note that all recursive calls to the μ sub-problem represent simpler problems: Either the number of elements is one less or the maximum weight is smaller (assuming that all the weights are positive). We must be careful to store the μ evaluations in a convenient place to eliminate unnecessary (and exponential) recursive calls. A hash table will work well when we create the key from κ and ω. At worst, we will have to evaluate (and store) μ for every possible combination of n and W. Therefore, we can say that the running time (and space) is $O(nW)$.

Can we solve the knapsack problem using the bottom-up method? Yes, but if we try to solve it naively, we will evaluate all nW values of μ, including many that will never be needed. Instead, we should determine the topological order, using *dfs*, and use that.

Conclusion

Dynamic programming is a general technique that enables the solving of problems in polynomial time that otherwise would likely take exponential time. Its fundamental method is based on recursion and the same principles of reduction as DnC but applies to a greater variety of problems. In particular, DP can be used on sub-problem/dependency relationships that cannot be expressed as a tree but that require a directed graph.

We have barely scratched the surface of dynamic programming, but it should be clear that it is an extremely powerful technique that will sometimes end up doing more work than is strictly necessary. The key to using DP successfully and efficiently is in the choice of sub-problems, their dependencies, and the function that optimally merges these dependencies. With a good understanding of the relationships between sub-solutions, it should be quite easy to determine the bounds on the running time and memory required.

There is a good deal of mystique in many of the available descriptions of dynamic programming. It is important to remove any mystery from your understanding of the general technique of DP. However, do not underestimate the difficulty of properly modeling any particular problem, because a poorly modeled solution may end up running in exponential time, or perhaps giving you incorrect results.

Takeaways

Following is a list of the main ideas to take away from this chapter:

- A lazy ADT is often more efficient than the equivalent eager ADT.
- When seeking the optimal solution to a problem, try, try, and try again.
- Dynamic programming deserves an entire book to itself—try to understand the main concepts from this chapter but never stop being curious for more examples and better explanations.
- Dynamic programming is more than just memoization.

Chapter Review Questions

Directions: Refer to what you learned in this chapter to respond to the questions and prompts:

- Under what circumstances can you implement dynamic programming using the bottom-up method?
- Does dynamic programming guarantee a more efficient solution than other methods?
- Do you think that, in the future, it will be possible to have a union-find data structure that answers the connectivity question in constant time and constant memory?
- Is the log*(x) function the same as the Ackermann function?
- What considerations affect whether you should use a top-down or a bottom-up approach in dynamic programming?

Reference

Hopcroft, J. E., & Ullman, J. D. (1973). Set merging algorithms. *SIAM Journal on Computing*, *2*(4), 294–303. https://doi.org/10.1137/0202024

www.ingramcontent.com/pod-product-compliance
Ingram Content Group UK Ltd.
Pitfield, Milton Keynes, MK11 3LW, UK
UKHW050141280726
14058UKWH00006B/767